LEGITIMACY AND TRUST IN CRIMINAL LAW, POLICY AND JUSTICE

Legitimacy and Trust in Criminal Law, Policy and Justice
Norms, Procedures, Outcomes

Edited by
NINA PERŠAK
University of Ghent, Belgium

Routledge
Taylor & Francis Group
LONDON AND NEW YORK

First published 2014 by Ashgate Publishing

Published 2016 by Routledge
2 Park Square, Milton Park, Abingdon, Oxfordshire OX14 4RN
711 Third Avenue, New York, NY 10017, USA

First issued in paperback 2016

Routledge is an imprint of the Taylor & Francis Group, an informa business

British Library Cataloguing in Publication Data
A catalogue record for this book is available from the British Library

The Library of Congress has cataloged the printed edition as follows:
Peršak, Nina, editor.
Legitimacy and trust in criminal law, policy, and justice : norms, procedures, outcomes / by Nina Peršak.
pages cm
Includes bibliographical references and index.
ISBN 978-1-4724-2604-8 (hardback)
1. Criminal law--European Union Countries--Philosophy. 2. Effectiveness and validity of law--European Union Countries. 3. Trust--European Union Countries. I. Title.
KJE7975.P47 2014
345.24001--dc23

2013037780

ISBN 13: 978-1-138-27059-6 (pbk)
ISBN 13: 978-1-4724-2604-8 (hbk)

Contents

Notes on Contributors

Thomas Elholm is a professor of law at the University of Southern Denmark. After graduating from Law School (LLM in 1997) he worked as a lawyer for a few years. Since his PhD in 2002 he has been working as a scholar, specialising in substantial criminal law, comparative criminal law, criminal procedure and EU criminal law. He is President of the Danish Association of European Lawyers and a member of the European Criminal Policy Initiative.

Anže Erbežnik is employed at the European Parliament, at the Civil Liberties, Justice and Home Affairs (LIBE) Committee. He is a doctor of law (European Faculty of Law, Slovenia) and the author of several articles and monographs in the area of criminal procedure law, constitutional criminal law and EU law. He participates as a lecturer at different national and international fora, such as the European Faculty of Law (Nova Gorica, Slovenia) and the European Judicial Training Network (EJTN, Brussels).

Nina Peršak holds a doctorate in law from the University of Ljubljana and an LLM and MPhil (Social and Developmental Psychology) from the University of Cambridge. She is a research professor in the field of criminology and sociology of law at the Faculty of Law, Ghent University. She has previously been Assistant Professor of Criminology, University of Ljubljana, teaching victimology at the University of Maribor. Her research interests lie in the field of criminology, criminal legal philosophy (in particular criminalisation theory), criminal law, victimology, sociology of law and social psychology.

Jože Štrus received his LLM from Harvard Law School, United States. He works for the European Commission (Directorate-General for Justice) where he has been previously mainstreaming the EU Charter of Fundamental Rights into EU legislative proposals and is now evaluating the independence, efficiency and quality of national justice systems.

Tom Vander Beken is a lawyer and a criminologist and holds a PhD in law. He is a professor at the department of penal law and criminology at Ghent University (Belgium) and one of the directors of the Institute for International Research on Criminal Policy (IRCP). He teaches on criminal law and criminal justice. His research interests are in organised crime, criminal policy and criminal justice-related issues.

Freya Vander Laenen is a professor of Criminology at Ghent University and a co-director of the Institute for International Research on Criminal Policy. She has a background in social work and criminology, and has between 1998 and 2000 acted as a drug policy coordinator of the city of Ghent, Belgium. She publishes mostly in the areas of drug prevention, harm reduction, drug policy, forensic mental health and qualitative methodology.

Joanne van der Leun is Professor of Criminology at Leiden Law School (the Netherlands) and a co-founder of the new research programme at the Leiden Law School 'Criminal Justice: Legitimacy, Accountability and Effectivity'. She has a background in sociology and social sciences. Her research interests lie in the field of metropolitan problems around crime and migration.

Maartje van der Woude is a PhD fellow at the Institute for Criminal Law and Criminology of the Leiden Law School (the Netherlands) and Assistant Professor at Leiden Law School. She has a background in criminology and criminal law. Her research interests lie in the field of (anti)terrorism, public order and safety, social and political effects of legislation, and migration.

Christophe Vandeviver is a criminologist and holds an MSc in Quantitative Analysis in the Social Sciences. He is a PhD student at the department of penal law and criminology at Ghent University (Belgium) and a member of the Institute for International Research on Criminal Policy (IRCP). His research interests include quantitative research methods and their application in criminology and the social sciences, offender mobility and the fear of crime.

Gert Vermeulen is Professor of (European and International) Criminal Law at Ghent University, co-director of the Institute for International Research on Criminal Policy (IRCP), and Extraordinary Professor of European and International Evidence Law at Maastricht University. His scholarly expertise lies mainly in the areas of (European and international) criminal law and policy, particularly police and judicial cooperation in criminal matters in the EU, organised crime, terrorism, trafficking in human beings, sexual exploitation of children, prostitution, witness protection, human rights, rights of the child and data protection.

Chapter 1

Beyond Procedural Justice: Some Neglected Aspects of Legitimacy of Criminal Law, Policy and Justice

Nina Peršak

The 'legitimacy crisis' of the state, legal institutions, and in particular in the criminal justice system, has become a much-observed phenomenon that is said to be plaguing several European democracies. Trust in advanced industrial democracies has similarly been reported to be in decline since the 1960s (Putnam 1995, Dalton 2005), with recent declines aggravated by the effects of the global financial crisis. The connection between the two notions is not accidental: when people lose trust in the state, government, legal institutions or the rule of law, they tend to perceive the last as less legitimate.

Trust in law, in the legal system and authorities behind it, is important in several ways. Law participates in the creation of normative culture, which is considered given and stable and is thus contributing to the balance of the social system. If law or the legal system are perceived as not functioning properly, this not only causes significant imbalances within the social system but also destabilises the normative culture by shaking the public belief in its stability and immutability. This may trigger great distress among the public and become a source of fears and insecurities, which can in turn fuel various negative social phenomena, such as crime and xenophobia. The lack of trust can create a breeding ground for populist and extremist movements and invite the criminalisation of 'the other', the anti-social, marginal or migrant. Lack of trust, fears and insecurities may also further decrease the public trust in the legal system and stimulate disrespect towards authorities. The non-functioning or malfunctioning of the legal system thereby impinges on trust in the 'order of things' and on the trust in those who were entrusted with maintaining this order.

From the viewpoint of society (and democracy, in particular), at least minimal trust in political institutions is required to enable their functioning. Even though no government enjoys – and perhaps even ought to – enjoy the absolute trust of its citizens, it must enjoy at least a minimum of public confidence in order to operate effectively. Trust enables governments to function properly without having to seek approval from citizens for every decision or resort to coercion. Trust is also crucial for the establishment of civil society, the creation of the sense of community and successful participation of individuals in the public life and collective institutions, be they political, such as political parties, economic or social (Mishler and Rose 1997). Trust, furthermore, facilitates coordination and cooperation. In the area of criminal justice, cooperation takes shape mostly through compliance: trust leads to the perceived legitimacy of an authority, which is one of the reasons why people comply with it and its decisions or the reason why people obey the law.

Regardless of the type of trust, it has to be remembered, however, that the trust itself – be it interpersonal or institutional – need not be necessarily a 'good thing'. If others conduct themselves dishonestly, trust turns into gullibility (Letki 2006). Since trust is an effective strategy only if others are trustworthy (Letki 2006), it follows *a contrario* that trusting institutions is not an effective strategy (i.e. equals gullibility) if those institutions are not trustworthy. What is therefore needed, in addition to trust, is a certain more objective quality, actual inner legitimacy, of the institution in order for it to deserve this trust and in the long run be able to maintain it. Considering 'legitimacy is the recognition of the right to govern' (Coincaud 2002: 10), the lack of legitimacy erodes the justification for the governance and acceptability of its power, which should be reflected in our trust towards it.

Until about a decade ago, issues of trust have been mainly ignored within the criminological literature (Crawford 2000). Legitimacy, too, being for a long time studied mostly within political science, has recently emerged or re-emerged as a research interest within criminology, although legitimacy has so far been mostly researched through the model of procedural justice and has mostly concentrated on the police or policing (e.g. Tyler 1990, 2003, Tyler and Wakslak 2004, Reisig 2007, Hough et al. 2010, Tyler 2012) and to some extent on prisons (e.g. Sparks, Bottoms and Hay 1996, Liebling 2004, Reisig and Meško 2009). This reinvigorated research in the study of legitimacy (problems) can at least partly be attributed to increasing concerns over legitimacy of criminal justice, and perhaps over legitimacy of state in general.

Legitimacy concerns in the area of criminal justice are, however, still in the process of being properly framed. The lack of agreed, water-tight definition of legitimacy in this area has at least partly to do with the fact that criminal justice scholars come from different disciplines – disciplines that use different conceptions of legitimacy, which consequently provide different points of departure. Some focus primarily on legitimacy conceptualised as public acceptance, agreement or consent to *x*. Enlightenment thinker John Locke (1995: 191), writing in the late seventeenth-century Britain, argued that the government is not legitimate unless it has the consent of the governed. If trust is breached, the consent is withdrawn and the power must 'devolve into the hands of those that gave it', i.e. the people. Weber (1978) laid the foundation for many a social scientist who studies legitimacy by defining legitimacy descriptively as 'a belief' in the acceptability and binding nature of a political or social order, and making a distinction between three types of legitimate authority (or sources of legitimacy): charismatic, traditional and rational-legal. The rational-legal authority, prevailing in modern democracies, is characterised by adherence to the requirement of legality, which encompasses the rationality of law. For moral philosophers, legitimacy is a normative concept, a question of providing good reasons to do (or omit doing) something. Political philosophers and jurists tend to view legitimacy through a similar normative lens. A legitimate political system is one in which certain objective criteria are met, such as the separation of powers, absence of corruption, sovereignty of people, and the democratic election of people's representatives. According to Beetham (1991), a state must fulfil, or appear to fulfil, three criteria to enjoy political legitimacy: (a) using power in accordance with established rules, (b) justifiability of the rules by reference to shared beliefs, and (c) the expressed consent of the people. A legitimate legal system has to do with respecting the values enshrined in the constitutional legal order and the prevailing, rational, fundamental (procedural and substantive) principles governing a certain area of law. If, for example, criminal law or a legislator or a judge complies with these demands, they are deemed legitimate, regardless of what the citizen on a street believes about it. Furthermore, legitimacy is distinguished from legality as requiring something more, some objectively 'good' contents of *x*, as opposed to legality, which is fulfilled when *x* is done according to the law, irrespective of whether the law is good (just) or not. While adherence to the law and rules is generally important, usually even necessary, for legitimacy (the Latin word *legitimus* means essentially lawful), it is not a sufficient condition for legitimacy. Classic textbook examples draw on totalitarian regimes, whose agents passed laws 'legitimating' their future actions, which, however, violated human rights. Some such lawful actions, directed towards minorities, even enjoyed support from a significant part of the population, as, for example, World War II painfully shows.

In the criminological literature so far, we mostly find issues of legitimacy and trust examined through the procedural justice paradigm, put forward by the American social psychologist Tom Tyler and his colleagues, where the ascription of legitimacy to an agent or institution depends primarily on how this agent or institution treats people. Procedural justice or procedural fairness comprises fairness of decision-making (neutral, unbiased, providing people with the opportunity to have their voice heard) and the quality of interpersonal treatment (treating people fairly and respectfully in the proceedings), and it is the latter of the two components that is said to be the most important, central factor in determining people's satisfaction, their trust and the perceived legitimacy of the relevant authority (Tyler 2009, 2013). This thesis has been empirically tested several times, mostly examining citizens' perceptions of the legitimacy of the police.

What is needed at this juncture is a look at the fuller, broader picture that exists. Procedural justice is one part of the legitimacy picture, but not the full picture. There are many important aspects that are still missing or remaining hidden/underexplored, including aspects that may differ from those that seem the most important in the context of trust and perceived legitimacy of law enforcement. It is this lack of examination of some other elements of trust and legitimacy issues in criminal law, criminal policy and criminal justice (courts), and a certain lack of normative and EU-oriented perspectives, that has provided a rationale for this book.

One underexplored aspect concerns the legitimacy of criminal law, of its legislation and application, and criminal policy in general. The legitimacy of criminalisation as a process of passing criminal law legislation (making some human conduct censure-worthy) as well as a process of turning some groups or individuals into 'criminals' that may happen in practice (e.g. by treating some groups as criminals) needs to be added to the examination of legitimacy. This aspect has ultimately to do with the legitimacy of state intervention in the individual autonomy, punitive interference with human conduct. Some other insufficiently explored legitimacy and trust issues can be found at the level of judiciary and its interaction, cooperation and communication with the public, parties and other authorities involved, including the challenges to judiciary posed 'from above' (by EU legal instruments), which may have legitimacy repercussions for both – judiciary and the EU.

The idea behind this volume was therefore to bring to light these various elements that influence trust and legitimacy in criminal law, policy-making and criminal justice in general – elements that have so far remained rather neglected or at least understudied. Our goal was to expand the current research on legitimacy by addressing also conceptions of legitimacy linked to the content of criminalisation, of criminal-law norms and sanctioning, and by examining some specific court-related issues of legitimacy and trust, through different perspectives and incorporation of some typically European (including EU policy-) aspects of the phenomena.

Structure of This Book

Part I addresses the topic of legitimacy and trust in criminal law and criminal policy. Chapter 2 draws on the knowledge of criminal law philosophy and criminalisation theory to address the question of the legitimacy of criminal law legislation (in the broad sense). It reflects, further, on the link between criminalisation and trust, and proposes that in order to comply with the classic criminal-law principles and to avoid legislating on the basis of mistrust or emotion alone, a principled approach – and in particular a harm-based one – should serve as the main guiding criterion for criminalisation, taking into account also possible cultural variability. Lastly, it considers the application of this approach 'at the border' of criminal law, i.e. in the law on violations, reflecting in particular on the recent trends in the penalisation of disorder (nuisance, incivilities, anti-social behaviour), which extend social control by prohibiting many a socially less desirable human conduct, irrespective of whether it is harmful or not.

Chapter 3 reflects on the legitimacy of incivilities regulation through the system of local administrative sanctions in Belgium. Vander Beken and Vandeviver provide a chronological analysis of the introduction and implementation of local administrative sanctions in Belgium from 1999 onwards and the analysis of Belgian newspapers on the issue of administrative sanctions. The authors argue that the concept and the idea to provide local governments with the power to define incivilities and react to them through their own sanctioning system stems from the options provided within the Belgian prevention policy in the 1990s, which was further shaped and developed by constitutional reform. Since then, the system has been implemented in many cities in the Belgium and has been until recently called a success. The authors assert that the possibility of establishing tailor-made rules for local policy-makers has, however, created a patchwork of sanctioning rules and practices throughout the country that have sometimes very little to do with the initial ambition of this measure. Moreover, their media analysis reveals that the system has begun to lose public support. The authors conclude that local administrative sanctions seem to have become a policy on their own and a repressive catch-all to deal with all kinds of societal problems or disorder, casting a shadow over the legitimacy of municipal reactions thereto.

In Chapter 4, Van der Leun and Van der Woude look more closely at another area of progressive criminalisation: migration. Although many regard the Netherlands as a tolerant country when it comes to immigration and a safe haven in terms of crime, the authors note a rather recent emergence of the culture of control and the development of a discourse in which minority groups are increasingly seen and addressed as 'dangerous others', comparable to criminals. This, they believe, is part of the country's broader process of crimmigration – the merging of migration policy and crime control. They situate this process within lingering apprehensions of the Dutch multicultural society and acute issues of immigration, integration, and the over-representation of non-Western ethnic minorities in registered crime statistics, which also appears to have played a role in the declining trust in the criminal justice system. The criminal justice system has reacted by becoming more preventive and increasingly oriented at detecting risky groups of persons as early as possible, and this 'actuarial justice' has been accompanied by a great deal of discretionary power in the hands of those who enforce the law. The authors examine whether and to what extent the above-mentioned social changes affect the legitimacy of the criminal policy, observing among other things that the risk that discretionary powers may be carried out (in part) on the basis of generalisations relating to race, ethnicity, religion or nationality rather than on the basis of individual behaviour or objective evidence have so far been rarely recognised.

Chapter 5 moves the debate on the legitimacy of criminal policy to the EU level and inspects the legitimacy of norms, i.e. norms of substantive criminal law and sanction provisions, and the national implementation of these norms from the European Union perspective. It clarifies why the legitimacy of norms is important, regardless of the underlying philosophical foundation of criminal law. Elholm fleshes out a number of elements that provide a basis for the legitimacy of criminal law at EU level, including legality, democracy or anchoring of norms in the population, effectiveness, proportionality, coherence, procedure or the application of norms, a justifiable outcome, trust and the cultural habit. Finally, he discusses the challenges of EU criminal law concerning the requirement of legitimacy.

Part II is dedicated to legitimacy and trust issues relating to criminal justice, more concretely to the judiciary. Here several additional challenges, including specifically European ones, are highlighted in a novel way. Issues of legitimacy of courts, inter-agency cooperation and mutual trust between states are critically as well as creatively examined with an eye on proposing solutions for the future. Chapter 6 first highlights the importance and factors of trust in judiciary, recognising the unsatisfactory state of affairs within the EU. Peršak and Štrus make a case for more objective, normative criteria of legitimacy that are more stable or less dependent on people's views, and focus on a few significant 'classic' factors of legitimacy (and culprits of reduced trust) of the judiciary, such as access to justice, problems with the quality of judicial decisions, communication, judicial independence and impartiality issues, drawing on existing research, secondary empirical data and recent cases of European Commission interventions towards some Member States, which reinforced the need to take a closer look at the national justice systems as a response to concerns regarding judicial legitimacy. Finally, the authors address current European justice-related challenges, particularly challenges of the effectiveness of national justice systems, owing to which the EU Justice Scoreboard has been developed, which will allow a progressively more detailed assessment of the functioning of justice systems in all Member States.

In Chapter 7, Vander Laenen inspects issues of legitimacy and power that play out in court when another agency is involved. She confronts and challenges legitimacy claims of criminal justice organisations when it comes to inter-agency collaboration between justice and health and social care services. The author observes that working across the care-control divide shows considerable differences between professional values and the ultimate goal of the agencies (a care-centred or client-centred orientation versus a public protection agenda) – differences that become particularly apparent in information sharing, with some health and care agencies reluctant to pass on client information to the justice partner. This reluctance, she adds, reflects a deeper value conflict and resulting distrust between agencies. The author proceeds with the analysis of the interaction between justice and health and social care services in inter-agency collaboration, employing a theoretical framework by Bottoms and Tankebe that perceives legitimacy as dialogic and relational in its character – the approach that may help to address some of the barriers in inter-agency collaboration.

In Chapter 8, Erbežnik examines the role of a judge and more concretely the effects of a mutual recognition mechanism, developed in EU criminal law, on the national judge. Mutual recognition is perceived as the ultimate solution to the creation of a common EU area of freedom, security and justice. However, the author notices that its practical application in criminal law shows substantial differences in the understanding of criminal procedure, where such differences and their accommodation (in cross-border cooperation) challenge the classic role of a judge in a modern democracy, which he mainly sees in protecting fundamental rights of the individual against the state in a fair procedure and reflecting the values and spirit of the national constitution. In the system of mutual recognition, the national judge, despite being sometimes confronted with substantial legal differences between Member States, is bound by enumerated, limited grounds for refusal. The author believes that this aspect bears the potential danger of transforming the judge in a kind of 'ticking boxes' automaton. Therefore, he argues for a 'balancing' theory of mutual recognition in EU criminal law – theory that would allow a national judge to provide fair procedure, safeguard national constitutional rights (including rights stemming from international covenants) as well as foster a pro-European understanding. Such a theory, the author asserts, has to establish equilibrium in a way that provides legitimacy to the national legal system, on one side, and helps to transform EU criminal law area into a coherent and functioning reality, thus legitimising EU legal system, on the other side.

In Chapter 9, Vermeulen exposes the reader to flaws and contradictions in the mutual trust and mutual recognition discourse for which the author wonders whether they do not cast a shadow on the legitimacy of EU judicial cooperation in criminal matters as well as on the legitimacy of EU criminal policy-making. For the European cooperation instruments in criminal matters to work there has to exist mutual trust between Member States and between competent authorities from different Member States. Since its official policy introduction in 1999 as the new cornerstone or bedrock of EU judicial cooperation in criminal matters, the principle of mutual recognition has been linked up with either the (assumed) existence or the (perceived) lack of mutual trust. Mutual recognition, despite being presented as an unambiguous, streamlined and coherent notion, has, however, many faces – as many as the mutual trust in the EU's and the Member States' discourse(s). Drawing on over a decade-long research on mutual trust and mutual recognition, the author unravels these mutual trust discourses, unveiling their often contradictory, instrumental, biased or one-sided underlying assumptions and their policy outcomes. The chapter, lastly, assesses the impact of this development on the legitimacy of EU efforts in this domain, and particularly on the legitimacy of judicial cooperation in criminal matters.

Chapter 10 is a concluding chapter in which an attempt is made to identify the themes that have emerged from this volume, consolidate the key debates and share some suggestions for future research.

Legitimacy as well as trust, even if narrowed down to criminal law, policy and justice, is of course a manifold and complex topic that is impossible to exhaustively cover in a single volume, and this has never been our goal. The purpose of this book is much more modest; it aims to contribute to the increasing discussion on the importance of trust in legal institutions of modern democracies and reflect on the social and normative aspects of legitimacy of criminal justice, which have so far remained understudied, from multidisciplinary and European perspectives, thereby, hopefully revealing a little more of the overall legitimacy picture.

I would like to thank all those who contributed to the lively debate and discussion at University of Ghent which ultimately led to the development of this book.

References

Beetham, D. 1991. *The Legitimation of Power*. Basingstoke: Palgrave Macmillan.

Coincaud, J-M. 2002. *Legitimacy and Politics: A Contribution to the Study of Political Right and Political Responsibility*. Cambridge: Cambridge University Press.

Crawford, A. 2000. Situational crime prevention, urban governance and trust relations, in *Ethical and Social Perspectives on Situational Crime Prevention*, edited by A. von Hirsch, D. Garland and A. Wakefield. Oxford: Hart Publishing, 193–213.

Dalton, R.J. 2005. The social transformation of trust in government. *International Review of Sociology*, 15(1), 133–54.

Hough, M., Jackson, J., Bradford, B., Myhill, A. and Quinton, P. 2010. Procedural justice, trust and institutional legitimacy. *Policing: A Journal of Policy and Practice*, 4(3), 203–10.

Letki, N. 2006. Investigating the roots of civic morality: Trust, social capital, and institutional performance. *Political Behavior*, 28(4), 305–25.

Letki, N. and Evans, G. 2005. Endogenizing social trust: Democratization in East-Central Europe. *British Journal of Political Science*, 35(3), 515–29.

Liebling, A. 2004. *Prisons and Their Moral Performance: A Study of Values, Quality, and Prison Life*. Oxford: Oxford University Press.

Locke, J. 1995 (orig. 1689). *Two Treatises of Government*. Guernsey: Guernsey Press Co.

Mishler, W. and Rose, R. 1997. Trust, distrust and skepticism: Popular evaluations of civil and political institutions in post-communist societies. *The Journal of Politics*, 59(2), 418–51.

Putnam, R.D. 1995. Bowling alone: America's declining social capital. *Journal of Democracy*, 6(1), 65–78.

Reisig, M.D. 2007. Procedural justice and community policing: What shapes residents' willingness to participate in crime prevention programs? *Policing: A Journal of Policy and Practice*, 1(3), 356–69.

Reisig, M.D. and Meško, G. 2009. Procedural justice, legitimacy, and prisoner misconduct. *Psychology, Crime, and Law*, 15(1), 37–54.

Sparks, R., Bottoms, A. and Hay, W. 1996. *Prisons and the Problem of Order*. Alderley: Clarendon Press.

Tyler, T.R. 1990. *Why People Obey the Law*. Princeton: Princeton University Press.

Tyler, T.R. 2003. Procedural justice, legitimacy, and the effective rule of law. *Crime and Justice: A Review of Research*, 30, 283–357.

Tyler, T.R. 2009. Legitimacy and compliance: The benefits of self-regulation. *Ohio State Journal of Criminal Law*, 7(1), 307–59.

Tyler, T.R. (ed.) 2012. *Legitimacy and Criminal Justice: International Perspectives*. New York: Russell Sage Foundation.

Tyler, T.R. 2013. Legitimacy and compliance: The virtue of self-regulation, in *Legitimacy and Compliance in Criminal Justice*, edited by A. Crawford and A. Hucklesby. Oxford, New York: Routledge, 8–28.

Tyler, T.R. and Wakslak, C.J. 2004. Profiling and police legitimacy: Procedural justice, attribution of motive, and acceptance of police authority. *Criminology*, 42(2), 253–81.

Weber, M. 1978. *Economy and Society*, edited by G. Roth and C. Wittich. Berkley and Los Angeles: University of California Press.

PART I
Legitimacy and Trust in Criminal Law and Policy: Principles and Implementation

Chapter 2
Norms, Harms and Disorder at the Border: The Legitimacy of Criminal Law Intervention through the Lens of Criminalisation Theory

Nina Peršak

Introduction

State criminal law interventions must have good, valid normative reasons behind them in order to be legitimate. In the area of criminal law and criminal law philosophy, which has been a driving force behind the developments in the normative criminalisation theory, the notion of legitimacy has to do with the internal reasonableness and normative justification for criminalisation (understood in the broadest sense). What interests criminalisation theory, in other words, is what sort of human conduct, and for what reasons or under which conditions, it is legitimate to criminalise (and consequently punish) within a certain normative (legal, social, political, moral) orientation of a given society. This conception of legitimacy is therefore linked to the normative grounds for criminalisation and to the content of criminal law norms, and it is this notion of legitimacy that will be used in this chapter.

As criminalisation can be construed as an act or process through which the state interferes with the autonomy of an individual by proscribing certain types of conduct under the threat of punishment, the search for legitimate grounds for criminalisation is, however, connected not only to the question of the legitimacy of criminal law but also to the question of the legitimacy of the state.[1] The latter comes in particular under scrutiny in times of economic hardship. With many living on the border of poverty, it is unsurprising therefore that the state is said to be encountering 'legitimacy crisis', revealed also in the lack of reported trust and confidence in the government, police, courts and other state institutions, as well as in the dominant economic system, social security system, migration policy and

1 Dubber (2007: 2597) claims that punishment is the most severe form of state coercion and as such 'poses the most serious challenge to the legitimacy of the state'.

so forth.[2] Economic and welfare infrastructures are crucial for the maintenance of trust and feelings of security (Burney 2005). Criminalisation taps into this issue of trust and feeds from it.

Criminal law and trust are, in fact, related on many levels. The impetus to criminalise *x* may in itself be understood as an expression of trust in the power of criminal law, a testament to the faith that criminal law will be able to reduce or even prevent *x* from further occurring. Moreover, criminalisation can be considered a litmus test of interpersonal (dis)trust: the less we trust one another, the more we are inclined to regulate behaviour through criminal law prohibitions, to resort to criminal law in order to 'straighten' others out. The less we trust, the more we rely on formal, written rules, contracts and laws, and on punishing those who violate our trust. As such, criminalisation can also be seen as a sort of coping technique for countering people's insecurities and fears. The latter may be concrete or very abstract. Everyday ontological insecurities (be they economic, social or urban anomie and alienation) that have no single, clearly distinguishable 'cause' or enemy to pinpoint, often channel into fear of crime and consequently – as a means of regaining control – into appeals for punishment of some suspected or suspicious *y*.

Legislating on the basis of mistrust or similar negative emotions and beliefs cannot, however, be considered as a welcome trend. In order to avoid it, as well as comply with the classic criminal law principles (such as *ultima ratio*), a principled approach, and in particular a harm-based one, will be put forward as that which should serve as the main guiding criterion for criminalisation. Moreover, it will be suggested that a similarly principled approach should be applied 'at the border' of criminal law, i.e. in the law on violations (*Ordnungswidrigkeiten*), inspecting in particular the penalisation of disorder (or nuisance, incivilities, anti-social behaviour, etc.). The latter often extend social control by prohibiting and penalising many a human conduct that has been (by those in power) deemed less socially desirable, irrespective of whether it is harmful or not.

Legitimate Grounds for State Intervention through Criminal Law

Criminalisation is important as people's notions of crime depend on formulations in criminal law. It is one way of constructing our social reality (Hulsman 1986) and even criminological enterprise that promotes critical understanding of 'crime' very much relies on these state-constructed notions or categories of 'crime' and their application. Criminalisation is, furthermore, a powerful process because it 'mobilises popular approval and legitimacy in support of powerful interests within the state' (Scraton and Chadwick 1991: 299). It is also one of the usual, the most primary, powerful and symbolic tools used against the 'less-desirable', although

2 See, for example, the results of recent Eurobarometers, Almond 2008, Igličar 2012, Roberts and Hough 2005, etc.

the strategies towards such social groups (e.g. immigrants, beggars, homeless) are not exhausted by their criminalisation.[3]

In the eyes of the normative criminalisation theory, however, criminalisation represents one of the most repressive acts of state power, for it restricts the individual's freedom of action and inflicts undesirable consequences upon the individual if he transgresses. According to John Stuart Mill (1991), every limitation, interference with the liberty of action of the individual or restraint *qua* restraint is an 'evil' or a '*prima facie* wrong' (Brown 1999: 137). Within modern liberal criminal law systems, based on Enlightenment principles, this means that these state-imposed limitations need to be legitimate. Legitimacy is, in fact, the central notion of the system of criminal law, as people have to believe in the system and perceive it as legitimate (Lahti 2000). Simester and Sullivan (2003: 5) have described criminal law as a 'condemnatory response from the state' and as 'a bluntly coercive system, directed at controlling the behaviour of citizens', emphasising that nobody, not even the state, should be allowed to coerce people without good reason. In their words, '[t]he manipulation of people's conduct calls for justification, especially when it is accompanied by censorious and punitive treatment of those who do not comply. Unless there are compelling reasons, the criminal law should not be deployed by Parliament' (Simester and Sullivan 2003: 5).

Several authors to date have attempted to flesh out legitimate principles and models of how an ideal or preferable criminalisation should proceed (e.g. Feinberg 1984, Schonsheck 1994, Peršak 2007a, Simester and von Hirsch 2011, etc.), as have some countries, which have worked out their own legitimate grounds for criminalisation (e.g. Finland and Sweden). Similar efforts can be recently observed at the level of EU with several EU institutions publishing their own views on the strategy for future EU criminal law development. In many other European countries the general approach to criminalisation remains rather casuistic, following only nomothetic rules (general rules for drafting of laws) and adhering to a few basic (formal) criminal law principles (e.g. principles of legality, of proportionality, of last resort), while more substantive principles of criminalisation, which would give instruction regarding the substance of that which is legitimate to criminalise, are lacking.

According to modern criminalisation theory, one of the 'good reasons' or legitimate grounds for criminalisation is harm to others. The 'harm principle' claims that harm to others provides sufficient (or even necessary) condition for the state intervention through criminal law.[4] Other principles, discussed most

3 Further strategies employed against them include, for example, displacement, gated communities as the new enclosures of the rich, ethnic profiling in police practices, etc. See also Van der Leun and Van der Woude (in this volume).

4 The two most known formulations of this principle are Mill's and Feinberg's. Mill's (1991: 14) 'principle of liberty' asserts that 'the only purpose for which power can be rightfully exercised over any member of a civilised community, against his will, is to prevent harm to others'. Feinberg (1988: xix), on the other hand, formulates his harm principle

comprehensively by Joel Feinberg in his tetralogy on the moral limits to criminal law, are the offence principle, legal paternalism and legal moralism. Legal moralism, in short, allows the criminalisation of conduct that (only) violates some conventional morality, i.e. even if the conduct in question does not harm anybody (Devlin 1965, Feinberg 1988, Peršak 2004). In the past, it has been often used to criminalise prostitution, homosexuality, unusual styles of clothing, etc. Legal paternalism (Feinberg 1986), on the other hand, permits the criminalisation of conduct with which one only harms (physically or psychologically) oneself, not others. It can be used therefore to justify criminalisation of suicide and other self-harming behaviour. Although paternalistic criminal law intervention may rest on various justifications, paternalistic agents often claim they are intervening for the individual's own good (Peršak 2010). Lastly, the offence principle asserts that the conduct that is (merely) offensive provides a good reason for its criminalisation.[5]

The harm principle is currently the most widely recognised or widely accepted principle of criminalisation out of the mentioned four. This is not to say, however, that the definition of what counts as harm is easy. What counts or should count as 'harmful'?[6] In brief,[7] for the purposes of the harm principle not any sort of harm will do. For one, to be legitimately criminalised, the conduct must entail *wrongful* harm. Any sort of harm, e.g. harm caused by natural disasters, would therefore not qualify. Harm has been conceptually formulated as 'a set-back to an interest' (Feinberg 1984) and an interest as a resource, i.e. longer-term means or capabilities that someone possesses, over which one has a legitimate claim (von Hirsch 2003). One cannot be therefore harmed, in any criminalisation-relevant sense, if one had no legitimate claim over that which has purportedly been harmed (e.g. over bodily integrity of another adult person). The concept of harm as used in the harm principle includes only harm *to others* (not oneself) and is predominantly limited

---

in the following way: 'It is always a good reason in support of penal legislation that it would be effective in preventing (elimination, reducing) harm to persons other than the actor (the one prohibited from acting) and there is no other means that is equally effective at no greater cost to other values'. In contrast to Mill, Feinberg formulates it as a positive principle, i.e. principle providing grounds for (not against) criminalisation.

5 The proponents of this principle often try to make it as stringent as possible, allowing only certain kinds of offensiveness to count, distinguishing between 'mere affront' and 'offensiveness' or tying it to harm, albeit remote harm, in some way or another or by introducing mediating principles that would further limit criminalisation on the basis of this principle (see e.g. von Hirsch and Simester 2006, Simester and von Hirsch 2011: 91–138).

6 In the Continental criminal legal system of Germanic legal tradition, legal scholars would mostly speak of the infringement of, or injury to, the legally protected interest or legal good (*Rechtsgut*) when conceptualising harm. For more detail, see Peršak 2007a and Hefendehl, von Hirsch and Wohlers (eds) 2003 (in German).

7 Owing to space limitations and the scope of this article, only a very brief overview or a sketch of the main ideas on harm can here be provided. For a more detailed overview of the literature on the harm principle and a comparative study on the issue of criminal harm, see Peršak (2007a).

to other *individuals*. This harm is the general harm that results generally from a certain harmful conduct, not the actual harm that has resulted in the concrete case. The conduct that would fall under the ambit of the harm principle is, further, the conduct that causes or may cause serious or *significant* harm. The harmed person has had to experience a 'set-back', i.e. a more lasting change to the worse, to one or some of her interests (over which she had a claim); a temporary discomfort will not do. Psychological harm may therefore be acknowledged as 'harm' only when the conduct caused a set-back, i.e. when one's personal resources or coping abilities were in various ways impaired by the conduct (von Hirsch and Simester 2006). Momentary offendedness or the mere state of being affronted is insufficient.

Moreover, the harm should predominantly be actual or direct, not too remote or abstract.[8] The same was acknowledged, for example, by the Council of the EU (2009: 3), which in its *Conclusions on model provisions, guiding the Council's criminal law negotiations*, suggested that the criminal provisions should focus on conduct 'causing actual harm or seriously threatening the right or essential interest which is the object of protection; that is, avoiding criminalisation of a conduct at an unwarrantably early stage'. It specifically states that conduct which only implies an abstract danger to the protected right or interest should be criminalised 'only if appropriate considering the particular importance of the right or interest which is the object of protection'.

What differentiates the harm principle and other above-mentioned grounds for criminalisation from the many other criminal law principles, such as the principle of legality, principle of proportionality or the principle of last resort (*ultima ratio*), is that the former are *substantive* reasons, for they speak of the content of what can legitimately be criminalised. *Nullum crimen nulla poena sine lege previa*, one element of the legality principle, on the other hand, instructs about the requirement of having a certain conduct first defined as 'criminal' by the law before it can be punished, prosecuted or even truly named 'criminal'. The substantive principles, conversely, provide instructions as to the characteristics of the conduct that may be legitimately criminalised and as such belong to the 'first filter' of legitimate criminalisation procedure.[9] According to Schonsheck's (1994) 'filtering approach' to criminalisation, the first-level filter is the Principles Filter, where the legislator should determine whether the action in question falls within the moral authority of the state. At the second filter, the Presumptions Filter, the legislator should look into other possible means, less coercive and intrusive than the criminal statute, which could perform the same function satisfactorily enough, that is, reduce the occurrence of the negative conduct to an acceptable level. And, finally, at the third

8 Remote harm, for example, leads to questions of imputation of authorship, particularly when other intervening actors or events contribute to the harm eventually occurring (see von Hirsch 1996).

9 When the original Schonsheck's structure is filled with existing criminalisation or criminal law principles, the first filter can be found to contain the harm principle or the 'penal value principle' (Jareborg 2005, Peršak 2007a: 91–4).

filter, the Pragmatics Filter, the legislator should perform a cost/benefit analysis, inspecting the consequences of enacting and enforcing a prohibition. The ideal criminalisation process should, on his account, resemble a funnel with these three filters, and a legitimate, justifiable criminalisation presupposes that a particular piece of the proposed legislation has 'successively and successfully' (Schonsheck 1994: 25) passed through all of these filters in the three-step, filtering procedure.

Cultural Variability

Although the harm principle is proposed here as the fundamental (substantive) guiding principle in criminal law *stricto sensu* as well as in the punitive regulation of disorder, its underlying cultural or political assumptions should be acknowledged. The harm principle, and more concretely its articulation (what should count as harm), rests on a certain political-normative vision of society, concretely liberal[10] democratic society, which exposes it to challenges of cultural or political diversity between states, which may have implications for criminal law and criminal policy. Diversity and cultural particularities may, for instance, influence the decision regarding the selection of legitimate principles for criminalisation.

In countries with well-functioning welfare states, for example in Finland or Sweden, the state may be viewed as something predominantly positive and, similarly, communities, paving the way for the concept of 'community' and community values to take a more prominent role in policy-making than in some other EU countries, which are more individualistic or individual-oriented. While in the latter, the preferred conception of criminal law is centred around the individual (as a perpetrator or injured party), in more communitarian societies, ideas about e.g. including the community as a separate actor in the criminal law arena and criminal process[11] or ideas about criminalising various harms to community (harm that may be difficult to pinpoint to an individual 'other') may be introduced.

The orientation of some countries towards a more individual-based criminal policy may be due to their political orientation or their histories, e.g. war and experiences with totalitarian regimes. The latter often put the people as a collective entity or the state and the Communist Party in the forefront at the expense of human rights and liberties of the individual, whose interests were subjugated to those of the Communist Party (Mishler and Rose 1997). In this respect, the cultural differences have (again), at least partially, to do with trust, more concretely, with

10 Liberal in the classical sense of the word, i.e. respecting the individual's liberty and autonomy, and supporting a minimalist approach to criminalisation. As such it can be completely consistent with the social state.

11 Lernestedt (2012) thus argues that community should be, at least within the Swedish criminal law system, introduced as an independent, separate actor, posited somewhere between the two 'traditional' actors: the offender, on the one hand, and the state, on the other. For further comments on such an approach, see Peršak (2012b).

the differences in the levels of trust. These differences certainly play a part in the general policy outlook on criminalisation and in consequent legitimacy ascription to actors who are relevant in it.[12] The individualism of some other countries, such as the UK or USA, could be, on the other hand, derived from their long-standing tradition of liberalism and emphasis on civil liberties. The concept of the individual's autonomy provides a point of departure not only for American penal law (cf. Dubber 2007) but also for much of its political thought. The more individualistic character of English law can be observed, for example, in its criminal law, in its criminalisations as well as in its omissions of criminalisation. While many a European state criminalises, for example, the failure to rescue a person in grave danger when rescuing her would not involve putting oneself or others in danger, the law of England and Wales does not recognise such a duty to rescue and consequently does not criminalise the omission of such a rescue (Ashworth 2013).

Regardless of where these differences are coming from, be they related to trust (past or present) or to something else, it may be argued that those conceptions or representations of harm that are widely shared within a certain society construct its 'social reality'. It could further be argued that the latter should, at least to a certain degree, influence the criminal law theory. Lord Bingham has, for example, claimed that the law needs overhauling when it fails to match the expectations of ordinary people on a regular basis (in Lords Hansard 2009). Fagan (2008: 134) similarly observes that perceptions of citizens matter, as the legitimacy and effectiveness of the law (criminal, in particular) are deeply dependent on the 'moral credibility it has achieved in the eyes of citizens'.

While people's expectations and perceptions matter and while popular support is undoubtedly a good thing to have (as it, for one, facilitates compliance), this does not, however, mean that popular opinion should be the main driving force behind criminalisation, defining what and how to criminalise. As a rule of thumb, popular opinion of the day should not be trusted, as it is often too fickle, not based on real data and can easily be manipulated. Studies on the fear of crime have shown us, for example, that there exists a clear gap between the perception of threat (fear) that people report and actual threat or dangerousness (or likelihood of being victimised). In other words, people are bad at assessing real danger. Secondly, our views are often manipulated by media, politicians and other people. Social representations theory (Moscovici 1984) reveals that our individual representations of some issue, object, person, etc., occur in communication with others and their representations. The more powerful, 'lauder' representations tend to receive more weight. Moreover, today, our knowledge about the world is mostly conveyed to us via media, be they classical (TV, newspapers) or virtual (Facebook, Twitter,

12 Post-communist and post-socialist criminal codes often reflect an intentional shift from not only the normative but also rhetorical legacy of the past. The post-1989 Slovenian Criminal Code thus dropped any reference to 'social danger' due to its past abuses and socialist connotations (Peršak 2012a).

other social networking sites). This process of mediation never occurs without some changing, co-constructing of the object, which often entails manipulation. It can fuel phenomena such as 'moral panic' (Cohen 1972), which has been known to have clear and unwelcome links to criminalisation. Yet, while popular opinion is fickle and therefore not to be entrusted with powers of steering criminalisation, the more general social beliefs, representations and values that are legitimate (e.g. not violating human rights) and rather stable over time could, it may be argued, be taken into account when legislating, therefore allowing for some society-specific or country-specific nuances in criminal policy or criminalisation. Should this be acknowledged, however, the reference point ought not be popular opinion as such but rather legitimate (i.e. human rights-respecting) and more stable (i.e. developed over time and in line with the principles of modern criminal law, less prone to changing overnight) values and beliefs, shaped by particular country-specific elements.

The specificities and differences between countries and societies are not to be neglected, but they should not be overstated either. They need to be acknowledged but so do commonalities between them. Within EU or Western liberal democratic societies there is some stability found, some consensus on the common agreed principles, Enlightenment heritage, basic values that penetrate into criminal law as well as on the similarity in ranking them (the values, and consequently the harms). One can, for example, safely say that, in general, crimes against sexual inviolability (e.g. rape) are everywhere within the said society perceived as more harmful and blameworthy, and hence more severely sanctioned, than crimes against property. Furthermore, despite the cultural variability, which requires from us to be careful in assuming a consensus, it is noticeable that, at least within EU, there are several fundamental values[13] and common grounds on which the EU criminal law is being built in a more consistent way or as a more homogeneous type of law. Various EU institutions have to date put forward their vision for future criminal law development at EU level. The Council of the EU (2009) has thus on 30 November 2009 issued its *Conclusions on model provisions, guiding the Council's criminal law negotiations*, suggesting the model on which the future proposals in the area of criminal law should be based. In September 2011, the European Commission (2011: 12) followed with a landmark Communication

13 Fundamental values of the EU are referred to in many EU legislative documents. The Preamble to the Charter of Fundamental Rights, for example, refers to values of human dignity, freedom, equality and solidarity. The Preamble of the Treaty on European Union (hereafter: TEU) confirms Member States' attachment to the principle of liberty, democracy, respect for human rights and fundamental freedoms, to the rule of law and fundamental social rights. Art. 2 of TEU stipulates that the Union is founded on the values of respect for human dignity, freedom, democracy, equality, the rule of law and respect for human rights, including the rights of persons belonging to minorities. It further claims that these values are common to the Member States in a society in which pluralism, non-discrimination, tolerance, justice, solidarity and equality between women and men prevail.

Towards an EU Criminal Law Policy, calling it 'the first step in the Commission's efforts to put in place a coherent and consistent EU criminal policy by setting out how the EU should use criminal law to ensure the effective implementation of EU policies'. Therein the Commission stressed, for example, that seriousness and character of the breach of law must be taken into account when choosing among different types of regulation. The European Parliament (2012) issued its own document on the topic in May 2012, emphasising among others that necessity of new substantive criminal law provisions must be demonstrated by the factual evidence making it clear among others that criminal provisions focus on the conduct causing significant pecuniary or non-pecuniary damage to society, individuals or a group of individuals. Furthermore, 19 June 2012 saw the inaugural meeting of Commission's expert group on EU criminal policy, tasked with assisting the Commission in 'designing and delivering an EU criminal policy' (Reding 2012).[14] All these developments attest to the EU-wide acknowledgment of the need to develop some shared, unified, common standards for employment of criminal law at EU level as well as show at least implicit recognition that there is enough common ground, shared values and willingness among EU Member States to make further steps in this area. Considering trust depends (or depends also) on value similarity – we tend to trust those whom we believe share similar values as us[15] – these EU developments can be considered as attesting not only to the similarity of values but also to a certain trust (or at least certain potential for trust) among Member States.[16]

Perhaps cultural variability, regional and local differences and specificities come (or ought to come) more into play in the area of the law on violations (regulatory offences) than in criminal law in the strict sense, particularly when the legislating body is regional or local government. As long as criminal law *stricto sensu* represents only the 'ethical minimum' (Jellinek 1878) of a given society, expressing 'our shared beliefs of what is truly condemnable' (Robinson 2000: 1869), cultural variability within a fundamentally similar western liberal democratic society should perhaps not make much difference in terms of the selection of basic principles of criminalisation.

14 Many members of this group are authors of the *Manifesto on European Criminal Policy* in which they have in December 2009 put forward a set of general principles for legislative proposals in the area of EU criminal law. See European Criminal Policy Initiative (2011) for the latest, updated Manifesto, and Elholm (in this volume).

15 Some distinguish between trust and confidence: trust is founded upon perception that salient values are held in common, whereas confidence is based on performance (Siegrist et al. in Breakwell 2007).

16 For more on mutual trust between Member States and its problems, see the chapters by Erbežnik and Vermeulen (both in this volume).

The Borderland of Criminal Law: Law on Violations and Regulation of Disorder

Disorder is regulated differently in different countries, and even under different names. The conduct (an act, object or practice) that, generally, interferes with another's interests by being offensive, annoying, dangerous, obstructive or unhealthy is sometimes referred to as 'nuisance'. In the UK it is regulated under the term 'anti-social behaviour' and in Spain and France as 'incivilities' or 'uncivil' conduct. Elsewhere they are also known as 'public order violations' (e.g. in Slovenia) or 'quality-of-life offences' (USA). In some jurisdictions these offences may be considered crime proper, while in others merely violations or regulatory offences. The latter in some countries belong to administrative law, in others they form part of the criminal law in the broad sense (as in Germany or Slovenia). In all, they penalise the offender.

What counts as disorder (or nuisance, incivility) varies across time and space as well as between societies and people. In part, this is due to sensitivities that differ from one person to another. Some people may be offended by a group of young men speaking loudly on a train or by a young couple publicly kissing, others may only shrug or even smile at them. Sensitivities may have biological roots, they can be acquired through socialisation, be culture-specific and media-manipulated. Media certainly help construct the 'problem of incivilities'. They influence public perceptions of harmfulness and of the 'law and order' problem (Levi 2008). They also act as a bridge between the official line of reasoning (on which they report) and the public, and are through this process influenced themselves by the official political and legislative stances.[17] In today's atmosphere of reduced tolerance, the temptation to expand the notion of disorder to trivial misconduct in order to regulate it (or earn money from it through fines imposed) is especially pronounced.

Content

In terms of criminalisation, i.e. in terms of content of that which is prohibited, however, what are particularly important are the reasons why some conduct is problematic to the extent that it warrants penal intervention. Is some disorderly conduct harmful or seriously offensive? Do people have good reasons to be offended, and society good reasons to criminalise the conduct? Obstructing a public road, polluting air and water and similar conduct may jeopardise health, safety or welfare of others, possessing therefore truly harmful dimensions. On the other hand, there are many incivilities that may also cause nothing but a slight inconvenience, such as youngsters hanging about.

17 This was confirmed in a relatively recent study on representations of 'anti-social' (Peršak 2007b), where it transpired that the meaning of 'anti-social' as used in British national press (broadsheets and tabloids) changed through time in line with the meaning of 'anti-social' as formulated by legal regulation and official policy documents.

Even when many people find certain conduct offensive, they may consider it that way for different reasons. These reasons are important in assessing the conduct's 'criminalisation potential'. While some may find *x* merely annoying, others may feel insecure and experience fear. Should all emotions be legally endorsed? Are emotions such as fear, worry, anger, disgust, alarm, resentment all equally deserving of protection? When it is merely 'alarm', that people experience, is this really sufficient to warrant criminal prohibition? Alarm as 'anxious awareness of danger' (Oxford Dictionary) may not be more than temporary minor discomfort as opposed to someone being intimidated or kept in fear for hours. On the other hand, when it is 'resentment' what people or victims feel when confronted with uncivil behaviour – as Bottoms (2006) observed when reading people's responses in the British Crime Survey regarding the anti-social behaviour[18] – the question arises also as to whether the state should really endorse this negative emotion quite in the same way as it endorses 'fear'. Not all emotional reactions seem to be equally deserving of law's protection or be equally legitimate to represent the prima facie[19] legitimate basis for criminalisation. Furthermore, criminalising some conduct on the sole basis of a negative emotion (resulting in others) without first inspecting whether such (an experience of) emotion is appropriate, would render it similar to criminalising 'mere affront', which has been appropriately argued as not constituting wrongdoing in itself and therefore not qualifying as a legitimate criminalisation ground even under the offence principle (von Hirsch and Simester 2006).

In order to avoid criminalisation based primarily on mistrust, mere affront, temporary discomfort or on negative emotions that should not be legally endorsed; in other words, in order to avoid problematic disorder regulation, harm should be our first concern. Harm, although perhaps not as stringently defined as in the criminalisation *stricto sensu* where only 'significant' harm should qualify, would certainly be legitimate. Anything else? Should perhaps some limited legal paternalism be allowed, for example, due to purported lack of censure in the

18 The respondents of the British Crime Survey reported annoyance, anger and frustration as experienced emotions to anti-social conduct. Based on Barbelet's theory, Bottoms realised that this mix of emotions amounts to 'resentment', which is a purely normative emotion, 'an emotion rooted in the view that others have behaved in a way that is normatively unacceptable, and that have thus violated the acceptable conditions of social living' (Bottoms 2006: 261).

19 Even if negative emotional reactions from some people were to be deemed a legitimate ground for criminalisation, there are other filters, mentioned above, through which a proposed piece of legislation should go before it really qualifies for criminalisation (Schonsheck 1994), one of them being the likelihood of success in preventing such behaviour. If the likelihood is too small to pass through the filter, criminalisation is not warranted. Passing through the first filter makes the conduct therefore only a prima facie good candidate for criminalisation.

sanctioning of violations?[20] Should the barrier for criminalisation here be dropped if not due to the lack of censure then perhaps due to less severe punishment – a minor restriction of the individual's liberty or autonomy? Could perhaps the so-called offence principle in the area of violations feature more prominently? If the offence principle is to be accepted as a legitimate grounds for criminalisation, the penal intervention on its basis would, on von Hirsch and Simester's account (2006: 120), have to be limited to the conduct that 'treats others with a gross lack of respect or consideration' and be based on good reasons, provided by the proponents of criminalisation, as to why the conduct in question is 'wrongful', i.e. why the conduct in question in being grossly disrespectful or inconsiderate.[21] Even when wrongfulness requirement is fulfilled, however, von Hirsch and Simester offer a series of mediating principles that further restrict the scope for criminalisation for they believe that not all offensive behaviour should be criminalised. Social tolerance, a ready avoidability of the offence and non-immediacy of the offence could mediate against criminalisation (von Hirsch and Simester 2006). However, there is a lot to be said for keeping the harm principle at least as the main principle and allowing exceptions, e.g. based on the offence principle, merely as just that – exceptions, as punitive law is not an appropriate (or even most effective) way to educate or socialise people. Moreover, the further away from harm we go, the more in trouble (quite literally) we can get, for it becomes less likely that we would (or could) comply with such regulation (as further explained below).

What is manifestly clear in many an existing disorder regulation is that there is no principle guiding it, no order in the regulation of disorder, if you will. It seems that currently anything goes. In the UK, anti-social behaviour includes anything from littering to emitting noise, from hanging about to attempted suicide, etc. It encompasses anything that 'causes or is likely to cause alarm, distress or harassment to people not part of the same household'. The vague definition itself is highly problematic from the legality principle point of view, but if we just look at the content and some real cases of Anti-Social behaviour Orders or ASBOs (given out for pigs running amok, attempted suicide, opening doors in Eve's costume, etc.), we see how the net of social control has extended to cover all kinds of nuisance, from real crime to merely unusual behaviour, covering almost any little deviation from 'normality'.

---

20 Justifying legal paternalism in the law on violations if based on the claim that violations do not contain censure, i.e. moral reproach toward the offender that is inherent in the (criminal) punishment, can be problematic though, as many (of not all) violations are not 'ethically colourless' (see Peršak 2010).

21 They list several such reasons, pointing out, however, that the reasons may depend on the conduct in question. While some offensive conduct (for example, insistent or aggressive begging) may, on their account, be wrongful as it violates one's privacy, one's right to be left alone, other conduct (for example, playing portable radios loudly on public transport) may be wrongful due to the fact that it pre-empts public space and reduces the scope for others to pursue their preferences in peace.

What separates, concretely, 'anti-social' conduct from existing crime is the fact that this group hosts a variety of breaches of social convention regarding socially desirable conduct, some of which have already been criminalised in one way or another (cf. Burney 2005), some of which, however, were until recently seen as a normal side product of an urban society, admittedly not particularly pleasant for everybody, yet nevertheless not a legitimate subject-matter of criminalisation (cf. Roberts 2006). Although days may be numbered for the controversial ASBO orders, observers note that the two new powers that are supposed to replace it (the Criminal Behaviour Order and the Crime Prevention Injunction) 'represent little more than a "rebranding" of the pre-existing tools' (Crawford 2013: 186).

In addition to problems of substance of that which is prohibited as disorder, there are problems of 'form', of proportionality and of legal certainty. In order not to stray too far from the substantive-normative focus of this chapter, these problems will only briefly be mentioned at this point, yet they are worth mentioning, as they, too, have repercussions for the legitimacy of disorder measures.

Form

In terms of the type of regulation used to tackle incivilities, what is striking is that such conduct tends to be criminalised through 'the back door'; either through the civil law or through the law on violations and administrative offences.

As regards the first type: some call it two-step prohibitions (Simester and von Hirsch 2006) or hybrid procedure (Ashworth 2000). A clear example of such regulation is the English anti-social behaviour legislation.[22] Anti-social behaviour orders (ASBOs) are civil-law orders, which, when breached, regain criminal nature, as the breach may lead to conviction with a penalty of imprisonment of maximum 5 years. A public authority in the first part brings civil proceedings, which may then provide substantive foundation for a later criminal prosecution (Ashworth 2000). This confusion of the nature of the matter blurs the boundaries between the civil and criminal, which has repercussions affecting the scope of

22 The *Crime and Disorder Act* 1998 introduced so-called ASBOs (*Anti-Social Behaviour Orders*), which came into force in England and Wales in 1999. They are being used against individuals who act in improper, anti-social ways, which presumably negatively affects the quality of life in neighbourhoods (Budd and Sims 2001). 'Proceedings may be initiated by the police or by the local authority, who must prove to the civil standard (a balance of probabilities) that the defendant has acted "in a manner that caused or was likely to cause harassment, alarm or distress to one or more persons not of the same household as himself". The magistrates may then make an ASBO, prohibiting a person from "doing anything described in the order" for a minimum of 2 years. A defendant who breaches the terms of the order without reasonable excuse is liable to conviction of an offence for which the maximum penalty is five years' imprisonment, and for which a magistrates' court is not allowed to grant a conditional discharge' (Ashworth 2000: 231). The order can be issued to a child of at least 10 years and it often prohibits the person from entering or accessing certain areas or behaving in a certain way. See more in Burney (2002), Campbell (2002) and West (2005).

criminal law as it bypasses certain principles of modern criminal law (e.g. *ultima ratio*) and this is not just of academic, theoretical importance. On the contrary, it has very practical consequences, since if a matter is classified as criminal in nature, there are certain procedural guarantees (minimum rights) that must be granted to the defendant.

The second type, i.e. criminalising incivilities through the law on violations, can particularly be observed in civil-law systems (such as the criminal legal system of Germanic legal tradition) that know two areas of law that both comprise the so-called criminal law *lato sensu* (criminal law in the broad sense): one being criminal law proper and the other the law on violations. Violations fall somewhere between the criminal law and administrative law and a lot has been written on which area befits violations best. Most authors, however, conclude that owing to its penalties and similarities in procedure (subsidiarity of criminal procedure), it is a type of criminal law. At least some particular violations, furthermore, carry censure – a typical element of criminal law offences. Because they are traditionally considered less serious, violations, even in legal and scholarly circles, often remain below radar. However, they may be even more dangerous in terms of liberty infringements as they tend to spread (every new statute in Slovenia has, for example, a 'violations' part at the end) and become unintelligible. As the law on violations usually involves greater ease of enactment, less media and scholarly attention, prohibiting some conduct as a violation, instead of making it into a criminal offence proper, can often mean taking a shortcut. In other words, the law on violations can be easily abused – in the sense that the conduct that should not be proscribed at all (not be made criminal even in the 'broader sense', i.e. as a violation) can be easily enacted under the law on violations.

Proportionality

Tied to this is the sentencing issue, more concretely the question of proportionality between the offence and its penalty. As violations fall outside criminal law *stricto sensu*, the concerns regarding proportionality in violations or administrative, regulatory offences are often neglected. Yet, even where disorder violations are punished by fines alone, the pecuniary sanction has to reflect the gravity of the violation. Punishment should be allocated in proportion to the perceived harm in order for the law to be perceived as morally credible (Fagan 2008). The asymmetry between the harm entailed in the infringement and the severity of the fine raises distributive justice concerns, which jeopardises the legitimacy of law. Some may argue that fines (typical sanctions for violations), particularly when they are small, do not contain censure and are hence not on a par with the criminal sanction or 'punishment' proper,[23] which may have repercussions for the proportionality

23 Many see censure (or moral condemnation, disapprobation) as a typical or defining characteristic of a criminal sanction – as that which distinguishes 'punishment' from other types of sanctioning (see, for example, von Hirsch 1993, Simester and Sullivan 2003).

requirement, yet what is a minor or negligible fine for the well-off may be a significant penalty (and felt like a punishment) for those struggling to make ends meet. Moreover, punishment is not the only thing that defines what is 'criminal' and therefore it need not really be particularly harsh. In the case of *Öztürk v. Germany*[24] the European Court of Human Rights held that '[t]he relative lack of seriousness of the penalty at stake ... cannot divest an offence of its inherently criminal character' (§54).

It is clear that several existing disorder sanctions infringe the principle of proportionality. The breach of an ASBO – which may have been obtained for a trivial offence, such as 'hanging about' – could earn one an imprisonment sentence for up to five years. The fact that a prison sentence can be pronounced for such a violation (or perhaps any violation of a civil order) at all seems to be a violation of the proportionality requirement (cf. Duff and Marshall 2006). An ASBO, being a two-step prohibition, also seems to involve two-step proportionality problems: firstly, the problem of disproportionality between the original ASB conduct and the restrictions imposed by the ASBO issued (e.g. restrictions or prohibitions of certain activities, prohibition to return to a certain area, etc.) and, secondly, the proportionality problem between the breach of a civil order and the criminal sanction. Regarding the latter, Simester and von Hirsch (2006: 189) remind us that '[p]unishment ought, in principle, to be determined primarily by reference to the gravity and wrongfulness of D's actual conduct ... not by reference to the fact per se that it has been prohibited by the order'.

Moreover, some disorder sanctions raise relative proportionality concerns. Relative proportionality between sanctions should reflect the proportionality between offences. Offences of similar nature or similar seriousness merit relatively similar sanction. This problem can be observed in the case of the city of Brussels, for example. A fine between €50 and €250 can be incurred for littering as well as for leaving rubbish out on incorrect days or uttering insults. Clearly there are significant differences between the seriousness (harmfulness and, in particular, wrongfulness) of these offences, yet the penalty (or the penalty interval) is the same.

Legal Certainty

When it is local communities (sub-national level) that are invested with such criminalising powers, the temptation to use them is great. With the main centres of power being located at the higher, regional, national and even supranational (EU) levels, this 'whip' is invested with great expectations. At the first sight, it seems reasonable, even legitimate, to grant such powers (mainly) to local governments. The latter are presumably better equipped with the knowledge or awareness of the problems that are bothering people in their communities. They may also be more effective in prosecuting infringements. Yet, how far should such delegation of powers go? The delegation of criminalising (in the broad sense) and sanctioning

24 *Öztürk v. Germany* (1984) 6 EHRR 409.

powers, on the other hand, decreases legal certainty – a crucial element of the principle of legality. If one travels across the country or even within one city, when the latter is composed of several communities that have their own mayor and their own regulations in this regard (such as Brussels), one usually has no idea about what a particular local municipality or mayor has decided to penalise with administrative sanctions. Furthermore, accessing this information may not be easy, particularly for non-lawyers or visitors, who are, on the other hand, the most vulnerable and likely not to know the local custom. Additionally, the *lex certa* is violated by the vagueness of some offences: in the UK, by the vague definition of 'anti-social',[25] in Belgium (concretely, in the City of Brussels), by the ambiguous category 'other incivilities', which incurs the administrative fine of €250 maximum and the tax of €50.[26]

This brings up two important dilemmas of disorder regulation of today. Firstly, it is reasonable to expect that the further away from penalising some general wrongful and/or harmful behaviour these disorder prohibitions go, the less likely will people (be able to) comply with them. This provides an additional argument for keeping the harm principle as the main principle of penal intervention in the area of disorder. Secondly, one cannot even talk of compliance with regulations when one is not aware of them. The sheer fact that one has not violated some regulation (e.g. prohibition of littering) has to be then attributed solely to other factors, such as good upbringing, avoidance of informal social control mechanisms (shaming), etc., and not to the respect or compliance with the regulation.

Concluding Thoughts

Criminal law holds a special appeal in the minds of people and governments for reasons of its inherent morality, engagement of emotions and the promise of

25 Cornford (2012: 3) has recently suggested reframing the definition of anti-social conduct by limiting liability only to those who have caused 'justifiable anxiety'. This would, according to him, eliminate the possibility of making criminalisation 'contingent upon irrational judgements'. While this reduces some of the vagueness of the existing definition, 'anxiety' is – similar to resentment – a complex and compound emotion, which may not be a result of the preceding conduct of the other. (Anxiety can arise out of different situations: according to Kemper, it can be experienced when individuals lose power or status in a situation, according to Burke, when their identities are not confirmed and, according to Thamm, when, in view of the changes in power or status, one anticipates that one will lose or gain power/status (in Turner and Stets 2005).)

26 Taxes on the incivilities vary according to the committed offence and range from 50 to 150 euros. They are added to the existing administrative fines (City of Brussels 2013). 'Other incivilities' are described as 'anything that has as a consequence the making of the roads or public places dirty or infringing public cleanliness' ('tout fait ayant pour conséquence de salir les voies ou lieux publics ou d'y porter atteinte à la propreté publique'). See *Règlement-taxe sur les incivilités en matière de propreté publique*, OJ no. 20, 19 December 2011, Art. 2, point. 5 (Ville de Bruxelles 2011).

'blood' in the shape of punishment. Criminal law displays and operates with certain symbolism and rhetoric that captures people's imagination. As criminalisation is often seen as a tool for 'correction' of some social anomaly,[27] the criminal law as such provides a great litmus test of societal values, tolerance and insecurities. It addresses our values and emotions more than any other type of law. The changing or amending of the criminal law, and even the speed with which laws are amended, thus mirrors the changes in the societal value system. Moreover, it mirrors the changes in how 'others' are perceived and treated. Channelling these values, emotions and expectations into a rational and reasonable criminal policy requires filtering them through the criteria for criminalisation that have been found legitimate in the modern criminal law system.

The theory and philosophy on how criminal law norms ought to be made, the normative criminalisation theory, can be of help here, providing interesting insights and guiding principles to policy-making, which are particularly strong when reinforced with criminological observations. The application of the criminalisation theory to the area of disorder or incivilities is particularly lacking, which is partly also due to their 'borderline' status, falling between criminal and administrative spheres.[28] In preceding chapters I have attempted to sketch out the main tenets of the normative criminalisation theory, in order to draw some implications thereof for the legal regulation of disorder, the underlying concern here being one of the legitimacy of criminal law in the broad sense and legitimacy of criminalisation as a process. One of the conclusions has been that while additional principles of criminalisation such as the offence principle – particularly susceptible to taking into account cultural or regional variability – may be more justified in the area of disorder regulation than in the area of criminal law proper, sailing away from the harm principle or 'wrongful harm' as the basis for criminalisation entails risks of overreach and reduced legal certainty.

If criminal law has anything to offer to the liberal, democratic society in terms of solving its societal problems, it would be well advised to strictly adhere to its liberal, democratic principles. Failing to do that can only increase societal harm and add to the state legitimacy crisis. The slippery slope effect is not to be neglected, as once the expansion of punitive measures is left unchecked it becomes tempting to use them on anything and anybody who is 'different'. When criminalisation is no longer seen as the last resort of state intervention but rather, as Ashworth and Zedner (2008: 43) put it, 'as a routine system for managing disorder there is [also] little inhibition in employing it liberally to regulate minor forms of offence'.

27 People widely perceive crime (despite being a very 'normal' social phenomenon) as an anomaly, a deviation from 'normality'.

28 There have been some attempts, most notably by von Hirsch and Simester. Particularly insightful in this area are the studies that combine criminological, psychological and sociological findings with jurisprudential and philosophical reflections (see in von Hirsch and Simester (eds) 2006), based on an interdisciplinary approach.

This is confirmed by the expansive trend in the regulation of disorder, be it in the USA, UK, Belgium,[29] France or elsewhere in Europe. In many cases, this almost knee-jerk societal reaction to a problem that empirically may not be on the rise (Husak 2006) or may even be 'problematic', turns out to be inappropriate from the normative legitimacy point of view as well as in its effectiveness. Will penalising people for e.g. being rude on the street[30] really socialise them into becoming more polite, for example? When these sorts of considerations are not even taken into account when the government, be it national or local, decides to invoke penal law to deal with a certain type of disorder or nuisance, an additional shadow is cast over the legitimacy of disorder regulation and, ultimately, over the legitimacy of the state. This is unsurprising perhaps as states that lack legitimacy tend to 'devote more resources to maintaining their rule and less to effective governance' (Gilley 2006: 499). While there are clearly certain things or behaviours society should not tolerate, maintaining the rule purely for the sake of maintaining the rule and a general lowering of societal tolerance towards anything 'different', albeit harmless, leads to its brutalisation, rather than to its civilisation process. It may earn the state points on the authoritarian scale but adds nothing to the legitimacy of its legislative devices.

References

Almond, P. 2008. Public perceptions of work-related fatality cases: Reaching the outer limits of 'populist punitiveness'. *British Journal of Criminology*, 48(4), 448–67.

Ashworth, A. 2000. Is the criminal law a lost cause? *The Law Quarterly Review*, 116, 225–56.

Ashworth, A. 2013. Die Rettungspflicht im englischen Recht: Sinnvolle Einschränkungen oder 'Island Mentality'?, in *Solidaritätspflichten und Loyalitätspflichten als Kriminalisierungsgründe*, edited by A. von Hirsch et al. Baden-Baden: Nomos, 115–30.

Ashworth, A. and Zedner, L. 2008. Defending the criminal law: Reflections on the changing character of crime, procedures, and sanctions. *Criminal Law and Philosophy*, 2(1), 21–51.

BBC. 2012. Bad language fines and other travel news [Online, 12 September]. Available at: http://news.bbc.co.uk/2/hi/programmes/fast_track/9750622.stm [accessed: 20 October 2012].

29 On Belgian situation in particular, see more in Vander Beken and Vandeviver (in this volume).

30 Brussels authorities have decided to fine insulting language spoken on the streets in Brussels with a fine of up to 250 euros. The mayor has been reported as saying that the rationale behind this is to crack down on the everyday unpleasantness found in any big city (BBC 2012).

Bottoms, A. 2006. Incivilities, offence and social order in residential communities, in *Incivilities: Regulating Offensive Behaviour*, edited by A. von Hirsch and A. Simester. Oxford: Hart Publishing, 239–80.

Breakwell, G.M. 2007. *The Psychology of Risk*. Cambridge: Cambridge University Press.

Brown, D.G. 1999. Mill on liberty and morality. *The Philosophical Review*, 81(2), 133–58.

Budd, T. and Sims, L. 2001. Antisocial behaviour and disorder: Findings from the 2000 British Crime Survey. *Findings 145*. London: Home Office.

Burney, E. 2002. Talking tough, acting coy: What happened to the Anti-Social Behaviour Order? *The Howard Journal*, 41(5), 469–84.

Burney, E. 2005. *Making People Behave: Anti-Social Behaviour, Politics and Policy*. Devon: Willan Publishing.

Campbell, S. 2002. Implementing Anti-social Behaviour Orders: Message for practitioners. *Findings 160*. London: Home Office.

City of Brussels. 2013. Fight against incivilities [Online]. Available at: http://www.brussels.be/artdet.cfm/4034 [accessed: 15 May 2013].

Cohen, S. 1972. *Folk Devils and Moral Panics*. London: MacGibbon and Kee.

Cornford, A. 2012. Criminalising anti-social behaviour. *Criminal Law and Philosophy*, 6(1), 1–19.

Council of the EU. 2009. *Conclusions on model provisions, guiding the Council's criminal law negotiation*, 2979th Justice and Home Affairs Council meeting, Brussels, 30 November 2009.

Crawford, A. 2013. 'Sticks and carrots … and sermons': Some thoughts on compliance and legitimacy in the regulation of youth anti-social behaviour, in *Legitimacy and Compliance in Criminal Justice*, edited by A. Crawford and A. Hucklesby. Oxford, New York: Routledge, 181–214.

Devlin, P. 1965. *The Enforcement of Morals*. Oxford: Oxford University Press.

Dubber, M.D. 2007. Legitimating penal law. *Cardozo Law Review*, 28(6), 2597–613.

Duff, R.A. and Marshall, S.E. 2006. How offensive can you get?, in *Incivilities: Regulating Offensive Behaviour*, edited by A. von Hirsch and A.P. Simester. Oxford: Hart Publishing, 57–90.

European Commission. 2011. *Towards an EU Criminal Policy: Ensuring the Effective Implementation of EU Policies through Criminal Law*, COM(2011) 573 final of 20 September 2011.

European Criminal Policy Initiative 2011. The Manifesto on European Criminal Policy in 2011, *European Criminal Law Review (EuCLR)*, 1(1), 86–103.

European Parliament. 2012. *European Parliament resolution of 22 May 2012 on an EU approach to criminal law*, 2010/2310(INI) of 6 June 2012.

Fagan, J. 2008. Legitimacy and criminal justice: Introduction. *Ohio State Journal of Criminal Law*, 6 (1), 123–40.

Feinberg, J. 1984. *Harm to Others – The Moral Limits of the Criminal Law*. New York: Oxford University Press.

Feinberg, J. 1986. *Harm to Self: The Moral Limits of the Criminal Law*. New York: Oxford University Press.

Feinberg, J. 1988. *Harmless Wrongdoing: The Moral Limits of the Criminal Law*. New York: Oxford University Press.

Gilley, B. 2006. The meaning and measure of state legitimacy: Results for 72 countries. *European Journal of Political Research*, 45(3), 499–525.

Hefendehl, R., von Hirsch, A. and Wohlers, W. (eds) 2003. *Die Rechtsgutstheorie – Legitimationsbasis des Strafrechts oder dogmatisches Glasperlenspiel?* Baden Baden: Nomos Verlagsgesellschaft.

Hulsman, L.H.C. 1986. Critical criminology and the concept of crime. *Contemporary Crises*, 10(1), 63–80.

Husak, D. 2006. Disgust: Metaphysical and empirical speculations, in *Incivilities: Regulating Offensive Behaviour*, edited by A. von Hirsch and A. Simester. Oxford: Hart Publishing, 91–114.

Igličar, A. 2012. Normativna integracija in (slovenski) zakonodajalec ter sodnik, in *Tretja od suhih krav: razprave o razlogih za razsulo*, edited by B.M. Zupančič. Domžale: Samozaložba A. Komat, 211–43.

Jareborg, N. 2005. Criminalization as last resort (ultima ratio). *Ohio State Journal of Criminal Law*, 2, 521–34.

Jellinek, G. 1878. *Die Sozialethische Bedeutung von Recht, Unrecht und Strafe*. Vienna: Alfred Hölder.

Lahti, R. 2000. Towards a Rational and Humane Criminal Policy – Trends in Scandinavian Penal Thinking. *Journal of Scandinavian Studies in Criminology and Crime Prevention*, 1(2), 141–55.

Lernestedt, C. 2012. Victim and society: Sharing wrongs, but in which roles? *Criminal Law and Philosophy*, October 2012 (Online first). Available at: DOI 10.1007/s11572-012-9188-3.

Levi, M. 2008. White-collar, organised and cyber crimes in the media: Some contrasts and similarities. *Crime, Law and Social Change*, 49, 365–77.

Lords Hansard. 2009. 18 May 2009: Column 1273 [Online]. Available at: http://www.publications.parliament.uk/pa/ld200809/ldhansrd/text/90518-0011.htm [accessed: 25 July 2012].

Mill, J.S. 1991 (orig. 1859). *On Liberty and Other Essays*. Oxford: Oxford University Press.

Mishler, W. and Rose, R. 1997. Trust, distrust and scepticism: Popular evaluations of civil and political institutions in post-Communist societies. *The Journal of Politics*, 59(2), 418–51.

Moscovici, S. 1984. The phenomenon of social representations, in *Social Representations*, edited by R.M. Farr and S. Moscovici. Cambridge: Cambridge University Press, 3–69.

Oxford Dictionary. 2013. Alarm, in Oxford Dictionaries. Oxford University Press [Online]. Available at: http://oxforddictionaries.com/definition/english/alarm?q=alarm [accessed: 10 May 2013].

Peršak, N. 2004. 'Pravni paternalizem' in 'pravni moralizem' kot podlagi inkriminiranja. *Rev. krim. kriminol.*, 55(2), 119–26.

Peršak, N. 2007a. *Criminalising Harmful Conduct: Harm Principle, its Limits and Continental Counterparts*. New York: Springer.

Peršak, N. 2007b. *Representations of the Anti-Social* (MPhil thesis), University of Cambridge.

Peršak 2010. In den Nebengebieten des Strafrechts: Paternalistische Interventionen im Recht der Ordnungswidrigkeiten, in *Paternalismus im Strafrecht: die Kriminalisierung von selbstschädigendem Verhalten* (Studien zur Strafrechtstheorie und Strafrechtsethik 1), edited by A. von Hirsch, U. Neumann and K. Seelmann. Baden-Baden: Nomos, 173–91.

Peršak, N. 2012a. Building justice through criminal law: Issues of criminalisation and trust, in *Building Justice in Post-Transition Europe? Processes of Criminalisation within Central and Eastern European Societies* (Routledge Frontiers of Criminal Justice 2), edited by K. Goodall, M. Malloch and B. Munro. London: Routledge, 43–55.

Peršak, N. 2012b. Criminal law, the victim and community: The shades of 'we' and the conceptual involvement of community in contemporary criminal law theory. *Criminal Law and Philosophy*, October 2012 (Online first). Available at: DOI 10.1007/s11572-012-9189-2.

Reding, V. 2012. Using criminal law to support growth and economic recovery (press release) [Online]. Available at: http://europa.eu/rapid/press-release_SPEECH-12-461_en.htm [accessed: 10 March 2013].

Roberts, J.V. and Hough, M. 2005. *Understanding Public Attitudes to Criminal Justice*. Maidenhead: Open University Press.

Roberts, P. 2006. Penal offence in question: Some reference points for interdisciplinary conversation, in *Incivilities: Regulating Offensive Behaviour*, edited by A. von Hirsch and A. Simester. Oxford: Hart Publishing, 1–56.

Robinson, P.H. 2000. Why does the criminal law care what the layperson thinks is just? Coercive versus normative crime control. *Virginia Law Review*, 86(8), 1839–69.

Schonsheck, J. 1994. *On Criminalization: An Essay in the Philosophy of the Criminal Law*. Dordrecht, Boston, London: Kluwer.

Scraton, P. and Chadwick, K. 1991. The theoretical and political priorities of critical criminology, in *Criminological perspectives: Essential Readings*, edited by E. McLaughlin, J. Muncie and G. Hughes. London: Sage Publications, 294–309.

Simester, A.P. and Sullivan, G.R. 2003. *Criminal Law Theory and Doctrine*, 2nd edn. Oxford: Hart Publishing.

Simester, A.P. and von Hirsch, A. 2006. Regulating offensive conduct through two-step prohibitions, in *Incivilities: Regulating Offensive Behaviour*, edited by A. von Hirsch and A.P. Simester. Oxford: Hart Publishing, 173–94.

Simester, A.P. and von Hirsch, A. 2011. *Crimes, Harms and Wrongs: On the Principles of Criminalisation*. Oxford: Hart Publishing.

Treaty on European Union (TEU, Consolidated version). 2010. *Official Journal of the European Union*, C 83/13, 30 March 2010.

Turner, A.H. and Stets, A.E. 2005. *The Sociology of Emotions*. Cambridge, New York: Cambridge University Press.

Ville de Bruxelles. 2011. *Règlement-taxe sur les incivilités en matière de propreté publique*, OJ no. 20, 19 December 2011.

von Hirsch, A. 1993. *Censure and Sanctions*. Oxford: Clarendon Press.

von Hirsch, A. 1996. Extending the harm principle: 'Remote' harms and fair imputation, in *Harm and Culpability*, edited by A.P. Simester and A.T.H. Smith. Oxford: Hart Publishing, 259–76.

von Hirsch, A. 2003. Das Rechtsguts Begriff und das 'Harm Principle', in *Die Rechtsgutstheorie – Legitimationsbasis des Strafrechts oder dogmatisches Glasperlenspiel?*, edited by R. Hefendehl, A. von Hirsch and W. Wohlers. Baden Baden: Nomos Verlagsgesellschaft, 13–25.

von Hirsch, A. and Simester, A.P. 2006. Penalising offensive behaviour, in *Incivilities: Regulating Offensive Behaviour*, edited by A. von Hirsch and A.P. Simester. Oxford: Hart Publishing, 115–31.

von Hirsch, A. and A.P. Simester (eds) 2006. *Incivilities: Regulating Offensive Behaviour*. Oxford: Hart Publishing.

West, E. 2005. *A Little Book of ASBOs: Asbolent Behaviour from Around the Country*. Cheam: Crombie Jardine.

Chapter 3

When Things Get Serious: Reflections on the Legitimacy of Local Administrative Sanctions in Belgium

Tom Vander Beken and Christophe Vandeviver

Introduction

Research has shown that people obey the law and cooperate with legal authorities primarily if and when they believe those legal authorities are legitimate (Tyler 2006). Legitimacy can be formally defined as the right to rule and the recognition by the ruled of that right (Sternberger 1968). In that respect, legitimacy can be seen as a sort of quality label for authorities that is attributed by society as a whole. With this label authorities can justify their interventions and use of force against certain members of this society. Moreover, in theory legitimacy is, or could be, a normative discussion about certain standards that states and institutions ought to meet. In contrast to this, empirical legitimacy is believed to be easier to define and measure (Hough et al. 2010) as it does not focus on theoretical standards, but rather on the attribution of legitimacy to an authority or an institution.

There is a strong line of research that considers legitimacy a product of how authorities treat citizens and make decisions when they are exercising their regulatory power (Schulhofer, Tyler and Huq 2011, Jackson et al. 2012). Legitimacy is conceptualised in terms of procedural justice and fairness in decision-making, including neutral and non-discriminatory behaviour and fair interpersonal treatment (Tyler 2011).

In this chapter, we aim to explore discussions about legitimacy in the context of local administrative sanctions in Belgium. In 1999 a new sanctioning system was introduced in Belgium, allowing local municipalities to define, report and sanction certain behaviours that are perceived as public nuisance. So far, no specific questionnaires and survey questions that tap into the appreciation and trust of the general public in the local administrative sanctioning system in Belgium have been administered. For our current study, we have cursorily examined the 2,694 articles on local administrative sanctions that have been published in a selection of Flemish newspapers since 1999 until 2013.

With this scan we aim to capture the evolution of the perception of this new sanctioning system in a part of Belgium and feed this into the discussions on legitimacy.

The Background

To understand the introduction of the system of local administrative sanctions in Belgium, it is necessary to briefly introduce the political background in Belgium relating to issues of crime and safety.

In the last decades of the twentieth century, Belgium suffered under various events and scandals that shook the political institutions and challenged their authority to deal with issues of crime and safety. In the 1980s, there were the extremely violent raids and killings of the Brabant killers (Bende Van Nijvel), terrorist attacks of the Communist Combatant Cells (Cellules Communistes Combattante), the death of 39 football supporters at the 1985 European Cup Final in the Heysel Stadium and many other incidents that led to the image of a malfunctioning police apparatus and justice system. In combination with an emerging concern about the increased migration, a rapidly changing demographic situation in the major cities and the political success of the extreme right Vlaams Blok (in 1991) in Flanders (one of the three Belgian regions), the Belgian situation was described as a legitimacy crisis of politics and politicians (Huyse 1996). In 1996, the Dutroux case on the abduction, sexual exploitation and murder of children once again disclosed a serious malfunctioning of police and justice. In October 1996 more than 300,000 Belgians held a White March in Brussels to show their distrust and discontent with the current situation.

In this period, crime rates remained rather stable but showed a rise in (the reporting on) petty crimes. Especially in the major cities, feelings of insecurity became a political issue. Several safety questionnaires, the so-called Security Monitors, were conducted from 1997 onwards. The results showed that feelings of insecurity were not so much related to serious crime issues but rather and far more to all sorts of nuisances and petty crimes, the so-called incivilities. Consequently, tackling people's concerns about these incivilities became a prominent political issue. The introduction of a sanctioning system that could aptly and swiftly react to those incivilities perfectly fits within this political undercurrent.

There is, however, more to be said about the introduction of the system of local administrative sanctions in Belgium. Though, at the time, many aspects of Garland's (2001) culture of control could also be discerned in Belgium, research has shown that in relation to the context of the development of local administrative sanctions the Belgian situation seems to differ from what can be observed in the Anglo-Saxon context (Devroe 2012). Similar to findings on the Belgian penal policy (see Snacken 2007), aspects relating to social welfare seem to be able to keep its own place in this late modern society. Belgian society does not cover all features of a real culture of control (Devroe 2012).

There are arguments that the constitutional reforms since 1980 onwards that provide a partial explanation for this. The constitutional reforms have transferred certain policy domains and regulatory powers from the federal to the regional level (communities and regions). In this transfer, most social welfare (and preventive) instruments have been attributed to the regions and communities (education, environment, labour, urban planning, care, etc.). This implied a considerable loss of power for the federal level and made it impossible to keep all aspects of crime control and safety policy in the hands of the federal authorities. After the constitutional reform, the federal state was only left with issues of repression (Ministry of Justice) and public order (Ministry of the Interior). Confronted with the urgent call for action against feelings of insecurity in a country in which the demarcation between social preventive action (welfare) and public order and repression (penal) is firmly embedded in the constitution, the federal state developed the repressive part of the policy. Yet, this did not mean that the repressive line was the only policy line. Following, and maybe thanks to, the constitutional division, other actors explicitly took up and developed social welfare and preventive action. In a broad sense, the reaction to public insecurity was therefore not limited to public order and repression alone. In a strict sense, however, it mainly came down to a punitive reaction: a federal instrument sanctioning incivilities in the cities.

The System of Local Administrative Sanctions

The Act of 13 May 1999 introduced a system that empowered municipal authorities to define certain behaviour as public nuisance (incivilities) and to sanction such conduct with a local administrative sanction (mostly fines) and an option to appeal to the police court. The Act of 1999 allowed municipal authorities only to react to those types of behaviour for which neither the federal nor the regional Parliament has provided penalties. In other words, municipalities could only react to 'new' types of public nuisance that have not been already addressed by the existing legislation and sanctioning system. In practical terms, local administrative sanction legislation proved to be an empty barrel for the municipalities. As the overlap with existing provisions elsewhere was formally excluded, local councils had not much room for manoeuvre. Moreover, the Act of 1999 allowed municipalities to draft their own laws, but did not allow them to appoint designated enforcement staff. Incivilities could only be established by a report made by the police (Devroe 2008).

In 2004 and 2005, several acts[1] amended the initial local administrative sanctions legislation allowing municipalities to sanction certain 'mixed violations', i.e. behaviour that qualifies both as a criminal offence and a local incivility. 'Milder' mixed violations could only be sanctioned by the local authorities if the public prosecutor refrained from prosecution. More 'serious' mixed violations could only be the subject of a local administrative sanction if the public prosecutor deliberately transferred the case to the municipal authorities. From 2005 onwards, municipal officers could draft reports and establish incivilities in addition to the police. With the amended law, minors (16–18-year-olds) could also be subjected to a local administrative sanction; however, only after they have been invited to participate in the mediation (Vander Beken 2005).

---

1 The Acts of 7 May 2004, 17 June 2004 and 20 July 2005.

A bill was introduced in 2012 to lower the age limit for the application of local administrative sanctions and to increase the amount of the fines. If these proposed amendments are accepted,[2] it will be possible to subject 14-year-olds to a local administrative sanction and the minimum and maximum fines will be raised from €125 to €175 and €250 to €350, respectively.

Taking only the implementation rate in the municipalities into account – i.e. whether or not the municipal authorities have drafted a special set of local rules with definitions of incivilities and have set up a local sanctioning system – the legislation on local administrative sanctions can be considered a success. According to the umbrella organisation of Flemish municipalities, just 10 per cent of all Flemish municipalities had implemented the system in 2005 (VVSG 2012). In 2012, already 83.12 per cent (N=256) of the Flemish municipalities had implemented the local administrative sanctions. Only 28 (9.09 per cent) have not implemented the system to date, while 8 (2.60 per cent) are planning to implement it shortly and 16 (5.19 per cent) are still considering whether to implement it or not.[3]

A Small-Scale Exploratory Media Study

In order to substantiate our discussion about the legitimacy of local administrative sanctions in Flanders, a small-scale exploratory media study was set up using a quantitative and qualitative design.

The quantitative part of this chapter aims to gain insight in the number of articles on the local administrative sanctions that have been published in the Flemish newspapers and the evolution in publishing frequency throughout the adopted time frame. In a sense, it also allows for an initial substantive screening of the various topics that may be relevant for the discussion on empirical legitimacy and procedural justice. It focuses on general trends, rather than on specific content. A major critique regarding the procedural fairness of the local administrative sanctions has to do with the fact that the entire procedure is dominated by the municipal authorities, from the definition of undesirable behaviour down to the imposition of the sanction. In that respect, what is in particular mentioned is the fact that the municipal authorities act as judge while lacking the constitutionally

2 In its plenary session of Thursday May 30 2013, the Federal Parliament adopted the bill with ample majority. Currently, the text is to be evaluated one last time by the Council of State. It is expected that the law will be published in July in the Moniteur Belge and it will enter into force on the first day of the sixth month following publication.

3 For a geographical distribution of these four categories of municipalities, see VVSG 2012 (scroll down for a map 'GAS – invoering Vlaanderen – 1/8/2012'). Green coloured are the municipalities that have implemented the local administrative sanctions legislation, red represents those that have not implemented the local administrative sanctions legislation, light green ones plan to implement the local administrative sanctions legislation shortly, while those that are still contemplating the potential implementation are coloured purple.

required independence (Vander Beken 2004). This prompted us to adopt a series of search strings related to judges and courts.

In the qualitative part of this paper, we focused on a selection of editorials and opinion articles about the local administrative sanctions. The aim of this part is to get a deeper insight into the substantive discourses and the various critiques on the local administrative sanctioning system. In a sense, this section complements the quantitative part by trying to find out what the broader discussion is about; as the quantitative part of this paper especially seems to tell us what the discussion is not about – this will be further elaborated on later on.

Media Coverage on Local Administrative Sanctions Related to Procedural Justice

Design

The quantitative study used predefined search strings relating to local administrative sanctions, in general, and their legitimacy, in particular, to perform a cursory examination of the Mediargus database. Mediargus is an online, daily press-monitoring database that indexes the paper and online editions of all Flemish newspapers as well as a selection of paper magazines. For this exploratory study, however, we only took into account the paper editions of those Flemish newspapers that have been indexed uninterruptedly since the inception of the local administrative sanctions legislation. This strategy has the advantage that it excludes duplicate articles that have been published both in the online and paper edition of a particular newspaper and that fluctuations in the number of articles found are not caused by the discontinuation of certain newspapers during the study period (e.g. *Het Volk*). In particular, only the paper editions of *De Morgen*, *De Standaard*, *De Tijd*, *Gazet van Antwerpen*, *Het Belang van Limburg*, *Het Laatste Nieuws* and *Het Nieuwsblad* have been included, resulting in a mix of broadsheet and tabloid newspapers.

The media study spanned a total of 14 years and included articles that have been published between 1 January 1999, the year when the original Act on the local administrative sanctioning system was introduced, and 31 December 2012 inclusive.

The relevant topics were operationalised using search strings, while common Boolean search strategies were adopted to obtain the required information and further our goal to substantiate our initial claims.[4] First, we determined how many articles related to the local administrative sanctions have been published in the Flemish newspapers in the considered time frame. This helps to illustrate the

4 The search strings and strategies are (translated from Dutch): 'local administrative sanctions' OR 'local administrative sanction'; 'local administrative sanctions' +judge OR 'local administrative sanction' +judge.

presence or absence of local administrative sanctions in the media debate and allows linking the activity of the written media to the legislative process and the public debate. Second, the presence of specific procedural issues, such as the fact that local administrative sanctions are imposed by a municipal officer and not by an independent judge, was scrutinised.

Both the absolute number of articles that relate to a particular search strategy as well as the relative number of articles have been considered. The relative number of articles was obtained by dividing the number of articles that a particular search strategy yielded in a given time window by the total amount of articles that relate to local administrative sanctions in general for that same time window. Arguably, this latter measure is more appropriate to discuss the importance of a particular topic since it corrects for an inflation of the overall number of articles on the local administrative sanctions. If the total amount of articles on the local administrative sanctions increases, one could expect by the same token that the number of articles on a related topic would also increase. When scrutinising only the absolute number of articles on a related topic, one could erroneously conclude that this particular topic has increased in importance and presence in the media debate, while the relative number of articles could signal that, in fact, this particular topic only makes up a fraction of the total number of articles on the local administrative sanctions.

Results

We begin with gauging the total number of articles on local administrative sanctions that have been published in the Flemish newspapers since the introduction of the legislation on local administrative sanctions. Over the past 14 years, the local administrative sanctions have been well covered by the media: a total of 2,694 articles discussed the local administrative sanctions, with the majority of articles having been published in the past three years. Looking at the absolute number of articles related to local administrative sanctions in Flemish newspapers, three major periods can be distinguished, which correspond to the initial introduction of the legislation (1999–2004), the amendments resulting in a broader applicability (2005–11) and the suggested second amendments potentially resulting in a lower age limit and increased amount of fines (2012).

The first period covers the years 1999 to 2004 and corresponds to the introduction and the first hesitant steps towards the implementation of the local administrative sanctions legislation. Although the local administrative sanctions legislation was introduced in 1999 and empowered local authorities to sanction certain types of unwanted behaviour, its scope was rather restricted and limited until the adopted changes in 2005 and only a handful of local authorities decided to use these newly introduced sanctioning powers. The limited implementation seems to be reflected in the scant number of articles that are devoted to local administrative sanctions. During this six-year period, only 21 articles on local administrative sanctions have been published, averaging at just over three articles a year (concretely, three in 1999, two in 2000, seven in 2001, one in 2002, two in 2003 and six in 2004).

The second period covers the years 2005 to 2011. In 2005, the Federal Parliament amended the initial legislation and broadened its applicability. These amendments allowed local authorities to sanction additional types of behaviour, granted certain civil servants the right to draw up reports in addition to police officers and made it possible for minors between the ages of 16–18 to become subject to a local administrative sanction. The adopted amendments were clearly aimed at strengthening the legislation and resulted in a more widespread implementation, which seems to be mirrored by the steadily increasing number of articles on the local administrative sanctions that have been published in the paper editions of the Flemish newspapers during this seven-year period. A total of 2,075 articles have been published during this period (120 in 2005, 200 in 2006, 289 in 2007, 333 in 2008, 383 in 2009, 325 in 2010 and 425 in 2011), with an average of 296 articles per year. After the initial surge from 4 articles in 2004 to 120 articles in 2005, every following year saw the number of articles on the local administrative sanctions steadily increasing, culminating in a total of 425 articles in 2011. Although a small decrease can be observed in 2010, the overall trend is positive and shows that the number of articles on the local administrative sanctions increases year after year, signalling that the local administrative sanctions are a topic that is very present in the media.

The last period covers the last year (2012) and seems to coincide with the increased attention for local administrative sanctions following the proposed amendments to lower the age limit for the application of local administrative sanctions to 14-year-olds and to increase the amount of the fines. In 2012, an all-time high of 598 articles have been published that discussed the local administrative sanctions, denoting an increase of approximately 40 per cent in comparison to the year before. This highpoint in the number of articles on the local administrative sanctions suggests that they featured prominently in the media debate in the past year.

Next, we turn our attention to the salience of the fact that municipalities take the role of a judge in the application of the local administrative sanctioning system[5] in the surrounding media debate. Since the introduction of the legislation in 1999, 108 articles discussing this particular topic have been published. Relatively speaking, however, 4.01 per cent of all articles on local administrative sanctions touch upon judicial control in one way or another. Arguably, the (non-)involvement of a judge as a major critique related to the procedural issues seems of little importance in the media debate on local administrative sanctions.

Looking at the relative number of articles related to 'judicial involvement' and 'local administrative sanctions', published in selected Flemish newspapers between 1999 and 2012 more light is shed on the evolution of the relative importance of discussions about the judicial role in the media debate surrounding local administrative sanctions. Generally speaking, this 'judicial' aspect seems to

5 It should be pointed out that a judge *is* involved when an appeal is made.

be little present in the media debate surrounding the local administrative sanctions. In the initial period leading up to the first amendment of the legislation, the judicial role can be seen as an important theme in the media debate surrounding the local administrative sanctions. The relative number of articles shows that one out of three articles and half of all articles in 1999 and 2000 respectively focus on judges and their role in the local administrative sanctioning system. However, the theme quickly dwindles and becomes less important in the media debate. In 2012, just over 5 per cent of all articles are in some way related to the role of the judge. Although in the last three years there seems to be a small increase in the importance of this topic in the media debate, the relative number of articles stays well below the 2000 all-time high. In essence, the figures suggest that judicial involvement was an important media topic following the introduction of the legislation on local administrative sanctions but that it was later quickly forgotten and kept playing only a small role in the media debate. In a way, these figures show that the media debate does not heavily focus on the major procedural issues critique.

Evolution in the Media Discourse on Local Administrative Sanctions

Design

The qualitative study was also exploratory in nature and tapped into the Mediargus database. It focused predominantly on editorials and opinion articles discussing the local administrative sanctions. For the qualitative part, we included the paper editions of a selection of Flemish newspapers.[6] The adopted time frame for the qualitative part spanned a total of 14 years and is not different from the quantitative study.

The goal of the qualitative part was to unearth the substantive discussions on and criticisms of the local administrative sanctions. Using the results of the qualitative part, we intend to outline the media debate. We also aim to uncover how the media perceives the local administrative sanctions and how this perceptions shifts, if it shifts at all, in the past 14 years.

The initial results from the quantitative study were supplemented with a number of search hits in Flemish news magazines. The editorials and opinion articles that discussed the local administrative sanctions were scanned and a selection of relevant articles was made. These articles were synthesised and clustered according to three criteria: (1) the period in which they were published, (2) the discourse or the tone of the article, and (3) which group's opinion is being represented.

6 These are the same as the ones included for the quantitative part of this chapter.

A Well-Supported Idea with Only Some Conceptual Remarks (1999–2005)

In the initial period of the local administrative sanctions legislation, characterised by its inception and the rather hesitant steps taken by the Belgian municipalities to put the legislation in practice, the media debate primarily focuses on the aim and scopes of the local administrative sanctions legislation. Particular attention is paid to the central goals of the legislation and the reasons why this particular legislation is needed are outlined. The adopted discourse in the media can best be described as one that leaves little room for a thorough criticism of the local administrative sanctioning system. The local administrative sanctions are characterised as a much needed and very effective instrument that is not too expensive for the taxpayer.

> The safety monitor shows that citizens especially worry about so-called petty crime like problems with neighbours, dog poop in the public space, noise, flyposting, graffiti etc. This, however, remains unpunished. Luc van den Bossche, Minister of the Interior, wants to do something about this. (Geudens, *Gazet van Antwerpen*, 16 January 1999)

> There is indeed a cost for the municipalities [related to the local administrative sanctions (or LAS)], but if the system is applied well, it will be self-financing. (Tollenaere, *Gazet van Antwerpen*, 27 March 2004)

> The LAS [are] a strong weapon in the fight against petty crime. Lokeren should finish its homework and be able to start at once. (D.V.R., *Gazet van Antwerpen*, 2 October 2004)

Notwithstanding the broad media support for the local administrative sanctioning system, some critiques are observed in the debate. These pertain to the formal aspects of the local administrative sanctions. In particular, the system of local administrative sanctions is questioned for being conceived as a parallel system to the criminal justice system, which, however, lacks the same rigorous legal safeguards present in the latter, i.e. an impartial assessment by an independent judge. This is best illustrated by the words of Hugo Lamon, the president of the Flemish Bar Association:

> If the government believes that certain acts are so refutable that they have to be sanctioned, it should include them in the criminal code … Who guarantees that all municipalities will follow the same policy? … What guarantees an independent and impartial treatment? … Hopefully MPs will have enough common sense to realise that this bill will destabilise the policy of prosecutors, prosecutor-general and the minister. The local government as judge: it takes less to spit in a tram … (Lamon, *De Morgen*, 30 December 2002)

It Works! (2006–11)

In the wake of the 2004 and 2005 amendments of the initial local administrative sanctions legislation, more municipalities implement the local administrative sanctions legislation and the system of local administrative sanctions steadily starts to run at full speed. In their coverage, the Flemish newspapers focus on this widespread implementation, labelling it a 'success'. Other, critical voices remain rather absent from the media debate. This is vividly illustrated by the following selection of quotes:

> Almost no appeal against administrative sanctions (Van Wiele, *Gazet van Antwerpen*, 7 May 2008)
>
> Administrative sanctions work (Bosmans, *Het Laatste Nieuws*, 10 May 2008)
>
> Administrative sanctions widespread (P.C., *De Standaard*, 18 November 2008)
>
> Each year 20,000 administrative sanctions in Antwerp (K.R.G., *De Standaard*, 20 February 2009)
>
> 14-year-old criminals should be punished for nuisance (Van Cauwelaert, *De Morgen*, 27 February 2010)
>
> More and more administrative sanctions in Ghent (Vanden Bussche, *Het Laatste Nieuws*, 9 March 2010)
>
> 17 administrative sanctions for one person (Verheijen, *Gazet van Antwerpen*, 12 March 2011)
>
> Petty crime promptly sanctioned by administrative fine in Antwerp and Ghent (Somers, *De Morgen*, 10 March 2011)
>
> Ghent deals with impunity (Van Damme, *Het Laatste Nieuws*, 16 April 2011)
>
> Drastic rise in administrative sanctions (Willocx, *Gazet van Antwerpen*, 22 April 2011)

Misuse, Protest and Distrust throughout Society (2012)

The tone of the media debate changes drastically in 2012: critical reports of the local administrative sanctions seem the rule rather than the exception. Maybe the local administrative sanctions are too often used in cases when it is believed they are not really necessary and target people that do not really need to be subjected to such sanctions.

> We don't want to become sheriffs (Van den Broeck, *De Morgen*, 4 April 2012)

> Are we all more repressive? (Tegenbos, *De Standaard*, 12 May 2012)

> Already as many local administrative sanctions as in the previous year (Van Synghel, *Het Laatste Nieuws*, 9 October 2012)

> LAS is an instrument to hurt the young and socially vulnerable (Oeyen, *De Morgen*, 13 November 2012)

> LAS cost higher than revenues (Maeckelbergh, *De Morgen*, 22 November 2012)

> The most absurd administrative sanctions of the country (Van Bastelaere, *Het Laatste Nieuws*, 21 November 2012)

These critiques lead to remarkable protests where the legitimacy of the system itself is questioned:

> Flanders has become a strained old people's home. Local administrative sanctions are the end of civilisation (Jan Leyers, singer-songwriter and television personality, quoted in Van den Broeck and Dehandschutter, *De Standaard*, 12 November 2012)

It is noteworthy that the critiques comes from different actors, both in society and politics, and is broadly supported. For example, 30 social and cultural organisations published an open letter in several Flemish newspapers in which they challenge the local administrative sanctions, echoing the previously voiced concern by a major youth movement organisation:

> Local administrative sanctions threaten fundamental democratic rights. When peaceful protest actions can be considered as incivilities, we disgrace the democratic rights we have fought for. The presence of activism and movements is a good indicator for the democratic level of our society. Their existence shows the room (that needs to be) given to raise critical voices and is a condition to work in a democracy where injustice can be put on the agenda and action can be taken to create a viable society for all citizens. (Open letter of 30 social and cultural organisations reprinted in Kets, *De Standaard*, 11 October 2012)

> We dream of a society in which you can put your feet on the seats and party without fines ... Local administrative rules sanction these dreams and turn them into a nightmare. Being young has become a criminal act. (Chirojeugd

> Vlaanderen, a major Flemish youth movement organisation, quoted in Rommers, *De Standaard*, 4 October 2012)

The critique is not limited to civil society. Politicians also voice their concern about the system of local administrative sanctions. For example, the political 'father' of the local administrative sanctions legislation and a mayor of a midsized Flemish city, both, question the system:

> In this case effectiveness and principles of law should go hand in hand and balance each other … I would reduce the law to what I have submitted in 1999. That's what I believe in. Not in the amendments that followed. (Luc Van den Bossche, Minister of the Interior in 1999 who introduced the Bill on local administrative sanctions, quoted in De Coninck, *De Morgen*, 15 November 2012)

> An administrative fine for eating a sandwich was a mistake. (Bart Somers, Mayor of Mechelen, quoted in Légère, *Het Nieuwsblad*, 3 November 2012)

Conclusions

The local administrative sanctions have been created in response to legitimacy problems in the security arena with the intention of forming a repressive capstone of an overall security policy.

The media analysis shows, however, that the local administrative sanctions are currently facing a legitimacy crisis of their own. Although the local administrative sanctioning system initially enjoyed a broad support and was considered a proactive means to actually do something about local safety problems, it is now considered a derailed system and it is threatening to lose much of its initial legitimacy.

It is remarkable that discussions on procedural justice seem to take a limited place in the broader discussions on the legitimacy (crisis) of the administrative sanctioning system. Although concerns about procedure, rule of law and legality have been raised in the wake of the inception of the local administrative sanctioning system, in particular municipal authorities acting as judges and the vagueness of the definition of nuisance, they seem to have become less dominant than expected in the legitimacy debate. Currently, it seems as if the legitimacy of the local administrative sanctions is challenged much more for its consequences – all of us and not just 'the others' are affected – than for the lack of formal integrity of the system itself.

The local administrative sanctioning system has been able to develop outside and alongside other components of the Belgian security policy. The result of this development is that some local authorities have explicitly included their local administrative sanctioning policy in an overarching security policy while others have not. A possible explanation for the legitimacy problems and perceived derailment of the local administrative sanctioning system may be sought at that level. Although in many cities local administrative sanctions are part of a broader safety and prevention policy and treated as the repressive culmination of such a policy, an increasing number of municipalities adopt the local administrative sanctions as an autonomous instrument of a strict control policy. They are convinced that 'in a risk society there is no fear of control, but of chaos' (Van den Broeck 2012: 45). Clearly, they are mistaken.

References

Bosmans, K. 2008. Gemeentelijke sancties werken. *Het Laatste Nieuws*, 10 May, 37.

De Coninck, D. 2012. Huidige GAS-boete klopt niet. *De Morgen*, 15 November, 4.

Devroe, E. 2008. The policy approach of nuisance problems in public space in Belgium and the Netherlands, in *Governance of Security in the Netherlands and Belgium*, edited by L. Cachet. The Hague: Boom Legal Publishers, 149–75.

Devroe, E. 2012. *A Swelling Culture of Control? De Genese en Toepassing van de Wet op de Gemeentelijke Administratieve Sancties in België*. Antwerpen: Maklu.

D.V.R. 2004. Filip en Filip hand in hand tegen kleine criminaliteit. *Gazet van Antwerpen*, 2 October, 24.

Garland, D. 2001. *The Culture of Control*. Chicago: University of Chicago Press.

Geudens, P. 1999. Weg met herrie en hondepoep. *Gazet van Antwerpen*, 16 January, 4.

Hough, M., Jackson, J., Bradford, B., Myhill, A. and Quinton, P. 2010. Procedural justice, trust, and institutional legitimacy. *Policing: An International Journal*, 4(3), 203–10.

Huyse, L. 1996. *De Lange Weg naar Neufchâteau*. Leuven: Van Halewyck.

Jackson, J., Bradford, B., Hough, M., Myhill, A., Quinton, P. and Tyler, T.R. 2012. Why do people comply with the law? *British Journal of Criminology*, 52, 1051–71.

K.R.G. 2009. Antwerpen telt 20.000 overlastboetes per jaar. *De Standaard*, 20 February, 72.

Kets, J. 2012. 'GAS-boetes bedreigen democratische rechten'. *De Standaard* [Online, 11 October]. Available at: http://www.standaard.be/cnt/DMF20121011_00330289 [accessed: 20 January 2012].

Lamon, H. 2002. De gemeente als rechter: je zou voor minder op de tram spuwen. *De Morgen*, 30 December, 28.

Légère, B. 2012. Somers wil geen boete voor lunchende tiener in Mechelen. *Het Nieuwsblad*, 3 November, 5.

Maeckelbergh, B. 2012. GAS-boete kost meer dan ze opbrengt. *De Morgen*, 22 November, 2.

Oeyen, M. 2012. GAS-boetes instrument om jongeren en sociaal zwakkeren te treffen. *De Morgen*, 13 November, 4.

P.C. 2008. Overlasttaks wordt populair. *De Standaard*, 18 November, 2.

Rommers, W. 2012. Jeugdbewegingen woest over strengere overlastboetes. *De Standaard*, 4 October, 8.
Schulhofer, S., Tyler, T. and Huq, A. 2011. American policing at a crossroads: Unsustainable policies and the procedural justice alternative. *Journal of Criminal Law and Criminology*, 101, 335–75.
Snacken, S. 2007. Penal policy and practice in Belgium. *Crime and Justice*, 36(1), 127–215.
Somers, S. 2011. In Antwerpen en Gent leidt kleine criminaliteit meteen tot een boete. *De Morgen*, 10 March, 2.
Sternberger, D. 1968. Legitimacy, in *International Encyclopedia of the Social Sciences*, edited by D.L. Sills. New York: Macmillan, 244.
Tegenbos, G. 2012. Worden we almaar repressiever? *De Standaard*, 12 May, 2.
Tollenaere, C. 2004. Gemeente speelt rechter. *Gazet van Antwerpen*, 27 March, 4.
Tyler, T.R. 2006. *Why People Obey the Law*. Princeton: Princeton University Press.
Tyler, T.R. 2011. *Why People Cooperate: The Role of Social Motivations*. Princeton: Princeton University Press.
Van Bastelaere, L. 2012. De meest absurde GAS-boetes van het land. *Het Laatste Nieuws*, 21 November, 7.
Van Cauwelaert, F. 2010. Boefjes vanaf veertien jaar moeten boeten voor overlast. *De Standaard*, 27 February, 5.
Van Damme, S. 2011. Gent maakt komaf met straffeloosheid. *Het Laatste Nieuws*, 16 April, 37.
Van den Broeck, A. 2012. We willen geen sheriffs worden. *De Morgen*, 4 April, 6.
Van den Broeck, T. 2012. *Formalisering/Informalisering van Sociale Controleprocessen: 20 Jaar Politie en Veiligheidsbeleid in Perspectief*. The Hague: Boom Legal Publishers.
Van den Broeck, D. and Dehandschutter, W. 2012. GAS-boetes zijn einde van beschaving. *Het Nieuwsblad*, 12 November, 6.
Van Synghel, B. 2012. Al evenveel GAS-sancties als vorig jaar. *Het Laatste Nieuws*, 9 October, 17.
Van Wiele, S. 2008. Bijna niemand vecht overlastboetes aan. *Gazet van Antwerpen*, 7 May, 16.
Vanden Bussche, S. 2010. Steeds meer gemeentelijke administratieve sancties. *Het Laatste Nieuws*, 9 March, 20.
Vander Beken, T. 2004. Administratieve afhandeling: anders en beter?, in *Het Strafrechtssysteem in de Laatmoderniteit*, edited by T. Balthazar et al. Mechelen: Kluwer, 119–36.
Vander Beken, T. 2005. Minderjarigen en gemeentelijke administratieve sancties, in *Gemeentelijke Administratieve Sancties*, edited by L. Veny and N. De Vos. Brugge: Vanden Broele, 139–58.
Verheijen, T. 2011. Eén overtreder heeft 17 sancties op zijn naam. *Gazet van Antwerpen*, 12 March, 69.

VVSG 2012. *GAS en Handhaving* [Online: Vlaamse Vereniging voor Steden en Gemeenten]. Available at: http://www.vvsg.be/veiligheid/%20handhaving/GAS/Pages/WelkomGAS.aspx [accessed: 14 January 2013].

Wet van 7 Mei 2004 tot Wijziging van de Wet van 8 April 1965 betreffende de Jeugdbescherming en de Nieuwe Gemeentewet. 25 June 2004. Brussels: Belgisch Staatsblad.

Wet van 13 Mei 1999 tot Invoering van Gemeentelijke Administratieve Sancties. 10 June 1999. Brussels: Belgisch Staatsblad.

Wet van 17 Juni 2004 tot Wijziging van de Nieuwe Gemeentewet. 23 July 2004. Brussels: Belgisch Staatsblad.

Wet van 20 Juli 2005 Houdende Diverse Bepalingen. 29 July 2005. Brussels: Belgisch Staatsblad.

Wetsontwerp van 30 Mei 2013 Betreffende de Gemeentelijke Administratieve Sancties. 30 May 2013. Brussels: Belgische Kamer van Volksvertegenwoordigers.

Willocx, C. 2011. Aantal overlastboetes neemt drastisch toe. *Gazet van Antwerpen*, 22 April, 16.

Chapter 4

Legitimacy at Stake? Crimmigration Processes and the Criminal Justice System in the Netherlands

Joanne van der Leun and Maartje van der Woude

Introduction: Legitimacy and Procedural Justice

Legitimacy is a broad term, which is used differentially across disciplines (Coicaud 2002, Bottoms and Tankebe 2012). The roots of the modern discussion of legitimacy are usually traced back to the seminal writings of Weber on the social dynamics of authority (Weber 1968), in which he argues that the ability to issue commands that will be obeyed does not rest solely upon the ability to use power. Not only are there rules that people will voluntarily obey, there are also authorities whose directives will be voluntarily followed. Legitimacy is not something an organisation can demand; it is, as Merelman (1966: 548) puts it, '… a quality attributed to a regime by a population'.

It goes without saying that the legitimacy of the criminal justice system is critical to its proper functioning (Meares 2005). In this respect, Tyler's procedural justice model cannot remain unnoticed (Lind and Tyler 1988, Tyler 1990, 2004). According to Tyler and colleagues, people are more likely to comply with the law when they view the law and the criminal justice actors enforcing the law as legitimate (Tyler and Blader 2005). From this social value perspective, a rule or an authority has legitimacy when others feel obligated to voluntarily defer to that rule or authority (Tyler 1990, 2006). A legitimate authority is regarded by people as entitled to have its decisions and rules accepted and followed by others (French and Raven 1959). Research has shown that legitimacy shapes everyday compliance with the law, a conclusion supported by more recent studies (Sunshine and Tyler 2003, Brockner and Siegel 1996). The internal value of legitimacy shapes law-related behaviour (Tyler 1990, Tyler and Huo 2002) and has more influence on compliance than sanction risks.

Whereas the procedural justice model seems rather straightforward, some of the social and legal developments over the past decades in the Netherlands seem to have complicated matters for criminal justice authorities. Criminal law and the criminal justice system as a whole have had to adapt and respond to increasing pluralism, insecurity, fragmentation and social conflict within advanced societies (Garland 2001). Among other things, this has led to an ever increasing scope and a diversification of functions of criminal law (Lacey 2008), including an instrumental one. Yet, criminal law still legitimises itself as the fair and equal application of rules to all suspects in society (Peršak 2007). Nevertheless, the question rises as to how this claim is to be reconciled with criminological findings on differential arrests and differential treatment along lines of gender, race, ethnicity, age, place of residence and so forth (Lacey 2008). While trying to explain this apparent discrepancy, one obviously has to take into account that, as Reiner (2006) and others have pointed out, practices of policing and punishment, and *mutatis mutandis* also practices of criminalisation, take place against the background of prevailing societal concerns about patterns of crime and safety issues. These concerns impact upon both rules and practices, as can be seen in the case of various societal concerns resulting from globalisation, including international migration and economic restructuring.

We will focus in this chapter on the police, who are crucial gatekeepers of the criminal justice system, in particular where it concerns individuals with a migrant background.[1] Police officers are the ones who conduct stop and search actions and who are seen as the ones who have to tackle migrant crime. They are also the first agents of internal migration control who have the powers to check a person's residence status whenever doubts arise as to the lawfulness of his or her stay (Aalberts 1989, Van der Leun 2003, Boekhoorn, Speller and Kruyssen 2004). In times of rapid social transformations, the police are increasingly under pressure to monitor and control 'suspect populations' and this is often accompanied by new actuarial powers and technologies which help them in fulfilling this task (Feeley and Simon 1992). At the same time, disproportionally targeting minorities might cause serious problems for their organisation, which for a large part of their work has to be able to rely on citizens (Cao, Frank and Cullen 1996). To be effective, police officers continuously need support and cooperation from the public and their willingness to cooperate in investigations. The perception of police practices as unfair may lead to more severe confrontations between police and citizens and finally to greater distrust of the police (Weitzer and Tuch 2004, Tyler 2003, Brown and Benedict 2002, Tyler and Wakslak 2004), which undermines legitimacy.

In Focus: Challenges for Legitimacy in the Dutch Cultural Security Complex

We will attempt to demonstrate that the reality of law enforcement in current European societies is more complex than the procedural justice model seems to

1 We use *migrants* or *minorities* as general terms for individuals who or whose parents have moved to the Netherlands, and ethnic minorities as a synonym. This is the Dutch meaning of the word and the authors are aware that the meaning of *migrant* in English is broader and includes immigrants as well as emigrants. We use *immigrants* only for individuals who have migrated themselves. Migrants without residence rights are usually dubbed *illegal immigrants* in the Netherlands. As many scholars object to the term, we will use *illegally residing immigrants*. For a more thorough discussion of terms in this area of study, see Schrover et al. 2008.

suggest. After all, the model tends to downplay the complex and two- or even multiple-way processes that often appear to go beyond procedures and interactions per se (cf. Smith 2007). We take the Dutch case as an illustration to further explore our assumption that given the present situation, a complex stage is set for policy makers, police officers and migrants. Growing concerns about migrants and crime cannot be ignored by politicians and policymakers, which often results in policy measures that are difficult to enforce. The recently expanding discretionary powers for police officers to stop and search potential criminals or illegally residing immigrants are an important example of these legislative changes. As will be elaborated below – depending on the choices made – this can be potentially damaging for the legitimacy of the criminal justice system. As we will also discuss, the currently pending legislative proposal criminalising illegal residence in the Netherlands, seems to bring about further pressures on the perceived legitimacy of the criminal justice system. Whereas this far-reaching 'crimmigration measure' (Stumpf 2006) sends out a message that residing illegally will be deterred and discouraged, which might speak to those who are worried about migration; migrants more in general might feel treated unfairly and indirectly criminalised, thereby affecting legitimacy.

Since empirical research in this area is scarce in the Netherlands (Eijkman 2010), the central questions of this chapter are exploratory and primarily seek to understand to what extent there is increasing room for *de jure* and de facto criminalisation of migrants in the Netherlands. Secondly, we will focus on the question how and to what extent this is studied by researchers and monitored by the government. Lastly, we will discuss how all of this relates to the legitimacy of the criminal apparatus.

Changing Scenery for Crime and Migration in the Netherlands

Despite having a positive immigration surplus since the early 1960s, successive Dutch governments were reluctant to recognise officially that the Netherlands was a country of immigration. It was not until 1998 that the Dutch government started to acknowledge this, which was also reflected in the country's research agenda. Acknowledging negative sides of immigration also took long. It was not before the end of the 1980s that the first systematic research on ethnic minority groups and crime was carried out (cf. Junger 1990, Bovenkerk 1991). Compared to other European countries, however, the Netherlands was still rather quick in breaking the taboo on social sciences research into issues concerning migration and crime. As to public policy, swift turnarounds took place both in the domain of migration policy and criminal justice policy. In a short time, the country turned from having a mild and tolerant stance towards migration and being a safe haven in terms of crime, to a Garlandian-style culture of control (Garland 2001). Around the same time, policies with respect to ethnic minorities shifted away from combating disadvantages (such as low education and low incomes) to demanding more responsibilities of migrants (Scholten 2007). In society, crime became a major cause of concern and migrants became to be seen as symbolic suspects par excellence (Downes and Van Swaaningen 2007, Van der Woude 2010, Van Swaaningen 2004, Pakes 2004). Although Garland in his analysis does not explicitly address the ethnic dimension within a culture of control, one of the key indices of the Dutch version of the culture of control concerns growing negative sentiments about migration policy and migrants, both in public and political discourse (Pakes 2004, Cavadino and Dignan 2006).

The 2002 governmental elections in the Netherlands are often seen as a 'watershed' moment in discussions surrounding immigration and integration. The rise in prominence of Pim Fortuyn, an outspoken critic of 'multiculturalism', on the Dutch political spectrum revealed a sense of uncertainty, insecurity and dissatisfaction among the population. These issues are not exclusively claimed by right-wing parties and the fine-tuning of migration and integration policies still takes place within the present coalition. Three 'key' events strongly contributed to this development: the 9/11 attacks, Pim Fortuyn and the murder of the Islam-critic moviemaker Theo van Gogh (Engbersen, Van der Leun and De Boom 2007). Lingering apprehensions of the Dutch multicultural society were raised and issues of immigration, integration, and the over-representation of non-Western ethnic minorities in registered crime statistics were given a hitherto unknown acuteness. The development of a discourse in which minority groups are increasingly seen and addressed as 'dangerous others', comparable to criminals, is part of a broader process of crimmigration – the merging of migration policy and crime control – in the Netherlands (Stumpf 2006; Van der Leun and Van der Woude 2011, 2012).

Legitimacy at Stake I: Ethnic Profiling

The procedural justice model is useful in order to grasp the complex relationship between trust in policing and the perceived legitimacy of the criminal justice system. Nevertheless, the model seems to downplay marked differences between groups of citizens in this respect. A lack of cognitive capacities or self-efficacy, which is often linked to a low level of education and a low income, can easily translate into higher levels of distrust (Van den Bos 2011), putting many groups with a migrant background at risk especially when concerning trust and confidence in the system of justice. The procedural model has little eye for the complex and two-way processes that often appear to go beyond procedures and interactions per se (cf. Smith 2007). If, for instance, a migrant is stopped by the police in the streets time and again and if he or she experiences exclusion or discrimination in several domains of life, a concrete interaction may be polite and procedurally right, but the person may still start to question the right of the police to rule. In the next steps of prosecution and decisions of judges, this may be reinforced. Here we focus on the police.

The extensive body of literature on ethnic and racial profiling by police officers in the US and the UK and other countries explores this issue of perceptions of being targeted disproportionally (Jefferson 1988). Whereas a large part of this body of research focuses on finding empirical evidence as to whether or not racial profiling is taking place, a small yet growing group of studies highlights the importance of studying the public's perception of racial profiling by police officials (Reitzel, Rice and Piquero 2004, Rice and Piquero 2005, Rice, Reitzel and Piquero 2005, Weitzer and Tuch 2002, 2004, 2005, Wortley and Tanner 2005). The pattern emerging from these studies is that race and personal experience with police are the most important correlates of perceptions of racial bias. Perceptions about police and their behaviour are very powerful influences on police–community relations, which can generate distrust not only among those who are personally stopped (Kennedy 1997). In the UK the perceived disproportional impact of stop and search on black and Asian people has attracted attention over the years. The Stephen Lawrence Inquiry report of 1999 examined the matter in-depth and concluded that stop and search powers were necessary but also recommended safeguards to try to ensure their proper and consistent use (MacPherson 1999). This investigation has led to an intricate monitoring system based on stop and search forms, where every stop and search action, the reasons behind it and the person's ethnicity has to be recorded. Since 2011, stops are recorded with mobile technology (Home Office 2013).

The above-mentioned processes have attracted significantly less attention of researchers in European continental countries. One of the very few to have conducted participant observations with the police in the Netherlands is Punch, who used this method to study police practices in Amsterdam. Decades ago, he reported that negative stereotyping of non-Western immigrants was not uncommon among police officers in the 1970s (Punch 1979). A recent anthropological study corroborates the outcomes for present times (Çankaya 2013). In another small-scale (older) study, non-Western immigrants appear to be stopped by the police more often than Dutch citizens (Bovenkerk 1991). For a long time, however, most Dutch studies on crime registration practices and outcomes did not find convincing evidence of ethnic bias (Rovers 1999, Wittebrood 2004). Junger (1989) maintained that due to the liberal tradition with relatively good police–community relations, ethnic bias was not a plausible explanation for group differences in crime figures. The absence or near absence of riots in the country over the years, which still holds (Adang 2010), was seen as proof for good police–community relations. Across the research community the long-term consensus was that studying overrepresentation in crime was more important than continuing to look into potential police bias or discrimination, which came to be seen as minor issues. Authors explained the good police–community relations by the organisation of the police and by terms written into the Aliens Act and the Identification Act, which were designed to prevent discrimination of foreigners. Empirical studies on surveillance of aliens in practice, carried out in the 1990s, demonstrated that the police was at that time very reluctant to stop and question allegedly illegally residing migrants. This not only had to do with preventing discrimination, police officers also stressed the importance of maintaining good relations within neighbourhoods (Aalberts 1989, 1990, Junger 1989). These outcomes were corroborated years later in a study on aliens surveillance by the police (Van der Leun 2003). Since then, however, rapid changes in the penal climate have taken place (Downes and Van Swaaningen 2007, Pakes 2004) as we have pointed out above and these at least call for further study.

As indicated before, the most recent research on implementation practices in the Netherlands dates back to the mid and late 1990s. Registered data as to what happens in practice are not readily available, as no records exist. Unlike in the UK, there are no specific reporting procedures such as stop and search forms, the police are not held accountable for their decisions as long as no complaints are filed, which rarely happens, and politicians rely on the professional attitude of the police to prevent bias (Van der Woude 2010). Legally, the situation is clear. Ethnic profiling is in defiance of the right to equal treatment and the ban on discrimination as included in the first article of the constitution (Eijkman 2010). In addition, despite strict and exclusionary migration control and lower thresholds for surveillance, actively going after immigrants just because they are suspected to be residing illegally is not permitted. In the following, we will cast a look at how relevant laws and surveillance practices may have changed more recently.

Increased Discretionary Space and the Risk of Selectivity

There are several reasons to rethink the consensus that surrounded the issue of police–minority relations and the absence of ethnic profiling in the Netherlands for a long time. The development of actuarial justice and preventive stop and search powers with the consequential increase of discretionary powers for law enforcement officials seems to be an important reason to do so. A number of fairly recent legislative changes have broadened the scope for police officers on the beat to stop people. First of all, the introduction of preventive stop and search powers in 2002. Before 2002, law enforcement officials could carry out searches if there was a reasonable suspicion of a criminal offence (Art. 27 together with 55b Code of Criminal Procedure). The legal basis for the 2002 stop and search powers can be found in both the Municipalities Act (article 151b) and the Weapons and Ammunitions Act (articles 50–52). After having consulted the municipal council and the public prosecutor, the powers to stop and search are vested in the mayor, by means of a by-law. The mayor decides which areas can be designated as 'security risk zones' in which anyone can be subjected to a 'preventive search' by police officers during a period of 12 hours. The police are empowered by the authority of the public prosecutor to search any individual as well as goods and vehicles, without having grounds for suspicion. In April 2011, a Bill has been proposed to further extend the possibilities for preventive searches, which is still to be debated in Parliament. Another body of law enabling preventive searches is the Dutch counterterrorism legislation: in response to the 2004 terrorist attacks in Madrid the Act on expanding the scope for investigating and prosecuting terrorist crimes was implemented.[2] Under this act, without the necessity of a reasonable suspicion, the public prosecutor can give a verbal order to the police to exercise stop and search powers during a 12-hour period in designated 'terrorist risk areas', a period which may be extended indefinitely (articles 126zq, 126zr en 127zs of the Code of Criminal Procedure). Within the context of counterterrorism, it is also possible for police officers to perform preventive searches without a preceding order by the public prosecutor in specific permanent security areas.[3]

In addition to these stop and search powers, there are several more specific powers as exercised by police officers or by other law enforcement officials, which may have repercussions in the area of ethnic profiling. Cases in point are identification checks and immigration controls. Expanded powers in these areas may very well affect the position of (alleged) illegally residing immigrants. For instance, the most recent Aliens Act 2000, which came into force in 2001, includes several renewed provisions (sections 50 and 53) for immigration authorities to carry out house searches for illegally residing migrants and also broadened the scope for stopping people in the street to ask for their identity and nationality. This can happen either because there is a reasonable suspicion that such persons are illegally residing or in order to prevent illegal residence of persons after they have crossed the border (section 48). Moreover, the police are authorised to enter a dwelling without the consent of the occupant if there is a reasonable suspicion that an alien who is not a lawful resident is staying there (section 51). An independent evaluation in 2004 of the use of these powers under the renewed Aliens Act 2000 showed that these new powers were increasingly being used, which was indicated by rising numbers of immigrants being stopped and questioned (Boekhoorn, Speller and Kruijssen 2004). In addition, with the introduction of the Extended Compulsory Identification Act (Wet op de Uitgebreide Identificatieplicht in Dutch, hereinafter WUID) on 1 January 2005, investigating officers and supervisors have been given a general power to demand proof of identity from individuals aged 14 or older as part of the performance of their duties. Individuals who do not immediately comply with this demand are guilty of a criminal offence, as they are violating Section 447e of the Dutch Criminal Code.[4] Whereas in the past, many

---

2 Kamerstukken II 2004/05, 30 164. For an overview of Dutch counterterrorism measures see: http://www.coe.int/t/dlapil/codexter/Source/Working_Documents/2011/CT_Measures_Netherlands.pdf.

3 Examples of these permanent risk areas are the Houses of Parliament, all airports, the train stations of the four major cities – Amsterdam, The Hague, Rotterdam and Utrecht – the Media Park in Hilversum and the nuclear power station in Borssele.

4 The WUID is an extension of the requirement to identify oneself, as compared with the situation before 1 January 2005. It consists of amendments and additions to the Compulsory Identification Act (Wet op de identificatieplicht in Dutch, hereinafter WID), in force from 1 June, 1994, and a number of associated acts. The WID provided for a limited identification requirement: individuals had to be able to identify themselves in specific situations as part of the fight against football hooliganism, fare-dodging in public transport, fraud and illegal stay in the Netherlands.

Dutch citizens strongly opposed identification checks, often with reference to the German occupation in World War II, these expansions have been accepted without any significant protest.

Indications of Ethnic Profiling in the Netherlands

Whereas the mere existence of expanded stop and search powers does not automatically entail ethnic profiling, research seems to imply that when police officials are exercising investigative powers without the necessity of a reasonable suspicion or concrete indications, one has to resort to something other than concrete offender-information to base one's decision on. It is exactly at this point where, either consciously or unconsciously, stereotypes and categorisations based on a person's presumed ethnicity or religious denomination can come in. As long as decisions to apprehend someone are not solely based on racial bias, stereotyping and categorisation are inherent and necessary to police work (Brown 1988, Wilson 1989, Bowling and Philips 2007, Miller 2010). As already stated, in the US and the UK there is – in contrast to the Netherlands – already overwhelming empirical evidence that racial or ethnic profiling in the context of discretionary police powers is taking place. In recent years a couple of reports have provided indications that the risk of ethnic profiling is also not just a theoretical 'risk' for the Netherlands: the 2009 European Union Minorities and Discrimination Survey (European Union Agency for Fundamental Rights 2010) revealed that that a quarter of Dutch Muslims of Turkish origin interviewed had been stopped by the police at least once in 12 months prior to the survey and that of these individuals a quarter had the impression that the stop was based on ethnicity. The corresponding figures for Dutch Muslims of North African origin were 26 per cent and 39 per cent, respectively (European Union Agency for Fundamental Rights 2009: 13–14). A 2010 survey by EU-MIDIS shows that in the Netherlands both North African (66 per cent), Turkish (61 per cent) and Surinamese (67 per cent) respondents feel that discrimination based on ethnicity is widespread. The outcomes match the results of the Special Eurobarometer 296 in which a similar question was asked: for the Netherlands 79 per cent of the respondents were of the opinion that discrimination based on ethnicity is widespread (European Union Agency for Fundamental Rights 2010). According to a report of the Open Society Justice Initiative on police stereotyping in the Netherlands, France, Germany, Italy en other EU-states, ethnic profiling is exercised on a large scale within continental Europe (OSJI 2009). The European Commission against Racism and Intolerance expressed its worries about the increase of ethnic profiling in relation to preventing and fighting terrorism, but also gives of a more general warning about the changed tone in political and public discourse regarding minorities (ECRI 2008).

These indications have to be taken seriously, but some problems with these findings have also to be noted: (a) comparable figures for perceptions of 'native' Dutch people are unavailable, and (b) the empirical basis is often weak. Research on the practice of ID checks is scarce. Although the 2009 evaluative study of

Everwijn, Jongbreur and Lolkema did not give any indication of the power to ask for a person's ID being applied incorrectly in a discriminatory fashion, a 2011 report by Bureau Beke states that 'the large number of North African names registered is at least remarkable' (Kuppens et al. 2011: 54). Svensson, Sollie and Saharso (2011) reach similar conclusions in a study on potential differences among teenagers in their experiences with and perception of the police and ID checks. They did not find any evidence for the systematically unequal treatment of minority youth, but at the same time they did warn for selectivity on the basis of some of their findings. Recent research by Weenink (2009) also seems to support the notion of potential ethnic bias in Dutch prosecutorial decision-making in juvenile justice cases and Wermink, De Keijser and Schuyt (2012) draw similar conclusions with respect to judges in penal cases. In sum, whereas strong conclusions as to selective criminal justice practices are difficult to draw, there appear to be enough indications to conclude that the consensus of the past does not necessarily hold anymore.

Preventive searches have repeatedly been evaluated in terms of effectiveness and in terms of how these collective searches are carried out. Recent reports by the National Ombudsman (2009) and by Kuppens et al. (2011) have concentrated on how law enforcement officials perform their duties with regard to preventive searches. Although no shocking abuses of power are observed in either of the studies, the researchers do reach the conclusion that it is impossible to refrain from acting selectively. When for practical or operational reasons it is impossible to stop and search everyone present in a safety risk area, police officers have to make choices as to whom to search and whom not to search. Although the researchers deem some discretionary freedom necessary, they also acknowledge that in these situations there is always the possibility that an officer (un)consciously bases his decision on ethnic or religious features and – in doing so – distinguishes between certain (minority) groups (Nationale Ombudsman 2009, Kuppens et al. 2011).

Concerning the issue of trust, we have to rely on surveys among the public. In general, since the 1980s, surveys measured the decline in trust in public authorities in Western European countries including the Netherlands (Dekker, Halman and Van der Meer 2006). For the general population, trust in police and the criminal justice system varies (according to the European Values survey) between a grade from 2 to 8 on a 1 to 10 scale. Highest grades are given in Denmark (8), Finland (7) and Austria (7). With a 5, the Netherlands scores somewhere in the middle, leaving behind countries like the Czech Republic, Estonia, Latvia and Slovakia who score lower (around 4) (Van der Meer 2004). A recent survey on perceptions of the police within neighbourhoods revealed that in general many citizens are not very positive about police work in their neighbourhood. Only one in three thinks that police try to do well, offer protection in the neighbourhood and react to local problems (Statistics Netherlands 2009). Remarkably, scores are higher in urbanised areas, which are also areas with highest shares of people with a migrant background. Earlier research with respect to ethnic minority perceptions of the Dutch police (Bijleveld, Goudriaan and Malsch 2007) found mixed results. Qualitative research showed more distrust among minority populations compared to native Dutch, whereas large-scale quantitative surveys appeared to demonstrate the opposite. Bijleveld, Goudriaan and Malsch (2007) explained this contradiction by pointing to the fact that large surveys do not do well in reaching and ensuring cooperation (from) people with a migrant background. In addition, non-response is also problematic in certain segments of the population (Stoop 2005). Therefore there are reasons to be careful in interpreting survey results with respect to this issue. In sum, we can safely say that the evidence so far is mixed and does not warrant alarming conclusions. Although in general, trust in the public sector appears to be declining and the police are perceived critically, we cannot tell whether people with a migrant background are seriously more distrusting about the police than the general population. We also know that there is more room for the police to be selective, but we are not certain whether or to what extent this leads to a disproportionate stopping of individuals with a migrant background. It seems fair to assume, however, that growing negative political and public sentiments towards immigrants have influenced immigrants' perceptions on governmental authorities and therewith also on the criminal justice system, and that the attention to criminal migrants has influenced the police as well.

Legitimacy at Stake II: The Criminalisation of Illegal Residence

A second case of relevance is the governmental stance towards illegal residence and present steps to criminalise it. Since the early 1990s, the Dutch government promotes a comprehensive 'discouragement policy' towards illegal residence through intensified labour market controls, high fines for employers, blocking public services for people without a residence status and increasing emphasis on surveillance, detention and expulsion (Van der Leun 2003, Broeders 2009). Priority, at least on paper, is given to immigrants suspected of committing criminal offences or causing nuisance. In 1998 an important step was taken by introducing a comprehensive law, which blocked access to publicly funded services, the Linking Act (Pluymen 2007, Van der Leun 2006). The current Parliament is taking a next step. Despite societal objections, the Council of Ministers has agreed to submit a proposal to the House of Representatives to amend the Aliens Act in such a way that foreign nationals who reside illegally in the Netherlands are guilty of a misdemeanour, subject to the sanction of a fine or imprisonment (if the fine cannot be paid). Migrants who are fined at least twice for residing illegally in the Netherlands risk a severe entry ban for a maximum of five years (Cabinet Rutte/Samson 2012; Council of Minsters 2012). In fact, earlier plans in this direction were never enacted because of expected difficulties with the implementation. Studies on illegal migration in the Netherlands suggest that the discouragement policy of the last two decades appears to be to a certain extent reaching its aims (Leerkes 2009). According to estimates, the number of illegally residing migrants present seems to be decreasing or stabilising (Van der Leun and Ilies 2009, Van der Heijden, Cruyff and Van Gils 2011), although the decline is not only policy-related. The economic downturn and the enlargement of the EU, which has opened more avenues for legal job opportunities for individuals from Central and Eastern European countries, also seem to have played a part.

Yet, despite all efforts, problems still arise when trying to expel migrants from the country (Van Kalmthout 2007, Boone and Kox 2012) and this holds especially for those illegal immigrants who cause public order problems. After a period of detention they are often let back out on the streets: 'sent away in Southerly direction' or 'cobbled' as police officers call this euphemistically (Engbersen and Van der Leun 2001). Difficulties with expelling people are largely caused by factors outside the sphere of influence of the authorities; a lack of cooperation of both individual migrants and their countries of origin. In that respect, it is not surprising that in Belgium, the formal criminalisation of illegal residence, which came into force in 1980 (with the Belgian Aliens Act of 1980), was abandoned some years ago. As the prisons became packed, it began to emerge that using them as a means of migration policy was not the cleverest thing to do (Van der Leun and De Ridder 2013).

Research has revealed unintended consequences. A quantitative analysis over the years 1997–2003 showed that all the policy measures together have also led to rising crime figures of illegally residing migrants who did not leave the country (Leerkes, Engbersen and Van der Leun 2012). As a result of their marginalisation, all kinds of opportunities had been blocked, which in some cases stimulated unconventional modes of making a living in the informal and criminal economy. The main conclusion of this analysis was that the increase in internal border control by means of excluding illegally residing migrants from the formal labour market and public provisions had stimulated criminal involvement, predominantly in the form of subsistence crime and drug-related crime. There seems to be a cycle visible here: criminal involvement or the fear thereof stimulates stricter policies, which in turn can lead to rising crime figures and subsequently to more repression. There is no monitoring whatsoever of these effects. In fact, in the policy domain of migration control no attempts have been made to work evidence-based, nor to take into account the realities of illegal migration (cf. Staring 2013).

Discussion: A Cycle of Crimmigration?

Against the background of legitimacy concerns, we addressed the room for *de jure* and de facto criminalisation of migrants in the Netherlands, and how and to what extent this is studied by researchers and monitored by the government. These questions were triggered by the one-sidedness of the Dutch debate, which emphasises criminal involvement of migrants and the presence of large number of illegally residing migrants without paying systematic attention to potential selective law enforcement. For a long time, researchers in the Netherlands have primarily concentrated on high crime figures of certain migrant groups and have assumed that selectivity was not really an issue.

Summarising briefly, we have first shown a series of changes in legislation, which have increasingly opened up possibilities for selective enforcement. Secondly, we have paid attention to potential ethnic profiling. Although sound evidence is lacking so far, there are some indications that groups with a migrant background feel that they are watched more closely than nationals. Although this is not the same as saying that the traditionally good police–community relations are under threat, it does point to the need for better monitoring. With respect to policies regarding illegally residing migrants, stricter policies and control of illegal residence have stimulated rather than curbed criminal activities. Nonetheless, further steps along the same line will be taken with the formal criminalisation of illegal residence, which according to Stumpf (2006) is the final step of crimmigration: merging migration policy and criminal law. When illegal residence will be criminalised, this might also stimulate ethnic profiling, because the police will be more likely to check the identity of people in the streets. This will happen more often to people who look like migrants to them, thereby increasing the risk of engendering a vicious cycle, which we could dub a cycle of crimmigration.

So far researchers have found neither dramatic disproportionality nor findings of a deeply alienated minority youth, but it is clear (a) that discretion has expanded, (b) that there is no monitoring, and (c) that researchers have largely ignored these issues. If we take these observations seriously, the question what they imply in terms of legitimacy is not easy to answer straightforwardly. On the one hand, the police and the criminal justice system as a whole have to respond to prevailing concerns in society, including concerns about groups of young migrants who are overrepresented in registered crime and about the presence of illegally residing migrants. But on the other hand, if they do so too easily, they risk undermining their legitimacy in the eyes of a part of the population, from whom they also need trust and cooperation. As Terlouw maintained: when a government reacts to fears among the population for 'others', the same government risks reinforcing these fears (Terlouw 2009: 75).

Therefore, we conclude that there are enough reasons to pay more attention to the potential influence of crimmigration processes on legitimacy in a broad sense. The procedural justice model, which is a dominant one in the criminological research, puts emphasis on the police having to treat individuals in a fair and polite way in order to protect legitimacy (Tyler 2006). Albeit a crucial and well-founded insight, this also tends to obscure the deep and complex sociological processes that take place and that influence people's perceptions. Many people with a migrant background who live in the less well-to-do areas, find themselves stuck on the lower rungs of societal ladder and do not even have to be treated unfairly in concrete situations to feel excluded. The process of framing crime as a migration-related issue, a complex of legal changes with expanding power and limits to rights, including migration control and counterterrorism that limits immigrants' rights, may all influence perceptions of the police. Bottoms and Tankebe (2012) rightly point to the fact that most procedural justice model-based research, including the influential work by Tyler and colleagues, ignores the fact that the government is serving not one audience but many audiences. This holds even more in present societies with highly diverse and often polarised populations. Acknowledging the complexities of law enforcement and making unequivocally clear that equal, fair and even-handed application of rules holds for all audiences – which legitimacy implies – requires not only much more attention and energy of authorities in the Netherlands; this also holds for criminal justice researchers studying the legitimacy of criminal justice systems worldwide.

References

Aalberts, M.M.J. 1989. *Operationeel vreemdelingentoezicht in Nederland.* [Operational aliens surveillance in the Netherlands]. Arnhem: Gouda Quint.

Aalberts, M.M.J. 1990. *Politie tussen discretie en discriminatie.* [Police between discretion and discrimination]. Arnhem: Gouda Quint.

Adang, O. 2010. *Zijn wij anders? Waarom Nederland geen etnische rellen heeft.* [Are we different? Why the Netherlands does not have ethnic riots]. Apeldoorn: Politieacademie.

Bijleveld, C., Goudriaan, H. and Malsch, M. 2007. Ethnic minorities and confidence in the criminal justice system, in *Legitimacy and Criminal Justice: International Perspectives*, edited by T. Tyler. New York: Russell Sage Foundation, 277–302.

Boekhoorn, P., Speller, T. and Kruijssen, F. 2004. *Operationeel toezicht vreemdelingen: evaluatie van de bevoegdheden in de Vreemdelingenwet 2000 voor het vreemdelingentoezicht door de politie* [Operational aliens surveillance: An evaluation of powers under the Aliens Act 2000]. The Hague: Research and Documentation Centre of the Ministry of Security and Justice.

Boone, M. and Kox, M. 2012. What works for irregular migrants in the Netherlands? *European Journal of Probation* 4(3), 54–68.

Bottoms, A. and Tankebe, J. 2012. Beyond procedural justice: A dialogic approach to legitimacy in criminal law. *The Journal of Criminal Law & Criminology*, 102(1), 119–70.

Bovenkerk, F. 1991. Het vraagstuk van de criminaliteit der Marokkaanse jongens. [The issue of crime of Moroccan boys]. *De Gids*, 150(12), 8–28.

Bowling, B. and Phillips, C. 2007. Disproportionate and discriminatory: Reviewing the evidence on police stop and search. *Modern Law Review*, 70(6), 936–61.

Brockner, J. and Siegel, P. 1996. Understanding the interaction between procedural and distributive justice: The role of Trust, in *Trust in Organizations: Frontiers of Theory and Research*, edited by R.M. Kramer and T.R. Tyler. Thousand Oaks, London, New Delhi: Sage, 390–404.

Broeders, D. 2009. *Breaking Down Anonymity: Digital Surveillance on Irregular Migrants in Germany and the Netherlands*. Amsterdam: Amsterdam University Press.

Brown, B. and Benedict, W. 2002. Perceptions of the police. *Policing*, 25, 543–80.

Brown, M.K. 1988. *Working the Street: Police Discretion and the Dilemmas of Reform*. New York: Russell Sage Foundation.

Cabinet Rutte/Samson. 2012. *Coalition Agreement* [Online]. Available at: http://www.kabinetsformatie2012.nl/actueel/documenten/regeerakkoord.html [accessed: 12 February 2013].

Çankaya, S. 2013. *De controle van Marsmannetjes en ander Schorriemorie. Het beslissingsproces tijdens proactief politiewerk* [Controlling Martians and other scum. The decision-making process in proactive policing]. The Hague: Boom Lemma.

Cao, L.J., Frank, J. and Cullen, F.T. 1996. Race, community context and confidence in the police: Disentangling the relationship. *Justice Quarterly*, 11, 119–34.

Cavadino, M. and Dignan, D. 2006. Penal policy and political economy. *Criminology & Criminal Justice*, 6(4), 435–56.

Coicaud, J.M. 2002. *Legitimacy and Politics: A Contribution to the Study of Political Right and Political Responsibility*. Cambridge: Cambridge University Press.

Council of Ministers. 2012. *Illegal residence is now a crime*. Press release from the Council of Ministers, 21–12–2012. The Hague: Council of Ministers.

Dekker, P., Halman, L. and Van der Meer, T. 2006. Ontwikkelingen in politiek vertrouwen in Europa 1981–2004 [Development in political trust in Europe 1981–2004], in *Bouwen aan vertrouwen in het openbaar bestuur* [Building trust in public administration], edited by A. Korsten and P. de Goede. The Hague: Elsevier, 61–78.

Downes, D. and Van Swaaningen, R. 2007. The Road to Dystopia: Changes in the penal climate in the Netherlands, in *Crime and Justice in the Netherlands*, edited by M. Tonry and C. Bijleveld. Chicago: Chicago University Press, 31–72.

ECRI (European Commission against Racism and Intolerance). 2008. *Derde Rapport over Nederland* [Third report on the Netherlands]. Strasbourg: Council of Europe.

Eijkman, Q. 2010. Has the genie been let out of the bottle? Ethnic profiling in the Netherlands, public space. *The Journal of Law and Social Justice*, 5, 27–48.

Engbersen, G. and Van der Leun, J.P. 2001. The social construction of illegality and crime. *European Journal on Criminal Policy and Research*, 9, 51–70.

Engbersen, G., Van der Leun, J.P. and De Boom, J. 2007. The fragmentation of migration and crime in the Netherlands. *Crime & Justice: A Review of Research*, 35, 389–452.

European Union Agency for Fundamental Rights. 2009. *European Union Minorities and Discrimination Survey. Data in Focus Report: Muslims*. Brussels: EUAFR.

European Union Agency for Fundamental Rights. 2010. *EU-MIDIS 5 Data in Focus Report: Multiple Discrimination*. Brussels: EUAFR.

Everwijn, H., Jongbreur, W. and Lolkema, P. 2009. *Het functioneren van de WUID in de praktijk: Evaluatie van de Wet op de uitgebreide Identificatieplicht.* [The Expanded Compulsory Identification Act in practice]. Barneveld: Significant.

Feeley, M. and Simon, J. 1992. The new penology: Notes on the emerging strategy of corrections and its implications. *Criminology*, 30(4), 449–74.

French, J.R.P. and Raven, B. 1959. The bases of social power, in *Studies in Social Power*, edited by D. Cartwright. Ann Arbor, MI: University of Michigan.

Garland, D. 2001. *The Culture of Control: Crime and Social Order in Contemporary Society*. Oxford: Oxford University Press.

Home Office. 2013. *Stop and Search* [Online]. Available at: http://www.homeoffice.gov.uk/police/powers/stop-and-search/ [accessed: 18 February 2013].

Jefferson, T. 1988. Race, crime, and policing. *International Journal of the Sociology of Law*, 16(4), 521–39.

Junger, M. 1989. Between police and self-report data for Dutch racial minorities. *British Journal of Criminology*, 20(3), 273–84.

Junger, M. 1990. *Delinquency and Ethnicity: An Investigation on Social Factors Relating to Delinquency among Moroccan, Turkish, Surinamese and Dutch Boys*. Deventer/Boston: Kluwer.

Kennedy, R. 1997. *Race, Crime, and the Law*. New York: Vintage Books.

Kuppens, J., Bremmers, B., Van den Brink, E., Ammerlaan, K. and Ferwerda, H. 2011. *Onder het oppervlak. Een onderzoek naar ontwikkelingen en (a) select optreden rond preventief fouilleren.* [Under the surface: A study on developments and potential selection in preventive searches]. Amsterdam: Reed Business.

Lacey, N. 2008. Legal constructions of crime, in *Oxford Handbook of Criminology*, edited by M. Maguire, R. Morgan and R. Reiner. Oxford: Oxford University Press, 179–200.

Leerkes, A.S. 2009. *Illegal Residence and Public Safety in the Netherlands*. Amsterdam: Amsterdam University Press.

Leerkes, A.S., Engbersen, G. and Van der Leun, J.P. 2012. Crime among irregular immigrants and the influence of internal border control. *Crime, Law and Social Change*, 58(1), 15–38.

Lind, E.A. and Tyler, T.R. 1988. *The Social Psychology of Procedural Justice*. New York: Plenum Press.

Macpherson, W. 1999. *The Stephen Lawrence Inquiry: Report of an Inquiry by Sir William Macpherson of Cluny*. London: Home Office.

Meares, T.L. 2005. Everything old is new again: Fundamental fairness and the legitimacy of criminal justice. *Ohio State Journal of Criminal Law*, 3,105–23.

Merelman, R.J. 1966. Learning and legitimacy. *American Political Science Review*, 60, 548–61.

Miller, J. 2010. Stop and search in England: A reformed tactic or business as usual? *British Journal of Criminology*, 50(5), 954–74.

Nationale Ombudsman. 2009. *Onderzoek inval vreemdelingenpolitie in Amsterdams cafe, Report 2009–170.* [Investigation on a police raid in an Amsterdam cafe]. The Hague: Nationale Ombudsman.

OSJI. 2009. *Ethnic Profiling in the European Union: Pervasive, Ineffective and Discriminatory.* New York: Open Society Institute.

Pakes, F. 2004. The politics of discontent: The emergence of a new criminal justice discourse in the Netherlands. *Howard Journal of Criminal Justice*, 43(3), 284–98.

Peršak, N. 2007. *Criminalising Harmful Conduct: The Harm Principle, Its Limits and Continental Counterparts.* New York: Springer.

Pluymen, M. 2007. *Niet toelaten betekent uitsluiten. Een rechtssociologisch onderzoek naar de rechtvaardiging en praktijk van uitsluiting van vreemdelingen van voorzieningen.* [Non admission implies exclusion. A socio-legal study on the justification and practice of excluding foreigners from facilities]. The Hague: Boom Legal Publishers.

Punch, M. 1979. *Policing the Inner City: A Study of Amsterdam's Warmoesstraat.* London: Macmillan Press.

Reiner, R. 2006. Beyond risk: A lament for social democratic criminology, in *The Politics of Crime Control: Essays in Honour of David Downes*, edited by T. Newburn and P. Rock. Oxford: Oxford University Press, 7–49.

Reitzel, J.D., Rice, S.K. and Piquero, A.R. 2004. Lines and shadows: Perceptions of racial profiling and the Hispanic experience. *Journal of Criminal Justice*, 32, 607–16.

Rice, S.K. and Piquero, A.R. 2005. Perceptions of discrimination and justice in New York City. *Policing: An International Journal of Police Strategies & Management*, 28, 98–117.

Rice, S.K., Reitzel, J.D. and Piquero, A.R. 2005. Shades of brown: Perceptions of racial profiling and the intra-ethnic differential. *Journal of Ethnicity in Criminal Justice*, 3, 47–79.

Rovers, B. 1999. *Klassenjustitie. Overzicht van onderzoek naar selectiviteit in de Nederlandse strafrechtsketen.* [Class justice. A review of research on selectivity in the criminal law chain]. Rotterdam: Erasmus University.

Scholten, P.W.A. 2007. Constructing immigrant policies: Research-policy relations and immigrant integration in the Netherlands, 1970–2004 (PhD thesis), University of Twente Enschede.

Schrover, M., Van der Leun, J.P, Lucassen, L. and Quispel, G.C. (eds) 2008. *Illegal Migration and Gender in a Global and Historical Perspective.* Amsterdam: Amsterdam University Press.

Smith, D.J. 2007. The foundations of legitimacy, in *Legitimacy and Criminal Justice: International Perspectives*, edited by T. Tyler. New York: Russell Sage Foundation, 30–58.

Staring, R. 2013. *Moderne slavernij of gewoon werk?* [Modern slavery of normal work?] The Hague: Boom Legal Publishers.

Statistics Netherlands. 2009. *Web magazine, 6 oktober 2010: Multiculturele buurt meest positief over politie* [Multicultural neighbourhood more positive about police] The Hague: Statistics Netherlands [Online]. Available at: http://www.cbs.nl/nl-NL/menu/themas/veiligheid-recht/publicaties/artikelen/archief/2010/2010-3182-wm.htm [accessed: January 2012].

Stoop, I. 2005. *The Hunt for the Last Respondent: Non Response in Sample Surveys*. The Hague: Netherlands Institute for Social Research.

Stumpf, J. 2006. The crimmigration crisis: Immigrants, crime, and sovereign power. *American University Law Review*, 56(2), 368–419.

Sunshine, J. and Tyler, T.R. 2003. The role of procedural justice for legitimacy in shaping public support for policing. *Law & Society Review*, 37(3), 513–48.

Svensson, J.S., Sollie, H. and Saharso, S. 2011. *Proactief handhaven en gelijk behandelen*. [Proactive enforcement and equal treatment]. Amsterdam: Reed Business.

Terlouw, A.B. 2009. *Angst en regelgeving. Onderscheid door de overheid op grond van nationaliteit, afkomst en religie.* [Fear and regulations. Differential treatment by the government based on nationality, background and religion]. Nijmegen: Wolf Legal Publishers (inaugural lecture).

Tyler, T.R. 1990. *Why People Obey the Law*. New Haven, CT: Yale University Press.

Tyler, T.R. 2003. Procedural justice, legitimacy, and the effective rule of law. *Crime and Justice: A Review of Research*, 30, 431–505.

Tyler, T.R. 2004. Procedural justice, in *The Blackwell Companion to Law and Society*, edited by A. Sarat. Malden, MA: Blackwell, 435–52.

Tyler, T.R. 2006. Legitimacy and legitimation. *Annual Review of Psychology*, 57, 375–400.

Tyler, T.R. and Blader, S.L. 2005. Can businesses effectively regulate employee conduct? The antecedents of rule following in work settings. *Academy of Management Journal*, 48, 1143–58.

Tyler, T.R. and Huo, Yuen J. 2002. *Trust in the Law: Encouraging Public Cooperation with the Police and Courts*. New York: Russell Sage Foundation.

Tyler, T.R. and Wakslak, C.J. 2004. Profiling and police legitimacy: Procedural justice, attributions of motive, and acceptance of police authority. *Criminology*, 42(2), 253–81.

Van den Bos, K. 2011. *Vertrouwen in de overheid: wanneer hebben burgers het, wanneer hebben ze het niet, en wanneer weten ze niet of de overheid te vertrouwen is?* [Trust in the government: When do citizens have it, when is it lacking and when do they doubt it?] The Hague: Ministry of the Interior and Kingdom Relations.

Van der Heijden, P.G.M., Cruyff, M. and Van Gils, G.H.C. 2011. *Schattingen illegaal in Nederland verblijvende vreemdelingen 2009.* [Estimates of the number of irregular migrants in the Netherlands 2009]. The Hague: Research and Documentation Centre, Ministry of Security and Justice.

Van der Leun, J.P. 2003. *Looking for Loopholes: Processes of Incorporation of Illegal Immigrants in the Netherlands*. Amsterdam: Amsterdam University Press.

Van der Leun, J.P. 2006. Excluding illegal migrants in the Netherlands: Between national policies and local implementation. *West European Politics* 29(2), 310–26.

Van der Leun, J.P. and De Ridder, S. 2013. Het cumulatief punitief karakter van het migratierecht. [The cumulative punitive character of migration law]. *Orde van de Dag*, 61, 28–35.

Van der Leun, J.P. and Ilies, M. 2009. *Illegal Immigrants in the Netherlands: A National Expert Report for Clandestino*. Athens: Eliamep.

Van der Leun, J.P. and Van der Woude, M.A.H. 2011. Ethnic profiling in the Netherlands? A reflection on expanding preventive powers, ethnic profiling and a changing social and political context. *Policing and Society*, 21(4), 444–55.

Van der Leun, J.P. and Van der Woude, M.A.H. 2012. A reflection on crimmigration in the Netherlands: On the cultural security complex and the impact of framing, in *Social Control and Justice: Crimmigration in the Age of Fear*, edited by M.J. Guia, M.A.H. Van der Woude and J.P. Van der Leun. The Hague: Eleven International Publishing, 41–60.

Van der Meer, T. 2004. *Vertrouwen in de rechtspraak: empirische bevindingen.* Rechtstreeks 2004/1 [Trust in Justice: Empirical-findings]. The Hague: The Netherlands Institute for Social Research/SCP.

Van der Woude, M.A.H. 2010. *Wetgeving in een Veiligheidscultuur. Totstandkoming van antiterrorismewetgeving in Nederland bezien vanuit maatschappelijke en (rechts)politieke context.* [Legislation in a culture of control. The drafting of Dutch counterterrorism legislation seen from within a legal, social and political context]. The Hague: Boom Legal Publishers.

Van Kalmthout, A.M. 2007. Het regiem van de vreemdelingenbewaring: de balans na 25 jaar. [The regime of foreigners detention: A balance after 25 years]. *Justitiële Verkenningen*, 33(4), 89–102.

Van Swaaningen, R. 2004. Veiligheid in Nederland en Europa; een sociologische beschouwing aan de hand van David Garland. [Safety in the Netherlands and Europe: A sociological reflection based on David Garland]. *Justitiële Verkenningen*, 7, 9–23.

Weber, M. 1968. *Economy and Society: An Outline of Interpretive Sociology*, edited by G. Roth and G. Wittich. New York: Bedminster.

Weenink, D. 2009. Explaining ethnic inequality in the juvenile justice system: An analysis of the outcomes of Dutch prosecutorial decisionmaking. *British Journal of Criminology* 49(2), 220–42.

Weitzer, R. and Tuch, S.A. 2002. Perceptions of racial profiling: Race, class, and personal experience. *Criminology*, 40, 435–56.

Weitzer, R. and Tuch, S.A. 2004. Reforming the police: Racial differences in public support for change. *Criminology*, 42, 391–416.

Weitzer, R. and Tuch, S.A. 2005. Racially biased policing: Determinants of citizen perceptions. *Social Forces*, 83, 1009–30.

Wermink, H.T., de Keijser, J.W. and Schuyt, P.M. 2012. Verschillen in straftoemeting in soortgelijke zaken: Een kwantitatief onderzoek naar de rol van specifieke kenmerken van de dader. [Differences in sentencing in similar cases: A quantitative study on the role of specific offender characteristics]. *Nederlands Juristenblad*, 11, 726–33.

Wilson, J.Q. 1989. *Bureaucracy: What Government Agencies Do and Why They Do It*. New York: Basic Books.

Wittebrood, K. 2004. Van delictmelding tot officiële aangifte – sprake van sociale ongelijkheid? [Recording of reported crimes: Social inequality?] *Tijdschrift voor Criminologie*, 46, 56–71.

Wortley, S. and Tanner, J. 2005. Inflammatory rhetoric? Baseless accusations? A response to Gabor's critique of racial profiling research in Canada. *Canadian Journal of Criminology and Criminal Justice*, 47, 581–609.

Chapter 5
Legitimacy and EU Criminal Law Regulation

Thomas Elholm

Legitimacy of Criminal Law Standards

What is legitimacy? The answer will probably depend on the context and is bound to vary from one subject and discipline to the next. A philosophical exposé is different from a legal one. Even within different law disciplines, different answers are given, in this author's view, as to when something is deemed to be legitimate. Below, this author offers his view of legitimacy from a legal, criminal law perspective.

The demand for legitimacy may be directed towards different parts of the state apparatus. Legitimacy can be claimed from the legislator, the courts or the administrative services. Demands may concern the design of legislation or specific decisions and procedures. The focus of this chapter is limited to the legitimacy of legislation, i.e. of the legal norms that lay down criminal liability, and additionally, of the legal norms regarding sentencing. Incidentally, this chapter is limited to the EU's criminal law legislation, i.e. to the part of EU legislation, which is designated as criminal law by the EU itself or which is directed explicitly towards the criminal law of the member states. By definition, some parts of EU legislation are not criminal law; this applies, for example, to administrative sanctions or fines in competition law. These are not dealt with here.

In many cases – in law and in other subjects – legitimacy is associated with a specific *procedure*. Laws or decisions are legitimate if they have been produced in accordance with specific procedures and have been adopted by a legitimate body. In our part of the world, where the state is based on democracy and rule of law principles, requirements with regard to legitimacy will include a democratic, parliamentary basis for decisions, separation of powers, citizen involvement and transparency.

I am convinced that the procedural aspect of this is significant. A legal norm adopted by an institution that is deemed to be legitimate will have a certain amount of legitimacy. But is this enough? Can a legitimate legislator adopt any kind of legislation and automatically assume that such legislation will be or should be deemed legitimate? In this author's view, that is not the case. Below, it is argued that there must also be requirements as regards the *content* of legislation. This applies in particular to criminal law legislation.

Philosophical and Criminological Aspects

In philosophical and criminological research, legitimacy is often defined as requiring a certain amount of backing for the legislation or decision concerned – from those subject to the law or from those in power, or both. Legitimacy of a legal norm or a decision is said to be achieved if citizens deem it to be 'in some way right and proper and something which ought to be followed' (Bottoms and Tankebe 2012: 124). Theories based on this assumption may be either descriptive or normative. Incidentally, it is assumed – and, in a descriptive context, it can probably be documented – that compliance is more likely if legal norms or decisions are deemed to be legitimate (ibid.: 37). Furthermore, in a philosophical and criminological context, arguments are often made to say that, to a certain extent, a shared value base is a precondition for legitimacy. Some even believe that this value base should be shared by those subject to the law and those in power alike (ibid.: 141ff., referring to Beetham).

Basically, this author agrees with the assumption that if legal norms are to have legitimacy, a certain amount of backing or acceptance is required from those subject to the law and possibly also from those in power. A certain degree of shared value base forms a basis for legitimacy can also be found. Below, this author shall assume that the shared core values have to do with a wish to live in a state (and a European union) that is based on ideals relating to democracy and the rule of law. Full compliance is not a must, but the ideals are nevertheless present and make up the basis for the formation of the state. Other core values may lead to other state formations; this is bound to materially change the question of legitimacy. If we wish to have a state formation like in the former Eastern Europe or enlightened despotism, the assumptions put forward below will not be valid. In such cases, legitimacy is something radically different. In other words, these arguments are based on the assumption that we share certain core values rooted in the concepts of democracy and the rule of law. On that basis, it will be argued below that legitimacy calls for the use of certain fundamental, legislative principles.

Principles are a Must in a *Rechtsstaat*

On the basis of experiences from different regimes of terror, a number of philosophers started thinking during the Enlightenment in the 1700s that the use of punishment as a steering tool would have to be subjected to certain limitations. Punishment can so easily be abused by those in power to fight political opponents. Consequently, criminal laws should be adopted in accordance with democratic principles and used while observing a number of procedural guarantees. Even if those in power only use punishment while observing specific procedures, punishment is still, however, difficult to justify. This is because punishment interferes with the basic rights of citizens (freedom and property) and has a stigmatising effect. Punishment imposes suffering on citizens for the purpose of making them feel agony. It is difficult to find legitimacy in such an approach. The philosophers of the Enlightenment thus indicated that certain requirements should be imposed in regard to the content of criminal law. Conduct should only be deemed criminal if solid reasons for this existed. Punishment must be a suitable, necessary tool and to be used while observing a requirement for proportionality between means and ends. In addition, the wording of criminal law must be clear and precise.

These requirements concerning *content* apply irrespective of which body adopts the specific legal norm and irrespective of the procedures used. Even lawfully elected popular assemblies that adopt standards in accordance with specific, legitimating procedures may adopt standards which – in the long run – are bound to be deemed illegitimate, since they violate basic principles regarding content.

As mentioned above, the state may not always live up to these ideals. However, a penal system or penal provision does not necessarily or automatically become illegitimate because principles are violated. Citizens in their daily lives cannot keep an eye on whether principles are observed. They may not even know these principles. However, if the shared core values of a society comprise ideals of democracy and the rule of law, it will become clear over time that the legislation concerned is not backed by the people. Consequently, it is the legislator's duty to continually ensure that these principles are not violated. A number of examples of such violations can be quoted. Nazi Germany, for example, adopted a number of changes to criminal law that violated these principles. These changes made it possible to punish individuals who offended public morality. This allowed those in power to persecute everybody they did not like, such as prostitutes, homosexuals, disabled people, etc. Such legislation may very well have been adopted by a democratically elected assembly following a legitimate procedure. However, such legislation is still not legitimate. Consequently, the question is: what requirements should be set as regards the content of legislation?

Most jurists – even across national borders – will probably agree that legislation should be based on some basic principles. However, it is more doubtful whether they can agree on *which* principles and *how* these principles are to be used. For example, it is very likely that criminal law jurists will disagree with administration jurists or EU law jurists on the specific content and use of such principles. Based on administrative law, there will be a tendency to focus on the system and to use criminal law as a tool for regulation (Greve 2008: 110 et seq.). Criminal law jurists often focus on the individual rather than the state or the system, and will find criminalisation unfounded or problematic, while jurists from other law disciplines may consider the use of punishment to be appropriate. Obviously, these are rough generalisations and simplifications, but the tendencies are noticeable. The attitudes of EU law jurists and criminal law jurists also clash, e.g. when the EU finds that there are no problems in adopting administrative measures which resemble penal sanctions, but does not provide the same legal guarantees for these measures (Elholm 2002: 232 et seq.).

In 2009, 14 criminal law researchers, including the writer of this chapter, from 10 different EU countries published 'A Manifesto on European Criminal Policy' (hereafter: the manifesto). This manifesto forms the basis of the thoughts put forward in this chapter. The work process for preparing the manifesto showed that criminal law researchers were able to agree on the principles, while they had more difficulties reaching agreement with researchers from other fields of law.[1]

Criminal Law Ideologies

The application of criminal law means that the state uses its monopoly on power to agonise citizens. If this is to be legitimate and find the backing of citizens, the state must have good reasons to use punishment. In different punishment ideologies, explanations are given for the good reasons that may exist for using punishment. The analysis is often divided into legislative level, sentencing level and serving-of-sentence level.[2] The rationale behind using punishment may very well vary depending on the level concerned. As mentioned, this author will focus only on the legislative level in this chapter.

It is assumed that the answer to the question of why the state should impose punishment is general prevention. The state introduces penal law rules in order to influence citizen behaviour. Criminalisation is based on a wish to protect one or more rights, such as property rights, the rights of sexual self-determination, life and health, etc. This author takes this to be the case in all EU countries to a certain extent, and also assumes that general prevention (both as a deterrent and as a morality booster) represents a 'good reason' for criminalisation, i.e. 'the general justifying aim'. Incidentally, the principles addressed below fit best with such basic assumptions.

In a criminal law context, the opposite of Utilitarianism is often the Ethics of Duty, which is based in particular on Kantian ideas expressing the view that effects of actions are not so important, but rather the fact that a person has 'ill will'. This is an extensive discourse, which will not be dealt with any further in this chapter. Suffice it to say that even if the ideology of punishment may have an influence on the question of legitimacy, this author actually finds that the following principles make criminal law legislation more legitimate, regardless of whether the underlying ideology of punishment is based on Utilitarianism or the Ethics of Duty. In actual fact, most EU countries have a mixed – or at least not a particularly clear – ideology. The normative account of legitimacy given in this chapter should apply to the penal legislation of all EU countries.

The question of duty or utility is a question of 'why', offering an idea of why we punish and giving a reason for using punishment. Different from this question

1 For the latest – most updated – version of the manifesto see European Criminal Policy Initiative (2011).

2 See also Jareborg (1992).

– although with a clear connection – is the question of 'how'. How do we design our penal system? Or, more specifically, how do we design criminalisation? The following principles are 'how' principles.

Protection of Fundamental Interests

According to the writers of the manifesto, the state should use punishment only to protect fundamental societal interests. Obviously, the definition of fundamental interests is a relative matter. Certainly, this definition will vary from one person to the next, from one country to the next and from one time to another. That makes this principle difficult for the legislator to use as a guiding principle. Put simply, it might say too little or be too unclear.

However, most people might be able to support the two following statements. Firstly, not all unwanted or offensive actions should be subject to punishment; put differently, not all such actions are worthy of punishment. Societal interest of a certain weight or value must be involved to make something a criminal offence. Secondly, the limit for what is worthy of punishment varies from one country to the next. Many countries restrict their criminal law to rather serious violations and use a kind of administrative sanction for minor offences. In Denmark, punishments (fines) are used for even very minor offences. This would be difficult to accept for a number of other countries. Hence, there are important differences between the countries.

In this author's view, if these two statements are correct, this means that the EU legislator must show some reluctance when it comes to insisting on having various actions designated as a criminal offence. The EU legislator should essentially insist on having only rather serious violations – i.e. involving significant societal interests and a need for protection – designated as criminal offences. If this is not ensured, there is a risk that the public support for legislation may be weakened in those countries, where criminalisation is not considered necessary.

This author is well aware that national legislators, too, do not always comply with such a principle. The social state often tends to make every minor offence criminal. This is a widely used counter-argument against imposing such requirements on the EU legislator. However, lack of compliance at the national level does not mean that the specific point could be a good idea at EU level. In addition, the national legislator is also seen to run into legitimacy problems for the same reason. For the EU, this is worth avoiding. In addition, cooperation in the EU involves special dynamics that may accelerate the problem. If the EU interferes in the criminalisation of even minor offences with a view to greater harmonisation of EU state legislations, there is a risk that a system, which shows the least tolerance to socially undesirable behaviour, even if they are only minor transgressions, would win the day. If one country makes a specific minor offence criminal and the EU chooses this as a starting point for criminalisation (and, in fact, the EU criminal law legislation concerns precisely such minimum harmonisation), the EU could contribute by introducing legislation for a great many minor offences in a number of countries. The EU will thus contribute towards more repression, which will weaken the legitimacy of EU legislation in a number of countries.

It is interesting to see that some attention is now starting to be paid to this problem in the EU. In a press release, Viviane Reding, Vice President of the European Commission, refers to the manifesto and points out that, in the future, the EU should comply with a number of fundamental legislative principles in its criminal law. In a new legislative proposal for a Directive on criminal sanctions for insider dealing and market manipulation the Commission has restricted the EU's claim for criminalisation to the more serious violations (the proposal defines what is to be understood by serious violations).

> However, criminal sanctions may not be appropriate for all types of violations and in all cases. The … Commission will assess whether … criminal offences and sanctions may prove to be essential in order to ensure the effective implementation of EU financial services legislation. The proposal follows the approach set out in the Communication of 20 September 2011 'Towards an EU criminal policy – Ensuring the effective implementation of EU policies through criminal law'. This includes an assessment, based on clear factual evidence, an assessment of the national enforcement regimes in place and the added value of common EU minimum criminal law codes, taking into account the principles of necessity, proportionality and subsidiarity. (European Commission 2011b: 2)[3]

This might mark a clear change of the course in the Commission's criminal policy. There has been a tendency for punishment to be applied for the protection of even the smallest or remotest interest or for punishment to automatically be considered an effective means.[4] However, much will depend on the future application of the principles mentioned. The proposal on insider trading and market manipulation has been put forward with Article 83(2) of the Treaty on the Functioning of the European Union (hereafter: TFEU) as the legal basis. The many framework decisions adopted in the past – where the EU has insisted on criminalisation – will be converted into future Directives with Article 83(1) of the Treaty on the Functioning of the European Union as the legal basis. Perhaps the Commission is merely cautious about Article 83(2), and perhaps the proposed directive on insider dealing is just an isolated occurrence. Time will tell. However, the message that in future the Commission will use the principles of the manifesto is interesting, at least on an ideological level.

---

3 See also the Communication *Towards an EU Criminal Policy: Ensuring the Effective Implementation of EU Policies through Criminal Law* (European Commission 2011a).

4 See also ground 117 of the Attorney General Ján Mázak's proposal in the decision of 28 June 2007 (Mázak 2007).

The example from the proposed Directive on criminal sanctions for insider dealing and market manipulation shows that the principle of protecting fundamental interests is actually more operational at EU level than one might think at first glance. Another witness to this is the manifesto itself. In an annex, the 14 criminal law researchers reviewed the EU's criminal law legislation over the last 10–15 years. They agreed on a number of examples of situations in which EU legislation infringes or does not infringe this principle. Thus, criminal law jurists seem to be able to agree on this across borders.

Incidentally, the manifesto recommends that the EU's criminal law regulation should only be applied to protect fundamental interests, provided that:

1. These interests can be derived from the primary legislation of the EU.
2. The Constitutions of the Member States and the fundamental principles of the EU Charter of Fundamentals Rights are not violated.
3. The activities in question could cause significant damage to society or individuals.

It is worth mentioning that the principle of fundamental interests (and other principles mentioned below) does not prevent EU from legislating on criminal law or set any absolute limits for such legislation. The principle seems rather to work as a starting point for deliberations and considerations which EU legislators should involve. One condition if this is to work is that the EU provides a detailed justification for its legislation, which includes 'a thorough explanation of why the interests in question shall be regarded as being of fundamental importance, and why the act marked as a criminal offence shall be considered to have a considerable negative impact on the interests concerned. Enforcement of the objectives and policies of the European Union cannot, by itself, legitimise the criminalisation of an act' (European Criminal Policy Initiative 2011: 87). The same line of argument can in fact be found in the decision of the German Federal Constitutional Court concerning Article 83(2) of the Lisbon Treaty. The Court says that the authority granted by Art. 83(2) is very broad and that if this is to be in accordance with the German Constitution, the interpretation must be restrictive; EU criminal law legislation must be necessary and specifically reasoned.[5]

5 Bundesverfassungsgericht, NJW 2009, recital 2288. See also Mázak (2007), ground 67: 'The criminal code is different in many respects from other fields of law. Through the toughest, most deterring means of social control – punishment – it marks the outer limits of acceptable behaviour, thus protecting the values that are highly prioritised by the population at large'.

Suitability, Necessity and Proportionality of Criminal Law

The manifesto includes a number of principles rooted in the thoughts of Enlightenment. Principles of the suitability, necessity and *ultima ratio* of the punishment are based on the line of thinking which believes that punishment imposes agony or suffering on citizens. Punishment interferes and stigmatises. Therefore, unnecessary suffering cannot be legitimised. Likewise, imposing agony on the citizen cannot be legitimised if it fails to have any (positive) effect. Consequently, punishment must be a necessary and suitable tool. If a less intrusive (suitable) means is available, punishment should not be used. These requirements, which are often proposed by the principle of proportionality – incidentally, also in EU law – are combined with a requirement that punishment should be used only as a 'last resort' (*ultima ratio*).

The principle of *ultima ratio* has been criticised for offering the legislator poor guidance (Böse 2011). This is mainly because of two features of the principle. Firstly, it is abstract; in connection with *ultima ratio*, the concept of punishment is used (punishment should be the last resort), but in reality punishment covers a wide range of interventions with widely varying intensity. Secondly, the concept is relative; according to the principle of *ultima ratio*, punishment must be the last resort, so it becomes all-important how other options are assessed. The concept of punishment typically comprises both incarceration and fines (as well as other types of punishment). However, the degree of intervention in these two types of punishment is widely different and there are bound to be other types of sanctions, which, in the circumstances, could be deemed to be more intrusive than punishment. A person who operates a business and who, because of a violation, has had his licence to operate the business withdrawn will probably see the fine as a minor sanction.

This criticism is justified and serves to further emphasise that the *ultima ratio* requirement is to be understood in connection with the principle of proportionality. In addition to the requirements that punishment must be a suitable and necessary means, the principle of proportionality also means there must be a reasonable relationship between the means and the end. In a criminal law context, this means that the punishment must fit the crime reasonably well. All in all, the *ultima ratio* and the proportionality principles lead to the following guidelines for the legislator:

- Firstly, the more serious the crime, the more legitimate would seem to be the use of punishment (always provided that the other criteria for using punishment are met, such as effectiveness and necessity).
- The less serious the crime, the less the use of punishment would seem to be justified – all other things being equal.
- Secondly, the more serious the crime, the more justified the use of intervening punishment (incarceration).
- The less serious the crime, the more legitimate would be to use fines (instead of incarceration).

These requirements contain certain guidelines for the EU legislator, who must consider and argue along the following points:

1. Is it reasonable at all in a given area (for a given act) to insist on the use of penal sanctions, i.e. is the violation of the law serious enough to warrant the introduction of penal sanctions?
2. If penal sanctions should be used, what would be a reasonable sanction, i.e. is the violation serious enough to warrant incarceration or only a fine (or other types of punishment)?
3. Is the penal sanction suitable for achieving the desired goal?
4. Is the penal sanction necessary to achieve the desired goal or could other, less intrusive means be used instead?

These considerations are no different from what the national legislator should consider. However, the special nature of EU legislation, i.e. the fact that EU criminal law legislation deals with approximation of member states' national criminal law via minimum harmonisation, makes it necessary for the EU to consider and argue also the following points:

1. Is a given area (a given act that violates EU law) *serious enough* for the EU to request approximation of criminal law sanctions in all EU countries?
2. Is the EU's requirement for criminal law approximation *suitable* to achieve the desired goal?
3. Is the EU's request for approximation of criminal law legislation *necessary* to achieve the desired goal?

In EU criminal law legislation, the tendency so far has been to automatically deem criminal law means as suitable and necessary. The EU should rather try to prove suitability and necessity of criminalisation, and should support it with empirical data.[6]

There has also been a tendency on the part of the EU to regard the failure to introduce criminal law regulation in a country as a weakness with respect to the implementation of specific legislation. The EU should give greater consideration to the fact whether this is actually the case. It may well be that a country refrained from introducing criminal law legislation in a specific field because violations in the said field were not deemed to be serious, or because punishment was not deemed to be suitable or necessary. The question is why, if this is the case, does the EU have to interfere in this member state's assessment by requesting that legislation be introduced? It may even be the case that other countries, too, could benefit from *not* criminalising the conduct concerned, consequently being in everyone's best interest that the EU actually proposes decriminalisation. This

6 Cf. the line of thinking in the Bundesverfassungsgericht, NJW 2009, section 2288 (German Federal Constitutional Court 2009).

would lead to a more balanced EU criminal law policy, to one that is not always pointing in a repressive direction.

Legality

In a country based on the rule of law, it is of a fundamental importance that the use of punishment is warranted by legislation. Such legislation must rest on a democratic basis. In the Age of Enlightenment, this requirement was called *nulla poena sine lege parlamentaria*. The parliamentary basis concerns the processing for adopting legislation, but the principle of *nulla poena sine lege* also makes demands on the contents of legislation. Legislation must be sufficiently clear and reliable as a basis for punishment and consequently – as a reflex of this requirement – it is important that criminal law legislation itself is worded clearly and precisely (*lex certa*). Criminal law provisions must provide a certain degree of predictability for citizens and draw the line between what is punishable and what is not. In addition, legislators may not adopt criminal law provisions that work retrospectively.

These requirements are the shared inheritance and shared core values of the EU countries. This can be seen, for example, from Article 7 of the European Human Rights Convention and the EU Charter, Article 49. This is not controversial. However, it is much more difficult to decide when a standard lives up to these requirements. The manifesto provides a number of examples of situations in which these requirements are not met. In this chapter, only particular elements that are specific to the EU legislator will be looked at. EU framework decisions and (after the commencement of the Lisbon Treaty) Directives concerning criminal law are in the form of framework legislation that binds member states in regard to the goal of such legislation, but leaves the member states certain room for deciding on the mode and means required for implementation. How does this relate to the requirements of *lex certa*? It could be argued that EU legislation is certainly not clear, precise and predictable, as it leaves the assignment of providing *lex certa* to the national legislator, when EU legislation is transposed into national law. Furthermore, it could be argued that EU legislation *should not* be clear and precise, because member states should be allowed some latitude so as to be able to adapt the requirements of the EU to their national criminal law. There is no doubt that this argument is significant.

On the other hand, the argument is too simplified. If the EU legislator does not provide a sufficiently clear, precise picture of what is to be criminalised, the national legislator is left with a problem. Firstly, the legislator may choose to specify the norm, the criminalisation, but this runs the risk of having national criminal law norms that do not adequately cover what the EU wants to have criminalised. Secondly, the national legislator may choose to adopt the EU's unclear criminalisation, but this violates the principle of *lex certa*. Thirdly and finally, the national legislator may choose a precise, but very broad criminalisation, so that the EU requirements have doubtlessly been met, but in a way that leads to an aggressive, unnecessarily repressive criminal law policy that violates the above-mentioned principles of proportionality and *ultima ratio*. Because of the shortage of time and resources, national legislators are often under pressure when it comes to transposing EU legislation. My impression is that, in a number of cases, member states directly adopt the wording of the EU legislation, which may lead to unclear penal provisions. The definition of terrorism in Danish law is a case in point. Parts of the wording of the EU framework decision have namely been directly transposed into the Danish criminal law. By trying to comply with the *lex certa* principle, EU legislation may therefore also contribute to enhancing the quality of national criminal laws.

Culpability

In a country based on the rule of law, the principle that citizens will only be punished within the limits of their own culpability is a fundamental principle (see further in relation to EU criminal law, Kaiafa-Gbandi 2011: 30–33). This requirement has an objective and a subjective side. The objective side is reflected in the requirement that citizens be punished only for actions (or omissions) they committed or to which they themselves contributed. One of the purposes of the rules on aiding and abetting is to delimit the scope of this liability.

The subjective side is a requirement that citizens should only be punished for actions they have committed 'with malice aforethought' or which they should have avoided or averted. This is the idea of *mens rea*. Citizens can only be culpable for crimes that comply with the subjective requirement. Since punishment is the state's way of expressing blame for the citizen's behaviour towards the citizen, the subjective requirement is also quite essential, while the rules on accountability set limits.

When it comes to the length of sentences, these requirements – combined with the proportionality principle – mean that the scope and roughness of the crime, including the perpetrator's accountability (intent or negligence), are important criteria for the determination of the length of the sentence. Generally speaking, EU criminal law seems to take the question of culpability into account, but there are exceptions, e.g. when the EU wants to put aiding and abetting on the same level as a 'completed' crime (European Criminal Policy Initiative 2011: 96f.).

Coherence and Subsidiarity

The following two principles are of a slightly different nature than those addressed above. They are not true Enlightenment principles. In my view, however, they are still indispensable for a country based on the rule of law if its criminal law is to be legitimate.

All principles mentioned in this chapter help to create coherence in the criminal law system of a country based on the rule of law. If a criminal law system is to be deemed legitimate – and work efficiently and effectively – major self-contradictions and value contradictions in the system must be avoided. This applies both at the overall, general level, i.e. the rules must reflect shared values to a certain extent, and at the specific level, i.e. the rules must be worded in such a way that they are consistent and not contradictory. This is the requirement of the principle of coherence.

Overall, coherence is important in a criminal law system, because '[s]uch inner coherence is necessary if the criminal law should be able to reflect the values held collectively by the society and if criminal law should be able to meet the understandings of justice held by individuals in the society' (Asp 2011: 47). Criminal law is a much-favoured management tool, but it is also a system of standards which communicate moral and ethical values and which via the punishment are linked to society's censure for the violating of norms. Without a certain amount of coherence in the system of norms and without a basic, shared set of values that are not too self-contradictory, punishment cannot fulfil this important function. Legitimacy is thus weakened. If citizens feel that the system is self-contradictory, this also impacts on the effectiveness of criminal law regulation.

At the specific level, i.e. regarding the individual Act or penal provision, a certain amount of coherence should be ensured. The rules of an Act of Parliament should not be self-contradictory or contradict the rules of other, related Acts. Coherence should extend to the terminology itself. The same elements or phenomenon should be called the same, while different phenomena should be named differently. In this connection, it is worth mentioning that the different levels in a criminal law system (legislative level, sentencing level and sentence-serving level) must satisfactorily interact. The legitimacy of a criminal law system is weakened, for example, if the minimum and maximum sentences for different types of crime are not proportionate in relation to each other, or if the application of law does not match the intentions of the legislation and so forth. If the legislator establishes rules that do not work in practice, the system seems self-contradictory and loses out on legitimacy. Consequently, a certain amount of coherence among the different levels must be ensured.

To the EU legislator, this means two things in particular. Firstly, the EU legislator must ensure that the EU's different legal norms and rules are connected and coherent. The EU is working continually to ensure that this is the case, but a greater degree of coordination in all cases where the EU uses criminal law should be sought. Proposals for EU legislation in which criminal law regulation is used are put forward by the different administrative units of the Commission;[7] coordination across the Commission's services should be ensured, so as to seek

7 Two Directorates General of the Commission in particular, i.e. DG Justice (at the moment led by Viviane Reding) and DG Home Affairs (at the moment led by Cecilia Malmstrøm), are involved.

coherence both generally and specifically in order to have uniform EU criminal law rules that are not contradictory. This could be called horizontal coherence. This means that the EU legislator must (1) take other EU instruments involving criminal law regulation into consideration when new punishment rules are issued, (2) use the same terminology for the same legal instruments and different terms for different instruments, and (3) use the same principles and solutions if, and only if, (a) the function and character of the two instruments are comparable, and (b) the intensity of the intervention towards the citizen is comparable in the two situations. On the abstract level one could say that Art. 7 TFEU does express the principle of coherence. However, Art. 7 is talking about coherence between 'politics and activities', while the above-mentioned requirements are rather more concrete.

What has been written here concerns relationships between different parts of EU legislation. However, in the EU context, coherence also means – as a secondary consideration – that vertical aspects must be considered as well, i.e. considerations about relationships between EU legislation and national criminal law. The EU legislator is in a special situation because EU criminal legislation must be transposed and work in 27 different countries. Each of these countries has its own penal system based on inner connections and coherence. When the EU makes criminal law regulations, there is a risk of disturbing this coherence. If the EU insists on higher minimum and maximum sentences in a given field, some countries will have to adjust their minimum and maximum sentences in other areas so as to maintain their inner coherence. The EU should pay attention to this aspect and allow the member states to adapt EU legislation to their own systems. One might say that this is expressed – although indirectly – in Art. 4(2) of TEU. According to this article, the EU must respect the 'national identities'. In the same way Art. 82(2) TFEU on judicial cooperation in criminal matters mentions that the EU must take different national legal traditions into account.

In this connection, the principle of subsidiarity becomes relevant. Article 5(3) of the EU Treaty says that the EU 'may intervene ... in areas which do not fall within its exclusive competence only insofar as the objectives of the intended action cannot be sufficiently achieved' by the member states. This principle relates to the principle of proportionality. This can be distinguished not only from the fact that the principle of proportionality is also mentioned in Article 5 but also from the fact that both principles concern *the necessity* of EU legislation.

Subsidiarity not only concerns the institutional and organisational aspect of how competences are to be divided between the EU legislator and the national legislator. In my view, this principle is closely associated with democracy and self-determination. All other things being equal, the closer to citizens decisions are made, the more democratic they are. Conversely, this means the further away from citizens they are, the less democratic they are. 'By respecting the principle of subsidiarity the citizens are given as much freedom to decide over their lives as possible' (Asp 2011: 46).

The principle of subsidiarity must be subordinate to the principles of proportionality and *ultima ratio* (ibid.). If the proportionality test shows that punishment is a suitable, necessary and reasonable tool, the question that follows is whether the EU legislator is the one to legislate, or whether should this be left to the national legislator? In many cases and perhaps more than any other type of legislation, criminal law is associated with a country's historic and cultural roots and shared ethical values. 'Criminal law more than other fields of the law widely reflects special cultural, moral, financial and other attitudes in society and is particularly affected by developments in society' (Mázak 2007: ground 105, see also ground 68). Acceptance by citizens of the criminal law rules, and thus their legitimacy, therefore depends to a certain extent on a country's history and culture. The principle of subsidiarity, which divides competences between the EU legislator and the national legislator, thus has special significance in criminal law. This is not to be understood to mean that the EU should not use criminal law legislation at all. In some cases, this is even useful and necessary; however, the EU criminal law legislation should take account of the special nature of criminal law and the close links to a country's culture and history. Yet, it should be mentioned that this link varies with the nature of the criminal law rules and the field of regulation. Certainly, much criminal law regulation does not involve a country's historical, cultural and ethical basis, e.g. some criminal law provisions within business law regulations.

One last point concerning subsidiarity: this principle should be analysed in relation to the specific elements of, or the specific provisions in, the proposed EU legislation, and not in relation to the overall objectives of a proposal. When the EU puts forward a proposal for a directive to fight insider trading across the borders, there is not much discussion about the principle of subsidiarity. It is easy to put forward a general argument saying that EU legislation, including criminal law rules, is necessary to fight this type of crime. However, it does not follow that requirements concerning maximum sentences are a necessary and suitable tool. Actually, it may well be that the individual countries are better able to ensure that the right, most effective minimum and maximum sentences and level of punishment are used. Incidentally, this is a view also presented by the Advocate General in the much-discussed case concerning the competences of the EU – prior to the Lisbon Treaty – when it comes to laying down requirements concerning minimum and maximum sentences in member states. In his view 'and in line with the principle of subsidiarity, member states are basically better equipped than the Community when it comes to "laying down" the concept of "sanctions that are effective, relate reasonably to the law infringement, and have a deterring effect" in relation to their respective criminal law systems and societal context' (Mázak 2007: ground 108, but see also grounds 104–108).

This is why – in my view – each aspect of a bill of law, each provision of a directive, should be discussed independently in regard to the principle of subsidiarity, and the question of criminalisation and requirements concerning minimum and maximum sentences should be discussed independently as they relate to the principle of subsidiarity. If the principle of subsidiarity is not used in a specific way, but only regarded as a general requirement on a EU instrument (for example a directive) as a whole, the practical impact of the principle is weakened; all EU legislation will automatically be in accordance with such a principle.

Why the Same Principles in the EU as in the Member States?

The above principles – perhaps with the exception of the principle of subsidiarity – are more or less inherited from the Age of Enlightenment. There is not always compliance with these principles and they are not always used in full, but in general the member states support the line of thinking involved, which is expressed in constitutions and international conventions, etc., which the countries have signed, including the EU Charter. However, one could ask why should the same requirements be imposed on the EU legislator? Are the situations comparable? As can also be seen above, there are major differences between a national legislator and the EU legislator; for example, the existing EU legislation (in the field of criminal law) basically consists of the framework legislation, which must be transposed and implemented in all member states. So, is it in fact possible to transfer the aforementioned principles to the EU legislative level? In this author's view, there are plenty of reasons to do so:

1. The invasive, stigmatising nature of penal sanctions is not affected by whether punishment is warranted via EU rules or under purely national auspices.
2. The EU adheres to the same basic democratic values and rule of law values as the member states.
3. As a consequence of the shared core values, EU legislation, too, must comply with these values. This contributes towards the legitimation of EU legislation.
4. As a consequence of the close link between the function of the EU's criminal law regulation and the member states' criminal law, it is necessary for the EU legislator to consider the aforementioned principles so as to avoid contradictions that would affect the effectiveness and legitimacy of the criminal law systems as a whole.
5. When the legitimacy of EU criminal law legislation is increased, the level of trust among member state authorities in cross-border criminal law cooperation will also increase, which includes the trust of users of the law, when it comes to using EU legislation as prescribed.

The latter reason, i.e. increased trust among authorities using the law in transnational cases, is perhaps the strongest political argument supporting the view that EU legislation should observe the aforementioned principles and ensure the legitimacy of EU legislation. The fact is that the Commission, in particular, is seeking to generate more trust in order to ensure that cooperation in the area of criminal law runs smoothly within the EU. EU criminal law that coherently and consistently builds on a number of rule of law principles has the best chance of being accepted by the citizens in the EU. Legitimacy and trust go hand in hand.

References

Asp, P. 2011. The importance of the principles of subsidiarity and Coherence in the development of EU Criminal Law. *European Criminal Law Review (EuCLR)*, 1(1), 44–55.

Böse, M. 2011. The principle of proportionality and the protection of legal interests. *European Criminal Law Review*, 1(1), 35–43.

Bottoms, A. and Tankebe, J. 2012. Beyond procedural justice: A dialogic approach to legitimacy in criminal law. *The Journal of Criminal Law and Criminology*, 102(1), 119–70.

Elholm, T. 2002. *EU-svig. En studie i dansk strafferet*. Copenhagen: Jurist- og Økonomforbundets Forlag.

European Commission. 2011a. *Communication from the Commission, Towards an EU Criminal Policy: Ensuring the Effective Implementation of EU Policies through Criminal Law*, COM (2011) 573 Final.

European Commission. 2011b. *Proposal for a Directive of the European Parliament and the Council on Criminal Sanctions for Insider Dealing and Market Manipulation*, COM (2011) 654 Final.

European Criminal Policy Initiative. 2011. The Manifesto on European Criminal Policy in 2011, *European Criminal Law Review (EuCLR)*, 1(1), 86–103.

German Federal Constitutional Court (Bundesverfassungsgericht). 2009. Judgment of the Second Senate of 30 June 2009, (BVerfG, 2 BvE 2/08 vom 30.6.2009, Absatz-Nr. (1-421).

Greve, V. 2008. Retsdisciplinernes sammenstød. *Juristen*, 4, 109–19.

Jareborg, N. 1992. *Straffrättsideologiska fragment*. Uppsala: Iustus Förlag.

Kaiafa-Gbandi, M. 2011. The importance of core principles of substantial criminal law. *European Criminal Law Review (EuCLR)*, 1(1), 7–34.

Mázak, J. (Attorney General). 2007. Proposal in the decision of 28 June 2007, case C-440/05, European Court Reports 2007, I-09097.

Treaty on European Union (TEU, Consolidated version). 2010. Official Journal of the European Union, C 83/13, 30 March 2010.

Treaty on the Functioning of the European Union (TFEU, Consolidated version). 2010. Official Journal of the European Union, C 83/47, 30 March 2010.

PART II
Legitimacy and Trust in the Judiciary: Contradictions and Challenges

Chapter 6

Legitimacy and Trust-Related Issues of Judiciary: New Challenges for Europe

Nina Peršak and Jože Štrus[1]

Introduction: Legitimacy Related to Public Trust and Beyond

The public trust in judicial authorities in many European countries has been a source of concern for quite some time now. As regards criminal courts and prisons, it has been observed that these 'low-visibility areas' of the criminal justice system receive the lowest confidence and satisfaction ratings from the general public (Nicholas et al., in Almond 2008). The latest Eurobarometer to record inter alia the trust in national justice systems showed that while in five Member States (DK, FI, SE, AT and NL) more than two-thirds of the public trusted the justice system, in six countries (in BG, LT, SI, RO, PT and SK) less than a third of the public expressed this trust (Eurobarometer 2010).[2]

Public trust (or distrust) in judiciary is important in various ways. Firstly, it affects compliance (Fagan 2008, Tyler 2006, 2009). Citizens who believe that, on average, 'institutions will prove to be trustworthy, i.e. will be fair, competent and bring about desirable outcomes' (Levi, in Letki 2006: 309) and therefore fulfil their obligations are significantly less likely to break the rules or cheat (ibid.).

1 The views expressed in this chapter are personal ones and cannot be considered as an official position of the Commission.

2 The cited Eurobarometer has shown that Nordic countries seem to trust the most, while among those that trust the least are mostly former Communist and socialist countries. In this context, specific problems of transitional justice can become particularly salient. Distrust may also have historic and cultural roots (and the above Eurobarometer findings seem to confirm this). Letki and Evans (2005) have, for example, observed that institutional trust has been significantly reduced under the Communist regime. The new democratic governments have inherited a citizenry with low levels of trust (Rose-Ackerman 2001). Distrust and cynicism have been labelled as 'the predictable legacy of Communist rule' as well as quite a natural consequence of living under Communist regimes as, even though some of the latter may have been more totalitarian than others, all were 'inclined to subjugate individual interests to those of the Communist Party' (Mishler and Rose 1997: 419, 420). This is said to have resulted in alienation from state institutions and a lingering distrust toward both, political and civil institutions (ibid.). Transition itself has, however, added to this through people's raised expectations that have not always been met and processes, such as privatisation, that caused certain social discontent (Peršak 2011).

A good image of some state institution therefore affects citizens' (law-abiding) behaviour, as well-performing institutions are likely to elicit support, confidence and compliance from citizens (Lind and Tyler 1988).

Secondly, it has important repercussions for the perception of violations of human rights. The more people distrust their own judicial system, the more they feel the violations of human rights abound. A study by Doise (2001) found that those respondents who distrusted their own judicial systems consistently broadened the domain of situations that they considered to be violations of human rights. They were also more often certain in their judgments about what a violation of human rights is and what it is not. This may mean that the representation of judiciary acts as a catalyst for the representation of the state of human rights.

Thirdly, from the perspective of judges (and other court officials) themselves, the legitimacy in the sense of public acceptance or trust in courts or good public opinion about their work is important for the self-image and work efficiency. The public opinion as an opinion of the 'Significant Other' importantly influences the self-image of judiciary and consequently the work motivation of the court personnel. While a good public opinion of one's work is stimulating, the negative opinion of others can negatively affect the performance of one's duties. Being a judge used to be considered a respectful profession, a profession that is nowadays often marred by the negative representation thereof in the eyes of the public and media. The circle becomes vicious when the constant vexation and negative labelling of their organisation negatively influences judges' self-image and consequently decreases their work motivation, which in the long run cannot, for example, help decrease the backlogs (Peršak 2005). Unfavourable public opinion may also stimulate political leaders (who are electively dependent on people's views) to put pressure on the courts, which may endanger judicial independence.

What affects trust can be attributed to several factors. Tyler (2006) has asserted that fairness of the process or procedural justice is the most crucial factor in establishing trust; fair and respectful processes are said to be the best ways for attaining trust in justice and consequent institutional legitimacy – the finding that has been particularly supported when studying the trust and legitimacy of the police. An experimental study by Van den Bos, Wilke and Lind (1998) has indicated that procedural fairness is particularly needed in the absence of information about an authority's trustworthiness. The old adage 'Justice delayed is justice denied', furthermore, indicates that the length of proceedings matter as well. A fair trial within a reasonable time is not only a fundamental right but also provides a basis for one's assessment of the courts' functioning.

While fairness and reasonable speed are the two factors commonly flagged as important, they are not, however, the only criteria, according to which people form their views on courts. In the context of courts, good functioning or performance could mean and depend on one, several or all of the following non-exhaustive factors: fairness, expeditiousness, efficiency and effectiveness, outcomes, as well as communication with clients and transparency. Some people may be, for example, satisfied with the court performance only insofar the outcome (the judgment) is in line with their expectations or, if personally involved, is in their favour. They may be even inclined to interpret something as 'fair' only insofar they are happy with the end result (Turner and Stets 2005). The 'fairness' here has more to do with the perceived fairness of decision outcomes (or distributive justice), rather than the fairness of decision-making processes though (Colquitt et al. 2012).

Trust may, further, also be affected by other, extra-judicial criteria, such as personal traits (some people have more trusting personalities than other), media representations of judiciary,[3] one's general outlook on life, knowledge and other personal experiences,[4] all of which are not necessarily equally worthy of consideration, i.e. should not be given equal weight when pondering about what to do or how to improve the judicial system. Trust can also be affected by the legal culture, or rather the degree of normative integration (integration of norms) within a society. Igličar (2012) thus believes that legal culture or degree of normative integration is reflected in people's reported degree of trust in courts, as the trust in courts is connected to the values that are prevailing in a certain global society. To understand this point, it is perhaps useful to distinguish here between identification-based trust and knowledge-based trust (or affect-based and cognition-based trust, respectively), a distinction often neglected by justice scholars, as psychologists point out (Colquitt et al. 2012). Igličar's trust in courts, related or even derived from the prevailing values, seems to be affect-based or identification-based trust, not really cognition-based trust that is based on our past experiences and 'reflects a confidence rooted in someone's track record and reputation for dependability, reliability, and professionalism' (Colquitt et al. 2012: 2). Rather than the conviction that concrete courts are trustworthy, it seems to comprise a belief that courts ought to be trusted and an expectation that they will do what they are supposed to do.

However, public acceptance or trust people may or may not experience vis-à-vis judiciary is not the be-all and end-all of legitimacy of courts. Not all public institutions are equally dependent on popular support. While democratic political leaders are much higher on the ladder of dependence, judiciary follows a different set of goals and values (pleasing the public not being one of them) and therefore much less relies on public support. Moreover, while the public perception of the courts as functioning well is of course important, what is more important is that they do, in fact, function well. In this light, it is particularly worrisome if the perception of the public and people's trust is based on actual dis-functioning of

3 Opinions about the courts, as research has shown (e.g. Dimitrijević 2006), are often received and moderated through the media. In today's environment this means that not only 'regular' media but digital media (social networking sites, Twitter, forum discussions, etc.) as well represent an important source of information – and not only for those who participate but also for others who merely visit the site.

4 On the other hand, it should also be noted that the general public is sometimes not very well informed about the organisation of the judiciary, which also influences their perceptions about the judiciary.

the justice system, which may relate, for example, to the quality, independence or efficiency of the justice system.

The question of legitimacy of the judiciary should therefore primarily be defined on normative grounds, i.e. as relating to a morally justified functioning as well as output of a justice system. This normative conception of legitimacy (as opposed to more external, public opinion-based one) derives the content of legitimacy from the internal characteristics of the object studied (in our case, the judiciary). Assessing such legitimacy of judiciary therefore proceeds from the viewpoint of legal standards, rule of law requirements and established substantive criteria that judiciary is supposed to meet, follow or implement. Considering that the main functions of a justice system are dispute resolution and implementation of public policies, embodied in law, the public has a vested interest in ensuring that the justice system delivers judgments and decisions that are independent of outside pressures, achieve a certain quality, are delivered in an efficient manner (mainly as regards to the costs and timeliness) and respect fundamental rights as guaranteed in national constitutions, the EU and international documents.

In what follows we shall limit ourselves to a few important 'classical' factors that affect the legitimacy as well as trust in the justice system (factors that are overlapping, when dysfunctional, with classical problems that stimulate distrust), i.e. access to justice, quality-related issues of justice (quality of judicial decisions), communication with parties, issues of impartiality and judicial independence. With respect to the challenges of the latter, we shall look more closely at the two recent European Commission interventions regarding two Member States, which highlighted the need to take a closer EU-wide look at the functioning of national justice systems. In the view of the EU Justice Scoreboard – a new initiative by the European Commission on the evaluation of national justice systems, which will allow a progressively more detailed assessment of the functioning of justice systems in all Member States, of their strengths and weaknesses –, we will then address the current European justice-related challenges, relating to the effectiveness of national justice systems and consequently effectiveness of EU law.

Factors Affecting Legitimacy of (and Trust in) the Justice System

Access to Justice

Access to justice is a fundamental right, enshrined, for example, in Article 47 of the Charter of Fundamental Rights of the EU (hereafter: the Charter) and in Articles 6 and 13 of the European Convention on Human Rights (hereafter: ECHR).[5] The Charter grants to everyone, whose rights and freedoms guaranteed by EU law are violated, the right to an effective remedy before a tribunal. It provides a right to a fair and public hearing within a reasonable time by an independent and impartial

5 As interpreted by the European Court of Human Rights.

tribunal previously established by law, and to receiving legal aid, if lacking sufficient resources, to the extent necessary to ensure effective access to justice. Article 6 of the ECHR also stipulates that the judgment shall be pronounced publicly but that the press and public may nevertheless be excluded from all or part of the trial in the interest of morals, public order or national security in a democratic society, where the interests of juveniles or the protection of the private life or the parties would so require, or in special circumstances where publicity would prejudice the interests of justice (but here only to the extent strictly necessary in the opinion of the court). Art. 6 also contains the presumption of innocence (para. 2) and lists minimum rights of a person charged with a criminal offence (para. 3). However, while the ECHR in Art. 6 only guarantees the access to an 'independent and impartial tribunal' concerning the determination of one's civil rights and obligations or of any criminal charge against him, and Art. 13 only provides for an effective remedy 'before a national authority' (not necessarily a court) against the violations of human rights and freedoms under the ECHR, the Charter guarantees access to a 'court' for any violation of a right under EU law, including the Charter itself (Praesidium of the European Convention 2007).

Access to justice, however, requires much more than just the existence of an independent tribunal to go to and a reasonable length of proceedings. Before an individual or a company even reaches a court, it is important that they are aware of their rights and informed about the body to which they should turn in case of a violation of their rights. Access to justice is also very much connected to the issue of cost of justice. The access is guaranteed also by not having too high or disproportionate a court fee or court tax (the initial fee for instigating a proceeding) as to preclude the poorer people from seeking justice. In 2010, 42 members of the Council of Europe required that court tax or fee be paid for initiating non-criminal proceedings. In Belgium, Cyprus, Portugal, Serbia, Switzerland and UK-Northern Ireland parties needed to pay taxes even for criminal-law proceedings. Following the introduction of court fees in France in 2011, Luxembourg appears to remain the only EU Member State that provides free access to all courts with the aim of facilitating a wide access to courts (The European Commission for the Efficiency of Justice of the Council of Europe (hereafter: CEPEJ) 2012). The rationale behind having a court fee is to dissuade trivial, unimportant complaints from reaching courts and from judges losing valuable time over trifles, as well as to fund the functioning of the justice system.[6] Disputes of lower value can be directed before a single judge using a simplified procedure or before another independent body, which operates in a less costly way than a court of law. However, the fee should not be as high as to stop important, serious cases from reaching courts.

6 Also, it is understandable that while criminal law cases may be without tax, the same should not necessarily apply for civil law cases. As emphasised by CEPEJ (2010: 112), it may be considered unjust if the cost of disputes, based on private interests, was borne by taxpayers.

The CEPEJ (2010) study, addressing the issue of access to justice, emphasised inter alia also the need to improve the 'social efficiency of the access to justice' such as the adaptation of proceedings to the needs of vulnerable people and victims (by e.g. hearing aids and special procedural rights). What is deemed generally important, however, is to make the party feel involved in the proceedings as a user, a citizen, as an active participant. This may go a long way to the democratisation of justice and generating trust in the judiciary. Being heard, having a voice in the matter, a voice that is actually heard is often felt as the most important element of justice and, for the victims, of their recovery. Listening to the party, not just seeing her as a bundle of potentially legally relevant information, shows her respect and alleviates the effects of secondary victimisation she goes through when she has to describe in the courtroom what exactly happened, re-experiencing, reliving the original victimisation.

Quality of Judicial Decisions and Related Issues of the Quality of Justice

Recognising that the quality of decisions is important for a large part of the quality of justice, CEPEJ in 2007 organised a colloquium on the quality of judicial decisions. The introductory paper highlighted the fact that the quality of judgment is a 'guarantee for the legitimacy of a judge and the confidence in justice on the part of the citizens' (Leyenberger 2007: 10). The trust and legitimacy of the justice system have therefore much to do with the quality of decisions or justice rendered. This quality is dependent, first and foremost, on the legal (substantive and procedural) knowledge of judges and their reasoning skills: ability to distinguish legally relevant facts from irrelevant ones, selection of the right legal rule to apply to the facts, syllogistic skills, absence of logical mistakes in reasoning, quality of argumentation, ability to assess proportionality and apply it in sentencing etc. However, when it comes to value decisions, as Perelman (1979) and Dworkin (1986) argue, the quality of a judgment moves further away from the quality of logic towards the quality of argumentation/persuasion. Value-laden judgment cannot be simply tested on formal logic; such a judgment is good when it is persuasive. A judge, however, need not only be a good lawyer and logician; judges need to have various other skills and specialised knowledge in the ever-increasing fields of human interaction. That is why training of judges and evaluation of courts' activities are so important that they have been included by the European Commission among the indicators of the quality of a justice system (cf. European Commission 2013b: 13 and 18).

This decision-quality element of the legitimacy of justice rendered is of course much more difficult to assess as one either has to know the law to re-evaluate decisions or rely on the external, formal indicators, such as the data on judgments overturned or annulled on appeal or recorded miscarriages of judgment.[7] The

7 These data are, however, also difficult to compare, as the comparability of justice systems at appeals level is lower than at first instance, owing to the different (ordinary and extraordinary) grounds of appeal (to the appeal courts and to the supreme courts).

quality of decisions is not, however, important only in the case at hand but also in terms of making good or bad law. This applies particularly in jurisdictions where a precedential system (doctrine of *stare decisis*) is in place; however, even in those (mostly Continental) systems where there is no formal obligation to take into account a precedent, in practice it is often followed. Even in the systems where on paper only the legislator, not judges, makes the law, the quality of judicial decisions is essential to the quality of the justice system as a whole. Low quality judicial decisions make low quality (case)law.

The quality of decisions is, however, dependent also on the quality of court-appointed experts. In complex cases, judges progressively rely on external experts to provide them with e.g. economic, financial or forensic details on the case. Although not legally bound by their summaries or evaluations, it seems that judges do very often follow the report of the court-appointed expert. If the latter is not very good or makes factual mistakes, the judge is usually in no position to spot them, so the errors provide the factual basis for a later judgment. To avoid such errors, experts need to be scrutinised. A second layer of protection would be, however, if the judge herself possessed some knowledge of the area in order to better understand and question, if necessary, the expert's report. This also touches upon the issue of continuous training of judges.

Mack, Roach Anleu and Wallace (2012), on the other hand, stress the importance of the right caseload allocation and, in particular, of taking into account special skills of judges. They suggest that caseload allocation processes should recognise and match judicial skills and abilities to specific work demands. They claim that Australian courts value the generalist judge, i.e. a judge that is 'able to do everything'; however, they also state that 'this preference for generalist judicial officers can create tensions in relation to the need to staff specialist lists, and to sometimes use particular skills in the general lists' (ibid.: 68). They suggest that judges as well as court users may benefit from a more clearly defined and transparent process to identify and develop skills and expertise, and allocate caseload accordingly.

Communication

The importance of availability and quality of communication – communication within courts, between courts, between courts and other agencies (e.g. social work agencies) as well as communication towards parties, the public and the media – cannot be overemphasised. Courts are not homogeneous entities, led by one-dimensional thinking and acting. On the contrary, within courts – as in other big organisations – 'multiple rationalities' (Eicher and Schedler 2012) exist, which are 'pursuing divergent goals and following different logical patterns' (ibid.: 20).[8] The same applies to the various agents that come before the court, be they individual

8 See also Vander Laenen, in this volume, describing how goals of judiciary and social care workers in a particular judicial case may (and often do) conflict.

parties to the case or agencies called to testify. Different goals and expectations undoubtedly pose challenges in terms of communication, yet sustained (respectful) communication is crucial in the attribution of legitimacy to judiciary.

Looking at the communicative dimension of the relationship between the judiciary and its public, one observes that in some countries it is very limited. The lack of communication often adds to the image of a distant judge – the image which, in itself, could also bear a positive connotation in the sense of being independent and impartial, and therefore disinterested (i.e. not having any particular personal interest in the decision of the case); however, one that may also give the impression that judge is possibly detached from reality and non-transparent in his or her work. For example, unwillingness to provide any information about the court process (that may be merely the explanation that no further information can be given at this point, as the case is still pending) could be perceived unfavourably by the individual or the public, casting a shadow over the institution, which is then projected on its employees.

Judicial communication is important not only as a vehicle for passing on bits of data but also as a method of contextualising the information and shaping public opinion on various matters. As such it can be taken (and perhaps increasingly so) as a litmus test of the quality (and trustworthiness) of the institution, which engages in it – or does not, as the case may be. The enhanced communication between courts or judicial administration and the public could certainly improve the trust in courts and their personnel. By opening channels of communication, the judiciary may be perceived less standoffish,[9] while keeping the appearance of independence and impartiality, and along the way improve people's knowledge about the functioning of the legal (particularly justice) system and convey a more accurate portrayal of the judges' work to the public. This 'opening' to the public, so to speak – either through the more active, visible role of the public-relations office(r) or through bigger engagement in public discussions on judicial matters – may add to a greater transparency and consequently better knowledge of, and higher trust in, judiciary. Parmentier and Vervaeke (2011), for example, suggest that one of the possible reasons for the sharp increase of the public confidence in the Belgian justice system (from 41 per cent in 2002 to 66 per cent in 2007)

9 A recent report by the Group of States against Corruption (GRECO) emphasised this aspect, concretely in relation to the prosecutors, suggesting a public communication strategy be adopted and relevant training provided to tackle the problem of poor communication of the prosecutors with the public. 'The public and the media often do not understand the reasons underlying decisions taken by prosecutors in some cases, especially as regards case dismissals. This poor communication gives the prosecution service the image of a closed and non-transparent body, and observers agree that this perception is one of the main explanations for the negative public image of prosecutors' (GRECO 2012: 52). Furthermore, while acknowledging the importance of confidentiality of information, it stated that confidentiality has to be balanced with the requirements of transparency, which is crucial for confidence in the justice system.

could lie in the efforts exhibited on the part of the Ministry of Justice to engage in more intensive communication with the public about concrete cases and the justice system in general. In France, the infamous Outreau case, which seriously tarnished the image of justice, demonstrated 'the importance of communication in legal cases and the need to handle it properly' (Jeuland and Sotiropoulou 2012: 132). In its aftermath (in 2003), a new position of 'a judge specialised in communication' (magistrat délégué à la communication or MDC), whose function was to improve 'the image and the credibility of judiciary', was created in each Court of Appeal (ibid.: 133).

The judges themselves are well aware of this issue. The President of the Supreme Court of the Republic of Slovenia, for example, has recently reaffirmed the need to openly, even critically, discuss the work of judiciary in society. He found unacceptable the ease with which justice and judges are labelled and denigrated in a way that has nothing to do with the reality of their work or with constructive criticism, but added that judiciary itself has to contribute to improving its image and authority by working better.[10] Engaging in respectful communication towards the parties involved as well as towards the public and the media is certainly one of its elements. Additionally, the communication is reflected in the reasons for judgment. If a judgment is well motivated and argumented, it goes a long way to showing the respect towards the parties, and in particular towards the party who lost the case or the defendant who was convicted. It indicates that time was taken and careful consideration given to the facts of the case. It provides the meaning to the judgment taken.

Jeuland and Sotiropoulou (2012: 134) claim that the traditional structure of French judgments does not provide much room for the argument and explanation. Judgments may be 'very elliptical and brief'. They find a possible explanation in the fact that in pre-revolution times judgments had no motivation at all as judges, representatives of the King, could not know what the King had thought of the case. They emphasise that this is an untenable situation for this day and age. Although a judgment of the Court of Cassation 'includes little if no argument in a few condensed lines', this tradition is, according to them, no longer tolerated by public opinion. The French supreme courts (the Court of Cassation, the Council of State and the Constitutional Council) have responded to this by publishing a special report, which explains the meaning of their judgments. However, Jeuland and Sotiropoulou (2012) suggest that this solution may not be the best, as this report becomes a new source of law that adds to the confusion and difficulties in the interpretation of the judgment. They conclude that although the report

10 'The functioning of judiciary has to be an object of discussion, even critical discussion, in the society. However, the unfathomable ease of labelling and denigrating of judiciary and judges, which has nothing to do with reality and constructive criticism, and thereby undermines their authority is unacceptable. Yet, the judiciary itself has to contribute, of course, to the improvement of its image and authority by functioning better' (Masleša, in Vukelić 2012).

(communiqué) serves as a substitute for the reasons of a judgment, it would be much better therefore to improve the judgments themselves.

Impartiality

There is ample empirical evidence that various biases penetrate into decision-making on account of impartiality. For example, in the so-called stranger rape cases (i.e. rapes by strangers) before a jury in the US, studies have found out that racial bias leads juries to convict black defendants more readily and harshly than white defendants (Bullock 1961, LaFree 1980). Mock jury studies revealed that when the criminal pair is mixed the readiness to convict and severity of the sentence depends on which race is victim's and which defendant's. In cases of black defendant / white victim combination, white jurors tend to convict and recommend a harsh sentence; however, where the defendant is white and the victim black, the fewest guilty verdicts and the mildest sentences are received (Johnson 1941, Bernard 1979, Hans and Vidmar 1986). In a study by Hymes, Leinart, Rowe and Rogers (2001), white American undergraduates deemed both white and black defendants as more guilty when the rape victim (whose consent was ambiguous on the transcript they were given to read) was of different race than their own. Identification of jurors with the victim increases the chances that jurors will vote for conviction (Miller and Hewitt 1978). Differential treatment has been observed also in the case when the perpetrator was a woman (Boritch 1992), although some emphasise that this is dependent on the type of a woman (traditional/non-traditional) on trial. In so far that a female perpetrator assumes the traditional gender role (married, with children, housewife, of traditional values), she receives a milder sanction, while the one not conforming to this stereotype does not. In this case, she may even forfeit those benefits that usually follow from her being a woman and receive a harsher punishment (Johnson and Schreuble, in Herzog and Oreg 2008). Although a student mock jury should not be equated with an actual jury and while a jury is not the same as a professional judge, social biases cannot be completely (if at all) eliminated through legal education.

Discriminatory treatment raises the question as to how 'blind' the justice really is. It is perhaps of some comfort to find out that bias mostly enters when the evidence is ambiguous (Hymes, Leinart, Rowe and Rogers 2001), suggesting that good, effective evidence gathering and quality evidence exposition and decision-making on its basis can significantly contribute to reducing the effect of bias. Continental justice systems that do not have a jury system may in this sense be less prone to bias – a trained professional should become immune – yet, many such systems still know lay judges, who are members of the public and thus arguably less immune. Furthermore, while judges ought to become aware of their potential biases, this does not mean that they, in fact, do become so. Unfortunately, as it is notoriously difficult to research the biases of actual judges, most studies tend to focus on mock jurors, often undergraduate students, which can only be an approximation.

In addition to the training of judges, well-established grounds for recusal of judges and having solid evidence, there are general principles of court administration that may help as well. While a good, transparent principle of caseload allocation cannot help reduce the internal biases of judges, it may help to maintain the perception of impartiality on the outside. In the case of Australia, Mack, Roach Anleu and Wallace (2012: 68) observe that the random distribution of cases among judges or the '"randomness principle" enhances public confidence in the impartial administration of justice'. It is true that actual impartiality and perceived impartiality are not the same things; however, the European Court of Human Rights has on more than one occasion emphasised that perceptions or appearances of independence and impartiality matter.[11]

New European Challenges and Approaches

Independence of Judiciary

In the case *Findlay v. The United Kingdom* (110/1995/616/706 of 25 February 1997) the European Court of Human Rights (hereafter: the ECtHR) emphasised that the concepts of independence and objective impartiality are closely linked. The ECtHR maintained that in order to establish whether a tribunal can be considered as independent, 'regard must be had, inter alia, to the manner of appointment of its members and their term of office, the existence of guarantees against outside pressures and the question whether the body presents an appearance of independence' (para. 76). Impartiality, on the other hand, has been described as having two aspects. The tribunal must be (a) subjectively free of personal prejudice or bias, and (b) objectively impartial, i.e. 'it must offer sufficient guarantees to exclude any legitimate doubt in this respect'. The assessment whether an institution presents an appearance of independence is an objective test depending on the rules governing the organisation of the judiciary and the existence of safeguards protecting its independence. According to the ECtHR, the appearance of independence and impartiality is crucial in order to maintain confidence in the independence and impartiality of the court on the part of the public and, above all, within criminal proceedings, on the part of the accused. What is significant is whether doubts about the independence or impartiality of the tribunal can be held to be objectively justified (para. 73). In *Findlay v. UK*, the lack of structural independence of the judiciary has been found to give rise to such a legitimate doubt (para. 75).

Independent judiciary is central to the process of democratisation; it plays an important role in the development of the rule of law (Ishiyama Smithey and

11 See, for example, cases *Bryan v. UK* (1995), *Cooper v. UK* (1999), *Campbell and Fell v. UK* (1984), *Incal v. Turkey* (1998), *Kleyn and Others v. The Netherlands* (2003), *Findlay v. UK* (1997), *McGonnell v. UK* (1995).

Ishiyama 2000). Particularly in the context of post-Communist and post-socialist systems, it has helped to develop and consolidate democratic governments, even if there are considerable differences among countries in the amount of power and independence they grant their judges. The limitations on judicial power can, in their view, partly be explained by authoritarian history and the differences among countries, specifically, by the differences in the willingness of the existing policy makers to limit their own powers (ibid.).

As witnessed by recent involvement of the European Commission regarding two Member States, judicial independence can be jeopardised where there are structural threats against the independence of the judiciary in the form of the absence of legislative safeguards (as in the case of Hungary) or when individual threats against the Constitutional Court and its judges can be distinguished (as in the case of Romania).

In the case of Hungary, the Commission has been particularly concerned regarding the powers (without appropriate safeguards) granted to the President of the National Judicial Office, i.e. a non-judicial authority, to designate a court in a given case and about the possibility to transfer judges without their consent. These measures were flagged as negatively affecting the effective application of EU law in Hungary and the fundamental rights of citizens and businesses to an effective remedy by an independent court in EU law cases, as guaranteed by Article 47 of the Charter.[12] Closely monitoring the amendments to the Hungarian legislation to verify compliance with the mentioned right to an effective remedy in Union law cases, the European Commission warned that it reserves the right to launch infringement proceedings in this matter in case it should not be satisfied that EU law will be applied effectively by independent courts in Hungary in line with the requirements of EU law (Reding 2012a). On 25 April 2012, the Commission referred Hungary to the Court of Justice of the European Union (hereafter: CJEU) for two infringement cases, one of them being the sudden reduction of retirement age for judges, prosecutors and notaries from 70 to 62 years, in which the CJEU in its ruling of 6 November 2012 confirmed the Commission's legal analysis and found the Hungarian forced early retirement of judges incompatible with EU law (European Commission 2012b). In 2013, some of the concerns expressed earlier were raised again, this time in relation to the draft Fourth Amendment to the Constitution of Hungary, which envisaged a constitutionalisation of the power of the President of the National Judicial Office to transfer cases.[13] The Hungarian

12 The Venice Commission of the Council of Europe issued three opinions on the justice issues in Hungary, which included concerns with regard to judicial independence (Venice Commission 2012a, Venice Commission 2012b, Venice Commission 2013), particularly linked to the 'unique system of judicial administration, which existed in no other European country and which threatened the independence of the judiciary' (Venice Commission 2012b: 16).

13 In a letter to the Hungarian authorities, the European Commission President Barroso has indicated that the Commission will have to take the necessary steps in order

government later expressed their willingness to remove the problematic provisions on the transfer of cases from the Constitution and legislation (MTI 2013).

In Romania, on the other hand, the Government and Parliament in the summer of 2012 adopted a series of extraordinary measures in the attempt to oust the President of the Republic. This combination of measures has been found as raising concerns with regard to the respect for the rule of law, democratic checks and balances and judicial independence[14] (Reding 2012b). In its report (European Commission 2012a), which is part of the Cooperation and Verification Mechanism (CVM) with which the Commission evaluates the progress of reforms in the judiciary and other areas in Romania, the Commission stated its concern with respect to the limitation of competences of the Constitutional Court relating to parliamentary decisions and urged the Romanian authorities to restore these competences. The pressure exercised by members of the Romanian Government and senior politicians on the Constitutional Court were declared 'unacceptable interventions against an independent judicial institution' (European Commission 2012a: 5). The lack of respect for the separation of powers was linked with the lack of respect for the independence of the judiciary.[15]

That judicial independence, or rather the perception of judicial independence, is an important issue within EU Member States was highlighted by the European Commission in its EU Justice Scoreboard (2013b: 21). The data from World Economic Forum and the World Justice Project, which were used for the 2013 EU Justice Scoreboard as regards the issue of judicial independence, show that even though several Member States are among the top 10 worldwide leaders in perceived judicial independence, there is a rather low level of judicial independence perceived in certain Member States (ibid.).[16]

---

to start infringement procedures where relevant, and also referred to concerns about the conformity with EU law of the powers given to the President of the National Office for the Judiciary to transfer cases (European Commission 2013c). In May 2013, the Commission sent to Hungary three letters requesting clarifications, including one with regard to the transfer of cases (*Die Welt* 2013).

14 Emergency decrees and laws were passed against constitutional practice with the aim to reduce democratic checks and balances notably by imposing sudden limits to the powers of Constitutional Court. At the same time, judges and prosecutors were subject to pressures and intimidation from political forces. The Vice President of the European Commission, Viviane Reding (2012b), emphasised that the pressure on the judiciary is 'unacceptable, regardless from which side of political spectrum it comes'.

15 On 30 January 2013, the Commission stated that while the Constitution and the Constitutional Court's role and decisions have been respected, commitments regarding the independence of the judiciary have not been adequately implemented (European Commission 2013a: 2).

16 Based on the World Economic Forum 2012/2013 report, which inspected the perception of judicial independence (from the influences of members of government, citizens, or firms) among 144 countries in the world, the ranking of EU countries revealed

Legitimacy as Effectiveness

It would be difficult to see the justice system as legitimate if it lacks effectiveness. If justice is neither effective nor efficient,[17] courts lose legitimacy. Judiciary has to work, achieve its set goals and without much time or effort wasted. In this aspect, the legitimacy has to do with 'outcomes', but not in the sense of the content of judgments but in the sense of results occurring and being clearly shown. If rights are not effective (and they are made effective through courts), they make no sense.

Effectiveness, firstly, ensures the enforceability of, e.g. contracts. Here an interesting, albeit counter-intuitive, observation regarding public trust in the legal system noted by researchers is also that '[t]he worst legal regime is not one in which contracts cannot be enforced but one with an intermediate level of enforceability' (Bohnet, Frey and Huck, in Letki and Evans 2005: 524). Both, high and low levels of law enforcement encourage trustworthiness as the best strategy, the most 'rational and efficient gamble', as in the former dishonesty is likely to be prosecuted, while in the latter trustworthiness between people is the only available framework for regulating contracts. At the intermediate levels, however, these conditions do not hold. So, in the complete absence of a credible state, trust among people is higher and forms a foundation for their contractual relationships, while in the states experiencing somewhat higher levels of democratisation (and consequent enforceability), this is not the case. This observation is particularly relevant for post-Communist and post-socialist states, as it helps explain why the effects of the better (clearer, more democratic or more certain) procedures and workings of some parts of law (the one dealing with the enforceability of contracts), acquired post-1989, need not 'spill-over' onto other parts of the legal system – why, in fact, the 'working better' can in some contexts, including the context of trust, be worse than 'not working at all'.

Secondly, the link between legitimacy and the effectiveness (in the sense of avoidance of delays) can be found in the old adage 'Justice delayed is justice denied'. Trial in a reasonable time is therefore not only a legal right (enshrined in, for example, the Art. 6 of the ECHR or Art. 47 of the Charter); it is also a prerequisite of justice. Lives are often 'suspended' during the period of waiting for the justice to be served. If this period is too long, a person's life may never get back to normal or resume its course. A judgment – be it as it may – provides for many

that half (13) of them are to be found in the bottom two-thirds and 6 of them in the bottom half of the judicial independence ranking among 144 states.

17 Although effectiveness is often used as an umbrella term for effectiveness, efficiency and efficacy, there is a distinction between the terms. In short, efficiency refers to how well you do something (in cost/benefit terms), to the (best or most economic) manner in which you do something, whereas effectiveness refers to how adequate a given instrument, body or tool is to accomplish a purpose or produce the intended result. Efficacy, on the other hand, is success in producing a desired or intended result, i.e. meeting targets. All these three concepts, however, add to the legitimacy of the object or action being taken.

a sort of 'closure', without which they feel they cannot move on. Pending trial is therefore not very much unlike a purgatory, where one is constantly replaying in his head the situation that led to this point without knowing how it will end or when it will end. This adds to the so-called secondary victimisation for the victims, but it is long-term just as untenable a position for the perpetrators.

In the context of the EU, the link has been made between the functioning of national justice systems and the effectiveness of EU law: if rights guaranteed in EU law are not effective (and they are made effective also when they are being applied by well-functioning national courts), they are tantamount to being non-existent. Whenever a national court applies EU legislation, it acts as a 'Union court' and must provide, as enshrined in Article 47 of the Charter, an effective remedy to everyone whose rights guaranteed in EU law were violated. Well-functioning justice systems are important for ensuring a stable and an attractive business environment, which contributes to economic growth. Effective justice systems are also relevant for strengthening the mutual trust between judicial authorities of Member States.

For these reasons, the newly established unit under Directorate General Justice of the European Commission, the 'General justice policies and judicial systems' unit, has been tasked with developing a new tool to promote effective justice and growth, the EU Justice Scoreboard, which aims at providing a systematic overview of the functioning of justice systems in all Member States. It recognises that objective, reliable and comparable data are necessary to support the national justice reforms (European Commission 2013b: 2). The objective is to help improve the effectiveness of the EU law through, first, the assessment of justice systems within the EU Member States and, consequently, improvements taken at national level when (and where) issues in some Member States arise. The task will not be easy though as European judicial systems – as recognised already by CEPEJ, which has 9-year tradition of assessing judicial systems across Council of Europe Member States – 'differ significantly, if not drastically, both in structure and in the conceptualisation of its elements and functions' (Johnsen 2012: 4), making even a pure data assembly a challenging enterprise.

The EU Justice Scoreboard coined a new term 'effective justice system' and stated that 'quality, independence and efficiency' are its 'key components' (European Commission 2013b: 3). All these parameters are important also for the effectiveness of the EU law and it is precisely there that the link with the EU law and the EU interest in the legitimacy of national justice systems is the strongest. The conceptual focus on the effectiveness of rights is also one of its distinguishing features, compared to the work of the CEPEJ, which has mostly focused on the efficiency and quality of justice. The EU Justice Scoreboard has a wider approach by including independence of the judiciary as the essential parameter of a justice system – judicial independence is perhaps even the central reason people and companies turn to the justice system for an independent and an impartial resolution of their disputes. The goal of the Scoreboard is not the good functioning of justice systems as such, but the effectiveness of rights, which is also ensured through independent justice bodies that work efficiently and deliver quality decisions.

The objective of the Scoreboard is, according to the Commission Communication, 'to assist the EU and the Member States to achieve better justice by providing objective, reliable and comparable data on the functioning of the justice system of all Member States' (European Commission 2013b: 3). It is focused on issues that matter most for the end-user of the justice system, e.g. the length of proceedings and availability of electronic systems of communication between courts and parties. The 2013 indicators are the following: the length of proceedings (disposition time, clearance rate, the number of pending cases), Information and Communication Technology systems for courts, the monitoring and evaluation of court activities, availability of alternative dispute resolution (ADR) methods, training of judges, resources of justice systems, and the perceived independence of the judiciary. The 2013 Scoreboard is based on data collected mostly by CEPEJ, who has been since 2004 collecting statistics on several similar topics through the European Judicial Survey (Johnsen 2012), and on data from the World Bank, the World Economic Forum and the World Justice Project.

Although the EU Justice Scoreboard indicators of the effectiveness of justice will be in the first year, year 2013, focused on civil and commercial justice, its potential and long-term aim is to include other judicial branches in the years to follow. Several of the charts included in the EU Justice Scoreboard, such as one on judicial independence (Figure 23), already reflect the results or people's views on judiciary in general. And it is worth remembering that people, when asked, have a hard time distinguishing between criminal and civil justice. In fact, as Van de Walle and Raine (2008: 46) remind us, '[w]hen citizens have been asked about the justice system in general, they have usually thought first about judges in criminal cases. This is an internationally significant tendency (e.g. very visible in the Dutch Justice Issues Monitor). In the same way, citizens tend to interpret the word court first and foremost as meaning "criminal court" (Genn 1999)'. According to the Commission Communication, the EU Justice Scoreboard is an evolving tool, one that will gradually expand not only in the areas covered, but also in the indicators and the methodology, with the objective of identifying the essential parameters of an effective justice system (European Commission 2013b: 3).[18]

18 While the EU Justice Scoreboard is focusing on the daily functioning of the national justice systems and is not meant to address extraordinary threats to the rule of law, it is nevertheless a useful addition to the existing tools in the field of justice in the European Union. President of the European Commission Mr Barroso in his State of the Union address acknowledged the need for 'a better developed set of instruments – not just the alternative between the "soft power" of political persuasion and the "nuclear option" of article 7 of the Treaty [on European Union]', which stipulates that the European Council may suspend certain rights, including voting rights from the Member State (its representative) in the Council if this country is found in serious and persistent breach of the values referred to in Art. 2 of the Treaty on European Union (Barroso 2012).

Conclusion

The negative public opinion of courts may affect the decision-making process, even if indirectly (or even unconsciously). Sentencing – as one type of decision-making in the context of courts – can be affected by legal and extra-legal factors[19] and a negative view of the judiciary can act as one such extra-legal factor. Judges do not live in isolation, detached from the rest of society, and are therefore as humans affected by how others view them. If the public, stimulated by media, cries for harsher penalties, the judiciary may be tempted (unconsciously perhaps) to give them what they want – jeopardising the principle of proportionality, perhaps even the culpability principle and standards of proof along the way. The problem thus becomes a larger social and legal problem, surpassing the issue of the judiciary's self-image. It affects the rule of law itself. The judiciary is directly affected when intimidation, political and other pressures are put on judicial officers to do or refrain from doing something they ought to do or not to do.

The two serious cases in two EU Member States, which engaged the concerns of the Commission in 2012, and the realisation of the importance of the functioning of national justice systems for the effectiveness of EU law and the economic growth led to the creation of the new tool – the EU Justice Scoreboard, aimed at evaluating the efficiency, independence and quality of the justice systems in all Member States. Although effectiveness of justice is not the be-all and end-all of the question of judicial legitimacy, it is understandable that the EU (European Commission) will approach the topic in this way. Not only does the 'effectiveness' provide a link with EU law, in view of the EU historical roots (origin), this approach is most likely to chime well with Member States. Additionally, as quality, independence and efficiency are said to represent the key components of an effective justice system, it is clear why the term effectiveness is an umbrella term for all the mentioned elements. In this sense, the effectiveness – whilst often on the opposite shore of legitimacy when it comes to the police – is in the case of judiciary rather the opposite side of the same 'justice' coin.

In this light the EU Justice Scoreboard is to be welcomed as a step in the (right) direction towards a somewhat more objective assessment of the functioning of justice systems across the EU. This is also an important step for the strengthening of 'mutual trust' between authorities of Member States – particularly when potential problems, spotted due to this tool, are rectified, or presumptions of how a national justice system works are dispersed by objective data.

Furthermore, it would be possible to imagine that some day a series of legal requirements on the functioning of a justice system will be developed within EU, similar to what already exists in the jurisprudence of the European Court of Human Rights regarding the 'reasonable time' of a trial. Since the European Court

19 This is even acknowledged by law: the Slovene Criminal Procedure Code, for example, lists grounds for the judge's mandatory disqualification (recusal) due to being e.g. a close relative of the accused.

of Human Rights has established a case law for the reasonable length of a certain type of proceedings, a party in a trial can now bring her country in front of the European Court for not delivering a judgment within a reasonable time. It is not impossible to imagine the future in which EU citizens will be able to legally rely also upon other parameters of an 'effective justice' in a similar vein and launch proceedings against a Member State in front of the Court of Justice of the EU for its failure to live up to those standards, ensuring the full effectiveness of their Union rights.

References

Almond, P. 2008. Public perceptions of work-related fatality cases: Reaching the outer limits of 'populist punitiveness'. *British Journal of Criminology* 48(4), 448–67.

Barroso, J.M.D. 2012. State of the Union 2012 Address [Online]. Available at: http://europa.eu/rapid/press-release_SPEECH-12-596_en.htm [accessed: 1 May 2013].

Bernard, J.L. 1979. Interaction between the race of the defendant and that of the jurors in determining verdicts. *Law and Psychology Review*, 5, 103–11.

Boritch, H. 1992. Gender and criminal court outcomes: An historical analysis. *Criminology*, 30(3), 293–326.

Bullock, H.A. 1961. Significance of the racial factor in the length of prison sentences. *Journal of Criminal Law, Criminology, and Police Science*, 52, 411–17.

CEPEJ. 2010. *Access to Justice in Europe*. Strasbourg: Council of Europe [Online]. Available at: https://wcd.coe.int/com.instranet.InstraServlet?command=com.instranet.CmdBlobGet&InstranetImage=1702042&SecMode=1&DocId=1657228&Usage=2 [accessed: 1 March 2013].

CEPEJ. 2012. *European Judicial Systems. Edition 2012 (data 2010): Efficiency and Quality of Justice*. Strasbourg: Council of Europe [Online]. Available at: http://www.coe.int/t/dghl/cooperation/cepej/evaluation/2012/Rapport_en.pdf [accessed: 1 May 2013].

Colquitt, J.A., LePine, J.A., Piccolo, R.F., Zapata, C.P. and Rich, B.L. 2012. Explaining the justice-performance relationship: Trust as exchange deepener or trust as uncertainty reducer? *Journal of Applied Psychology*, 97(1), 1–15.

Die Welt. 2013. Drei blaue Briefe an die Orbán-Regierung [Online]. Available at: http://www.welt.de/print/die_welt/politik/article115869011/Ausland-Kompakt-I.html [accessed: 5 May 2013].

Dimitrijević, V. 2006. The 'public relations' problems of international criminal courts. *Justice in Transition*, special edition. Belgrade: Center for Transitional Processes, 67–74.

Doise, W. 2001. Human rights studied as normative social representations, in *Representations of the Social*, edited by K. Deaux and G. Philogène. Oxford: Blackwell Publishers, 96–112.

Dworkin, R. 2003 (orig. 1986). *Law's Empire*. Oxford: Hart Publishing.

Eicher, A. and Schedler, K. 2012. Management responses to multiple rationalities in courts – A review. *International Journal for Court Administration (IJCA)*, Special issue, 20–34 [Online]. Available at: http://www.iaca.ws/files// ijca_2012_special_issue/ijca-2012-special_issue.pdf [accessed: 28 January 2013].

Eurobarometer. 2010. *Standard Eurobarometer 74, Autumn 2010, Annex* [Online]. Available at: http://ec.europa.eu/public_opinion/archives/eb/eb74/eb74_en.htm [accessed: 15 Jan. 2013]

European Commission. 2012a. *Report from the Commission to the European Parliament and the Council on Progress in Romania under the Cooperation and Verification Mechanism*, COM(2012) 410 final, 18 July 2012 [Online]. Available at: http://ec.europa.eu/cvm/docs/com_2012_410_en.pdf [accessed: 15 December 2012].

European Commission. 2012b. *Court of Justice rules Hungarian forced early retirement of judges incompatible with EU law*, Press release, 6 November 2012 [Online]. Available at: http://europa.eu/rapid/press-release_MEMO-12-832_en.htm [accessed: 5 May 2013].

European Commission. 2013a. *Report from the Commission to the European Parliament and the Council on Progress in Romania under the Co-operation and Verification Mechanism*, COM(2013) 47 final, 30 January 2013 [Online]. Available at: http://ec.europa.eu/cvm/docs/com_2013_47_en.pdf [accessed: 8 May 2013].

European Commission. 2013b. *Communication from the Commission to the European Parliament, the Council, the European Central Bank, the European Economic and Social Committee and the Committee of the Regions – The EU Justice Scoreboard: a tool for effective justice and growth*, COM(2013) 160 final, 27 March 2013 [Online]. Available at: http://ec.europa.eu/justice/effective-justice/files/justice_scoreboard_communication_en.pdf [accessed: 5 May 2013].

European Commission. 2013c. *The European Commission reiterates its serious concerns over the Fourth Amendment to the Constitution of Hungary.* Press release of 12 April 2013 [Online]. Available at: http://europa.eu/rapid/press-release_IP-13-327_en.htm [accessed: 5 May 2013].

Fagan, J. 2008. Legitimacy and criminal justice. *Ohio State Journal of Criminal Law*, 6, 123–40.

GRECO. 2012. *Fourth Evaluation Round: Corruption prevention in respect of members of parliament, judges and prosecutors. Evaluation report: Slovenia.* Strasbourg: GRECO.

Hans, V. and Vidmar, N. 1986. *Judging the Jury*. New York: Plenum.

Herzog, S. and Oreg, S. 2008. Chivalry and the moderating effect of ambivalent sexism: Individual differences in crime seriousness judgments. *Law & Society Review*, 42(1), 45–76.

Hymes, R.W., Leinart, M., Rowe, S. and Rogers, W. (2001). Acquaintance rape: The effect of race of defendant and race of victim on white juror decisions. *The Journal of Social Psychology*, 133(5), 627–34.

Igličar, A. 2012. Normativna integracija in (slovenski) zakonodajalec ter sodnik, in *Tretja od suhih krav: razprave o razlogih za razsulo*, edited by B.M. Zupančič. Domžale: Samozaložba A. Komat, 211–43.

Ishiyama Smithey, S. and Ishiyama, J. 2000. Judicious choices: designing courts in post-communist politics. *Communist and Post-Communist Studies*, 33, 163–82.

Jeuland, E. and Sotiropoulou, A. 2012. The role of communication in the French judicial system. *International Journal for Court Administration*, Special issue, 132–7 [Online]. Available at: http://www.iaca.ws/files//ijca_2012_special_issue/ijca-2012-special_issue.pdf [accessed: 28 January 2013].

Johnsen, J.T. 2012. The European Commission for the efficiency of justice (CEPEJ). Reforming European justice systems – 'Mission impossible?' *International Journal for Court Administration*, Special issue, 1–19 [Online]. Available at: http://www.iaca.ws/files//ijca_2012_special_issue/ijca-2012-special_issue.pdf [accessed: 28 January 2013].

Johnson, G.B. 1941. The negro and crime. *The Annals of the American Academy of Political and Social Science*, 217, 93–104.

LaFree, G.D. 1980. The effect of sexual stratification by race on official reactions to rape. *American Sociological Review*, 45, 842–54.

Letki, N. 2006. Investigating the roots of civic morality: Trust, social capital, and institutional performance. *Political Behavior*, 28(4), 305–25.

Letki, N. and Evans, G. 2005. Endogenizing social trust: Democratization in East-Central Europe. *British Journal of Political Science*. 35(3), 515–29.

Leyenberger, S. 2007. Propos inductif, in *La qualité des décisions de justice*, edited by P. Mbongo. Luxembourg: Editions du Conseil de l'Europe [Online]. Available at CEPEJ website: http://www.coe.int/t/dghl/cooperation/cepej/series/Etudes4Qualite_fr.pdf [accessed: 28 January 2013].

Lind, E. A. and Tyler, T. R. 1988. *The Social Psychology of Procedural Justice*. New York: Plenum Press.

Mack, K., Roach Anleu, S. and Wallace, A. 2012. Caseload allocation and special judicial skills: Finding the 'right judge'? *International Journal for Court Administration*, Special issue, 68–81 [Online]. Available at: http://www.iaca.ws/files//ijca_2012_special_issue/ijca-2012-special_issue.pdf [accessed: 28 January 2013].

Miller, M. and Hewitt, J. 1978. Conviction of a defendant as a function of juror-victim racial similarity. *The Journal of Social Psychology*, 105, 159–60.

Mishler, W. and Rose, R. 1997. Trust, distrust and scepticism: Popular evaluations of civil and political institutions in post-Communist societies. *The Journal of Politics*, 59(2), 418–51.

MTI. 2013. Hungary to withdraw option to transfer cases to another court to avoid 'attacks' on judiciary. *Politics.hu* [Online]. Available at: http://www.politics.hu/20130607/hungary-to-withdraw-option-to-transfer-cases-to-another-court-to-avoid-attacks-on-judiciary/ [accessed: 7 Jun 2013].

Parmentier, S. and Vervaeke, G. 2011. In criminal justice we trust? A decade of public opinion research in Belgium. *European Journal of Criminology*, 8(4), 286–302.

Perelman, Ch. 1979. *Logique juridique: La nouvelle rhétorique*. Paris: Dalloz.

Peršak, N. 2005. Učinkovitost sodišč v luči strukturnih in subjektivnih dejavnikov delovne uspešnosti [The court's efficiency in view of the structural and subjective factors of the individual's work efficiency], in *Potek kazenskih postopkov v Sloveniji: analiza stanja in predlogi za spremembe* [*Progress of criminal proceedings in Slovenia: analysis of the current situation and suggestions for the future*], edited by M. Bošnjak. Ljubljana: GV revije, 241–52.

Peršak, N. 2011. Managing Insecurities and Expectations: Social Trust and Judiciary in Transition, *Shaken Order: Authority and Social Trust in Post-Communist Societies (Case studies in Law) – CAS Working Paper Series*, no. 4. Sofia: Centre for Advanced Study, 3–33.

Praesidium of the European Convention. 2007. Explanations relating to the Charter of Fundamental Rights of the European Union, 14.12.2007, EU OJ C 3030/17. [Online, 15 December 2007] Available at: http://eur-lex.europa.eu/LexUriServ/LexUriServ.do?uri=OJ:C:2007:303:0017:0035:en:PDF [accessed: 15 February 2013].

Reding, V. 2012a. Hungary – infringements: European Commission satisfied with changes to central bank statute, but refers Hungary to the Court of Justice on the independence of the data protection authority and measures affecting the judiciary (press release). [Online, 25 April 2012] Available at: http://europa.eu/rapid/press-release_IP-12-395_en.htm [accessed: 30 April 2012].

Reding, V. 2012b. Speech at the European Parliament. [Online, 12 September 2012] Available at: http://www.europarl.europa.eu/ep-live/en/plenary/video?debate=1347455074438 [accessed: 9 December 2012].

Rose-Ackerman, S. 2001. Trust and honesty in post-socialist societies. *Kyklos*, 54(2/3), 415–44.

Turner, J.H. and Stets, J.E. 2005. *The Sociology of Emotions*. Cambridge: Cambridge University Press.

Tyler, T. 2006. *Why People Obey the Law*, 2nd edn. New Haven, CT: Yale University Press.

Tyler, Y. 2009. Legitimacy and criminal justice: The benefits of self-regulation. *Ohio State Journal of Criminal Law*, 7(1), 307–59.

Van de Walle, S. and Raine, J.W. 2008. Explaining attitudes towards the justice system in the UK and Europe (Ministry of Justice Research Series 9/08) [Online]. Available at: http://tna.europarchive.org/20081106074241/http:/www.justice.gov.uk/docs/explaining-attitudes-towards-justice-in-ukandeurope-full-report.pdf [accessed: 15 Dec 2012].

Van den Bos, K., Wilke, H.A.M. and Lind, E.A. 1998. When do we need procedural fairness? The role of trust in authority. *Journal of Personality and Social Psychology*, 75(6), 1449–58.

Venice Commission. 2012a. Opinion on Act CLXII of 2011 on the Legal Status and Remuneration of Judges and Act CLXI of 2011 on the Organisation and Administration of Courts of Hungary, adopted by the Venice Commission at its 90th Plenary Session (Venice, 16–17 March 2012) [Online]. Available at: http://www.venice.coe.int/webforms/documents/?pdf=CDL-AD(2012)001-e [accessed: 5 May 2013].

Venice Commission. 2012b. Opinion on the Cardinal Acts on the Judiciary that were amended following the adoption of Opinion CDL-AD(2012)001 on Hungary, adopted by the Venice Commission at its 92nd Plenary Session (Venice, 12–13 October 2012) [Online]. Available at: http://www.venice.coe.int/webforms/documents/?pdf=CDL-AD(2012)020-e [accessed: 5 May 2013].

Venice Commission. 2013. Opinion on the Fourth Amendment to the Fundamental Law of Hungary, adopted by the Venice Commission at its 95th Plenary Session (Venice, 14–15 June 2013) [Online]. Available at: http://www.venice.coe.int/webforms/documents/?pdf=CDL-AD(2013)012-e [accessed: 17 June 2013].

Vukelić, M. 2012. Branko Masleša: Zavračamo paternalističen ton drugih dveh vej oblasti, *Delo*. [Online, 6 February] Available at: http://www.delo.si/zgodbe/ozadja/branko-maslesa-zavracamo-paternalisticen-ton-drugih-dveh-vej-oblasti.html [accessed: 12 December 2012].

Chapter 7
Whose Claim is Legitimate Anyway? Negotiating Power in Inter-Agency Collaboration

Freya Vander Laenen

Background: Increased Cooperation between 'Justice' and 'Treatment'

In a comprehensive approach to (the reintegration of) offenders, the cooperation between law enforcement and treatment has become increasingly important (Bond and Gittell 2010, Williams 2009). This is particularly the case for problematic drug users and mentally ill offenders (Williams 2009, Morrissey, Fagan and Cocozza 2009). A merely repressive reaction to this type of offenders has not produced desirable results such as the reduction of substance use and drug related offences or the treatment of mental illness (Bull 2005, De Wree et al. 2009). The problems relating to substance use provide a clear illustration. Substance use is highly prevalent in prisons (Bullock 2003, Kanato 2008), and incarceration, as opposed to community sanctions, increases the likelihood of (drug related) recidivism (Bales and Piquero 2012, Mears, Cochran and Bales 2012). In contrast, imposing judicial alternatives to imprisonment on substance using offenders contains an opportunity to divert them to community (drug) treatment services. As a result, drug users are orientated to treatment by the law enforcement actors in order to divert (drug) offenders away from crime and drugs (De Wree, De Ruyver and Pauwels 2009). Consequently, the cooperation between criminal justice and health and social services has become increasingly important.[1]

Obviously, the intensity of the 'cooperation' can be rather diverse. The development of inter-agency relationships can differ in both level and intensity of cooperation and integration, and it can involve multiple inter-organisational

---

1 It should be pointed out that inter-agency collaboration is not restricted to the cooperation between law enforcement and treatment; it is also prominent between child welfare and juvenile justice agencies (Chuang and Wells 2010), and between health and social care services (Richardson and Asthana 2006). Moreover, it is stimulated by (local) governments in public services in general (Dickinson and Glasby 2010, Glasby, Dickinson and Smith 2010). For this chapter, no distinction is made between the different actors of the criminal justice system, e.g. the police, the public prosecutor's office and the courts (see below, 'Limitations of the Chapter').

dimensions (Fletcher et al. 2009, Schwalbe and Maschi 2012). Fletcher et al. (2009) conceptualised systems integration activities on a continuum, ranging from informal, less structured activities to more formalised, structured activities. The cooperation of criminal justice and health and social services seems to be situated in between 'cooperation' and 'collaboration' on the integration continuum.[2]

From a literature review on essential conditions regarding the cooperation between criminal justice and health and social services (De Ruyver et al. 2009, Vander Laenen, Vandam and Colman 2010), we identified several bottlenecks for this cooperation: cultural and ideological differences (Barton 1999a, Barton 1999b, Boyer et al. 2002, Bull 2005, Lough 1997), a lack of clarity in the demarcation of boundaries and roles (Stevens et al. 2005), a lack of knowledge and training (Pavis, Constable and Masters 2003, Turnbull et al. 2000), a lack of dialogue (Wenzel et al. 2001, Wenzel, Turner and Ridgely 2004, Bull 2005), a lack of motivation in the referred clients (McSweeney, Turnbull and Hough 2008, McSweeney et al. 2007, Seddon 2007), no clear legal position of the client (McSweeney, Turnbull and Hough 2002), a lack of a contact person within the justice and treatment services (Fletcher et al. 2009, Freeman 2002) and discussions concerning the professional secrecy (Marlowe 2003, Mears et al. 2002, Peters and Wexler 2005).

To overcome these bottlenecks, several recommendations have been made. The first recommendation is to 'balance' the goals and values of the different agencies (Taplin 2002, Treloar et al. 2004, Bull 2005, Holloway, Bennett and Farrington 2005, Nash 2005). Next, the differences in the ultimate goals between the agencies have to be respected. A clear demarcation of aims, boundaries, roles and responsibilities (Turnbull et al. 2000, Taplin 2002, Stevens et al. 2005), including an agreement on information exchange will further increase a positive collaboration (Mcleod and Stewart 1999, Lasker, Weiss and Miller 2001, Barton and Quinn 2006). Finally, communication and consultation between the several domains involved and training of the actors involved will increase the knowledge of the other agencies (Mcleod and Stewart 1999, Heale and Lang 2001, Lasker, Weiss and Miller 2001, Henderson et al. 2007).

However, although guidance indicates that inter-agency collaboration is not intended to require non-criminal justice agencies to perform a quasi-criminal justice role, tensions remain between care and public protection agendas and difficulties continue to exist, particularly regarding information sharing, with health and care organisations identified as 'reluctant partners' in crime and disorder reduction partnerships, in particular to pass on client information to the criminal justice organisations (Williams 2009). Next to this, from professional

2 Cooperation is conceptualised as: 'Agencies may work together to change the procedures and structures to help make programs more successful'. Collaboration is conceptualised as: 'Although temporary or brief collaboration can operate informally, ongoing collaborations are usually more structured. Autonomous agencies and programs work together with a common goal, product or outcome' (Fletcher et al. 2009: 556).

contacts with health and social services in Belgium,[3] it became clear that these essential conditions and recommendations, in particular in the case of professional secrecy, though not without merit, could not 'solve' *in practice* the bottlenecks and tensions identified in the literature.

The literature on legitimacy offers some guidance as to the further analysis of the difficulties in the collaboration between 'justice' and 'treatment' and might provide an impulse to mediate these difficulties. To this end, the chapter analyses the complex nature of inter-agency collaboration by means of the literature review on legitimacy. The experiences of health and social care professionals in Belgium when collaborating with justice, with a specific focus on information sharing and professional secrecy, will serve as an illustration of the interactions in practice.[4]

Inter-Agency Collaboration: Challenging Legitimacy

The literature on legitimacy within the field of criminal justice has focused for the most part on the police, citizens and to some extent on prisons (Tyler 2007, Van Damme and Pauwels 2012, Liebling 2011, Liebling and Arnold 2012). The dominant theoretical approach to legitimacy by criminologists and socio-legal scholars is that of 'procedural justice' (Bottoms and Tankebe 2012). Methodologically diverse empirical studies have identified the importance of procedural justice mechanisms in shaping both compliance with the law and cooperation with law enforcement (Huq, Tyler and Schulhofer 2011). In empirical studies, the importance of legitimacy in achieving law-abiding behaviour and cooperation from citizens has been established. A common element in legitimacy literature is that there is a 'power-holder' and an audience/citizens that might (or might not) recognise the power-holder's (moral) right to exercise that power (and consequently (not) obey) (Bottoms and Tankebe 2012).[5]

However, little attention has been paid in literature to legitimacy (claims) of criminal justice organisations in the case of inter-agency collaboration, i.e. collaboration between 'power-holders'. The article of Anthony Bottoms and Justice Tankebe 'Beyond procedural justice' that was recently published in *The Journal of Criminal Law and Criminology* will serve as a framework for the analysis of inter-agency collaboration in this paper. In their article, Bottoms and

3 On the basis of policy-driven research by IRCP on the cooperation between justice and (drug) treatment (e.g. De Ruyver et al. 2009, Colman et al. 2011, Geenens et al. 2005) and through consultation and training on professional secrecy in the context of inter-agency cooperation, in particular in the field of drug treatment and mental health care.

4 The collaboration between the criminal justice organisations and mandated social services such as probation officers or child protection agencies is excluded from the analysis; the focus is on autonomous health and social services (Davidov et al. 2012).

5 Other terms used in literature are on the one hand 'authorities' and 'leaders' and on the other hand 'followers' and 'subordinates' (van der Toorn, Tyler and Jost 2011).

Tankebe draw on insights from wider social science literature and apply them to criminal justice contexts.

From the research on problems in prisons, it has become clear that prisons present chronic problems of legitimacy and that legal officials sometimes have to consider their legitimacy in relation to more than one audience and that these audiences might have significantly different priorities (Sparks and Bottoms 1995, Liebling 2011). Bottoms and Tankebe (2012) add that this is also the case for the police in policing neighbourhoods where different groups have *conflicting interests*.

Starting from the theoretisation of Weber on legitimacy, Bottoms and Tankebe conclude that Weber's use of *claims* to be legitimate by political regimes implies that power-holders are addressing one or more audience(s), and that Weber's focus on the cultivation of legitimacy implies that there is a continuing relationship between the power-holder and the audience(s). This leads them to conclude that legitimacy should be perceived as always dialogic and relational in character. 'That is to say, those in power (or seeking power) in a given context make a claim to be the legitimate ruler(s); then members of the audience respond to this claim; the power-holder might adjust the nature of the claim in the light of the audience's response; and the process repeats itself' (Bottoms and Tankebe 2012: 129). As a consequence, legitimacy is like a perpetual discussion, an iterative process of claim and response.

As mentioned above, inter-agency collaboration is not simply a matter of power-holders and (individual) citizens. The relation between health and social services and the criminal justice services is of a more complex nature. On the one hand, health and social services are not just citizens; they are part of organisations and institutions that hold power as well (which will be discussed in detail below). On the other hand, it is clear that this type of collaboration cannot simply be considered 'as horizontal, trust-based relationships' either (Dickinson and Glasby 2010: 813). The consequences of the latter will be analysed in the following paragraph.

Legitimacy and Power

As regards the nature of the relationship in the collaboration between the health and social services and the criminal justice organisations, many concerns in inter-agency collaboration are linked to power disparities among participating organisations (Purdy 2012). From professional contacts with health and social services in Belgium,[6] it became clear that some health and care agencies feel less powerful than the criminal justice organisations. In particular they feel pressured

6 See footnote 3.

to give up their professional secrecy and share information with the criminal justice organisations.[7]

The concept of *discursive legitimacy* as an important source of power (Hardy and Philips (1998) as cited in Purdy (2012)) is useful for understanding this inter-organisational dynamic. Discursive legitimacy refers to the ability of an organisation to represent a discourse. Organisations exercise discursive legitimacy when they act on behalf of the values or norms of a society. An organisation with discursive legitimacy draws its power from the societal status of the value it represents. In the experience of some health and social welfare professionals,[8] the value of the protection of the society against (re)offending is more widely shared than the value of professional secrecy and the ability for a client to speak freely in a therapeutic relationship, in particular if this client is a(n) (potential) offender. Even more so, recently, due to scandals of child abuse (in the Church) the health and social care professionals feel an increased (political, media and legal) pressure to cooperate with the criminal justice system and exchange information (Kamer 2011).[9] An element contributing to the pressure that is being felt is that some social services in Belgium with a mandate to treat offenders are financed by the justice department. As a consequence, some health and care agencies experience an element of coercion in the collaboration (Vander Laenen 2011).[10]

The experience of coercion might lead to even more reluctance from health and social care professionals to cooperate (Sidman 1989). Dickinson and Glasby (2010) warned about the use of coercion in their article in the context of networking between health and social care organisations. They state that UK central government has produced coercive isomorphism by both explicit (a legal duty for health and social care services to work together) and subtler techniques (by making partnership a necessary feature for some sources of funding). As a result, 'partnership is starting to lose some of its legitimacy within the wider health and social care community. Once this happens, even when "true" partnership is the most appropriate response to a particular situation it may be dismissed out of hand due to the negative connotations it has acquired' (Dickinson and Glasby 2010: 824). In the inter-organisational dynamic between criminal justice and health and

7 In order to monitor compliance with the (quasi-)compulsory treatment, criminal justice agencies require information about whether offenders are attending (and engaging with) treatment (Seddon 2007).

8 The relational and perceptual aspects of power are important in collaborative contexts (Purdy 2012). Consequently, we cannot state that this perceived pressure and power imbalance are 'objectively' present, without empirical research.

9 Following the recommendations of a special parliamentary commission on sexual abuse and paedophiles within authority relationship in the Church, the Belgian law on professional secrecy (article 458*bis* of the Belgian Criminal Code) was changed to extend the exceptions to professional secrecy.

10 One author wrote, in 2004, that the cooperation between justice and drug treatment had evolved from a LAT-relationship into 'a shotgun wedding that is enforced by a security policy' (Todts 2004: 17).

social services described above, the societal status of the value of the protection of the society against (re)offending further adds to the (perception of) coercion.

Claiming Legitimacy

Notwithstanding the experienced power differences in inter-agency collaboration the relation between health and social services and criminal justice organisations is not simply a matter of power-holders and (individual) citizens. Health and social services have claims, too; claims that might conflict with the claims of criminal justice organisations.

Firstly, in inter-agency collaboration conflict can occur between several laws. On the one hand, some (criminal) laws are aimed at the prevention of crime and at crime control. On the other hand, laws on the rights of the patient/client safeguard the right to privacy, to confidentiality and the right to be protected from harm (McGrath, Cumming and Holt 2002). Secondly, in inter-agency collaboration, conflict can exist about the claim over the – ultimate/dominant – goal of the cooperation: a care (client-centred) orientation versus a public protection agenda.

Before the claim of the health and social services can be discussed, it is important to elaborate on the discussion regarding the professional ideology of human service organisations, since it is exactly the differences in professional values and their underpinning ideologies that which creates barriers in joint working with offenders (Williams 2009). The professional ideology of (a) human service organisation(s) is a belief system about the causes of human needs and problems, ways of dealing with these problems, and the values that serve as a basis for the modes of response. Ideologically, human service organisations seem to be divided between individualistic approaches (when the cause of human problems is mainly attributed to the individual) and socially orientated approaches (when the cause of human problems is mainly attributed to society) (Weiss 2005).[11]

---

11 The debate on the position of 'social work' (for this chapter, this term is used as an overall term to refer to health and social services and to health and social interventions) in relation to the criminal justice system and criminal justice is not new. In fact, it has been the subject of an ongoing debate since the 1970s. The general societal undercurrent in the 1970s was the switch from a consensus to a conflict approach in the definition of social problems; the recognition that diversity exists in the opinions on and the interpretation of social goals, norms and values (Vander Laenen, Vander Beken and De Bie 2012). From the 1970s onwards, social work has been critically questioning its own role in the preservation of social order. Rehabilitation and support turned out to be more repressive and in some ways more punitive than the punishment itself (Svensson 2003). For 'justice clients' in particular (people coming into contact with the police or justice) the subordinate role of social work in relation to justice is questioned. As a result, the goal of social work is no longer simply to instrumentally adapt (the clients) to economic and social control targets but to strive for social and economic justice as an integral part of social work (Hancock and Waites 2012). As a result, social work had to distinguish itself from power, criminal law and social control that were executed by law enforcement (Vander Laenen, Vander

An interesting study worthwhile discussing in detail with regard to the (ultimate) goal(s) of health and social services is the study of Hancock and Waites (2012). Hancock and Waites (2012) studied the views of social work students on the causes of the structural disadvantage of social groups and how they relate to students' perceived obligation to advocate for these structurally disadvantaged clients. Interestingly, they found a typology of three categories characterising how students' explanations of structural disadvantage were linked to distinct practice orientations.

The first category, students working from 'an ethic of conformity', comprised students that 'uncritically accepted the facts of structural oppression … and believed the oppression was necessary to preserve the social order'. These students viewed social justice as belonging to people who upheld their view of social order (Hancock and Waites 2012: 8). The second category, students working from 'an ethic of individualism', 'tended to deny … the structural nature of oppression'. Justice for this group meant 'treating everyone equally and with respect' (Hancock and Waites 2012: 8); and thus they saw no need for structural change interventions. The third category, students working from 'an ethic of care', were students who 'accepted the evidence of the social structural nature of oppression and viewed this arrangement as unjust. These students tended to view social justice as empowering people in subordinate positions to determine and attain what is in their best interests' (Hancock and Waites 2012: 8). The authors continue that these students were completely aware of the ways in which dominant members of social groups make life more difficult for less powerful subordinate others and that this awareness was grounded in deep empathy for others in subordinate positions and in a sense of fairness in view of the facts of structural inequality (Hancock and Waites 2012). Hancock ((2008) as cited in Hancock and Waites (2012)) further divides this third category into two subgroups: a subgroup willing to assist clients on a one-to-one basis (the care-orientated students) and a subgroup embracing advocacy and social change roles.

Why then is this an interesting study with regard to conflicting claims? First, the study clarifies the fundamental differences between the ultimate goal of some health and social professionals (empowerment and self-determination) and most criminal justice professionals. The wording used by the authors is deliberately cited here to illustrate these differences (e.g. 'structural oppression', 'structural inequality').

Beken and De Bie 2012). On the one hand, this era resulted in the emancipation of social work from justice and the formulation of separate goals, where the goals of social work were determined by the client – a care (client-centred) orientation – rather than by law enforcement, driven by a public protection agenda. In general, the goal of social work is twofold: the improvement of the well-being of the individuals and the promotion of 'social justice and reform' (Weiss 2005, Hancock and Waites 2012). On the other hand, the debate within social work about which goals should be part of the social work profession is ongoing and topical, particularly in the context of a growing societal focus on risk and risk management (Garland 2001).

Second, for some criminologists and socio-legal scholars it might seem surprising that some of the concepts used in this study are comparable to some of the concepts in the criminological legitimacy literature (e.g. 'justice', 'rights', the use of 'power' and 'fairness') albeit the meaning of the concepts is quite different, with (*social*) *justice* as the most striking example.[12] Thirdly, the study shows that individual differences exist between future social care professionals with regard to the goal of health and social interventions. It illustrates the divide between professionals using individualistic and socially orientated approaches. These (individual) differences further complicate the debate in inter-agency collaboration. Social workers working from a structural change perspective will very likely be highly critical towards cooperation with criminal justice organisations and will fundamentally question the claims for legitimacy made by criminal justice authorities. The latter brings us back to the potential conflict over the ultimate goal of the cooperation between criminal justice and health and social services.

From professional contacts with health and social services in Belgium,[13] when health and social services interact with the criminal justice organisations, it seems that they will seldom openly challenge the claims of legitimacy of criminal justice organisations. Rather, they will indirectly challenge the claims for legitimacy, as becomes clear from the following two examples.

The first example comes from a study on the provision of substitution therapy for drug users (OST) (Vander Laenen et al. 2012). In the focus groups, aimed at developing policy recommendations to optimise OST, the participants stressed that they regretted 'the growing focus on repression in society' and that, first of all, the general approach of opiate dependence and substitution therapy should be to focus on improvements in well-being and quality of life of clients, rather than based on the reduction of crime and the restriction of nuisance, 'especially as keeping client's confidence proves a very important success factor for substitution treatment' (Vander Laenen et al. 2012: 7). This quote illustrates that drug treatment providers stress the value of the well-being of the individual as the goal for treatment, rather than the goal of the protection of society. To support their claim, they indirectly stress the importance of professional secrecy by referring to the importance of the client's confidence in therapists. They go on to add that it is exactly this confidence, which acts as a success factor for treatment. The latter argument is linked to the growing emphasis (by governments) on evidence-based practice and policy (namely the effectiveness of their goal setting).

The second example comes from a report regarding 'the judicial support for the social worker in the case of information exchange with the police or justice for referred drug users' (VAD 2012), which was developed by the Flemish drug

12 The promotion of social justice is not limited to this study with social work students; it is also recommended for clinicians, advocates and researchers involving patients with mental disorders (Compton et al. 2011) and a framework for persons with disabilities (Stuart 2012).

13 See footnote 3.

treatment services in 2012. In this note, aimed at providing seemingly technical information on professional secrecy issues, the first essential condition for inter-agency collaboration is described as follows: 'When the justice official deliberately prefers an initiative aimed at improving the well-being of a particular client over a purely judicial measure, this signifies that he/she, in case of observing the conditions, entrusts his client to the expertise of treatment' (VAD 2012: 3). Moreover, this expertise aims to improve the individual's psychological and physical health. 'The treatment goals, which can be medical, psychological as well as social, are formulated within a welfare and health perspective. The client is centred in this treatment process. It is the task of treatment to stimulate the self-consciousness of the client and his well-considered choices in life' (VAD 2012: 3). From this part of the note, it becomes clear once more that drug treatment services claim legitimacy as well: treatment is client-centred and it is the client that has the power to make his/her choices in life. In this document, the professional expertise is referred to in order to support their claim.[14] Moreover, it is implied that when justice officials refer clients to drug treatment, the official recognises the *dominance* of the treatment goal and expertise (note that in the text, the expression 'in case of observing the conditions' is the only reference to the public protection agenda).

In sum, in inter-agency collaboration, health and social services will seldom openly challenge the claims of legitimacy of the criminal justice organisations. Rather, they will indirectly challenge the claims for legitimacy of the criminal justice organisations by stressing the values that are central to treatment (the well-being of the individual, the (em)power(ment) of the individual to determine the goal of treatment) or sometimes by claiming dominance of the treatment interventions over the public protection agenda. Another strategy that can be used is the referral to intangible resources of power: the professional expertise and the effectiveness of treatment interventions (Purdy 2012).

Discussion and Conclusions

Learning from Legitimacy Literature

As discussed above, the inter-agency collaboration is not simply a matter of power-holders and (individual) citizens. The relation between health and social services and the criminal justice services is of a more complex nature. On the one hand, power and perceived power disparities are an important element (of concern) (Purdy 2012). On the other hand, health and social services also have claims for legitimacy; claims that might conflict with the claims of criminal justice

14 This focus on professionalism has been criticised, in the aftermath of the 1970s discussed above, for it proclaims that this type of professional, expert intervention is 'neutral', while in fact it is highly power-driven (Apostel 1985).

organisations. From the discussion on the claims for legitimacy and the struggle over dominance in the debate it becomes clear that the criminal justice system and the health and social services do not necessarily derive authority from, and act within, the *shared* beliefs and values in a given society. There seems to be a gap between what criminal justice agencies believe the legitimacy of their own authority is and the assessment of the latter on the part of their audience (Bottoms and Tankebe 2012), in our case, of the health and social service.

In the literature it is stated that difficulties in inter-agency cooperation can be overcome by 'balancing' the goals and values of the different agencies (Taplin 2002, Treloar et al. 2004, Bull 2005, Holloway, Bennett and Farrington 2005). Some authors suggest the pursuit of a shared goal as a solution to the problem of collaboration (Bond and Gittell 2010). From our analysis it became clear that in the cooperation between 'justice' and 'treatment' the pursuit of a shared goal is quite unlikely to be attainable. The difficulties in sharing information across organisations are to some extent due to technical and confidentiality concerns (Bond and Gittell 2010). They also reflect deeper value conflict and resulting distrust between organisations.[15] For information sharing, there is a fundamental tension between practice driven by the respect for (the needs of) the individual and practice guided by the demands of the risk management of groups considered to be high-risk offenders (Seddon 2007, Barton and Quinn 2006). The central argument used by health and social care organisations in their refusal or at least reluctance to share client information is that the ultimate goal of the organisations involved is fundamentally different (Williams 2009), rather than arguments relating to the right of privacy for the individual client. By doing this they also try to maintain distinctive identities and protect their independence as professional bodies (Irvine et al. 2002).

From this analysis, it becomes clear that these ideological barriers between different agencies should be addressed. Since attitudes towards information sharing reflect underlying (conflicting) professional values, it will not suffice to develop joint working protocols, including protocols for the sharing of information, let alone impose them, since these are mainly designed to alleviate *procedural* problems (Williams 2009, Richardson and Asthana 2006). The divergent professional values are a hurdle that needs to be *negotiated* (Williams 2009). In the dialogic approach of legitimacy developed by Bottoms and Tankebe (2012), legitimacy needs to be perceived as always dialogic and relational in character. Within the dialogic framework, legitimacy is constantly in flux; it is a significant test for power-holders when it becomes clear that a relevant audience has rejected one or more aspects of their initial claim to legitimacy. Bottoms and Tankebe (2012) state that in contexts where shared values are in short supply, this might require skilful negotiation by power-holders if the legitimacy of the official law

15 The role of trust relationships is obviously more complex. Dirks and Ferrin (2001), for example, found that prior levels of trust frame the perceptions of the partner's behaviour and the motives underlying it.

is to be fostered. In the context of inter-agency collaboration, where values might diverge or even conflict and where the claims for legitimacy of the criminal justice organisations are challenged, this will require even more skilful negotiation and the establishment of cooperative social relations.

Limitations of the Chapter

With this chapter we only scratched the surface of the complex interactions between the health and social services and the criminal justice organisations. The divergence (in professional cultures) between health and social care services complicates matters further (Richardson and Asthana 2006, Salmon and Rapport 2005, Robinson and Cottrell 2005). The same goes for the differences (in goals) between different levels and interests within these organisations (such as the differences between management and staff or the improvement of services for patients versus organisational interests, as Dickinson and Glasby (2010) found). Moreover, differences in the decision-making process and conflicting values in different parts of the criminal justice system can also be established (Wong 2001, Roach 1999).[16]

Next to this, Bellamy et al. (2006) found that distinct styles of handling personal information can be discerned and that these differences can be explained by their consistency with the deeper *institutional* character of the organisational settings in which they were found. Among other things, they found that an element of hierarchy in the institutional mix tends to increase confidence that data are being shared appropriately and that confidentiality is being properly respected.

Finally, *individual* differences are important as well. Individual differences among perceivers may shape fairness judgments (Bianchi and Brockner 2012). Individual differences were also found in the study of Hancock and Waites (2012) on the views of social work students on the causes of the structural disadvantage of social groups and how they relate to students' perceived obligation to advocate for these structurally disadvantaged clients.

The main limitation of the chapter is that the analysis is not based on empirical research, but merely on the (survey) research on legitimacy and recorded experiences of Belgian health and social care professionals when collaborating with justice institutions. As such, it is predominantly exploratory in nature.

Implications for Policy and Practice

If conflict can sometimes be observed between the police and justice, which are supposed to be complementary social control institutions in the criminal justice system (Wong 2001), it is not surprising then that conflict over the claims for legitimacy and values can also be observed between the health and social

16 One clear example is the observed tension between the due process and crime control models in an adversarial system.

organisations and criminal justice organisations. In fact, in the cooperation between health and social organisations and the criminal justice organisations you have to deal with an intractable problem in the balancing of values. The values of one type of organisation cannot hold an upper hand over the other. In the context of inter-agency collaboration, neither the criminal justice system nor the health and social services can be considered neutral and disinterested authorities that can establish a fair outcome, as Tyler (2012) argues. So what is a way out of this conflict? For this, we can turn to the theory of Bottoms and Tankebe (2012) once more: making the differences in values explicit and not trying to sweep the differences under the rug – without doubt an unsettling process at the start – and recognising the legitimacy of both claims/sets of values, will enhance the cooperation in the long run. This would require a change in communication on the part of the health and social services in that they would have to communicate more directly what their professional values and ultimate goals are. On the part of criminal justice system, this would entail accepting the difference between the ultimate goals of health and social services. For both types of services, it would entail ultimately accepting the legitimacy of each other's values.

Interesting in this context was the testimony of Johan Put, during the hearings of the Belgian special parliamentary commission on sexual abuse and paedophiles within authority relationship in the Church. In his testimony, he advocates for 'some modesty and recognition from justice that the judicial settlement is not the only or single intervention strategy and the recognition from treatment that the therapeutic relationship cannot be the only point of reference either' (Kamer 2011: 245). Indeed, I agree with Gray (1989, as cited in Purdy 2012) that collaboration is 'a process through which parties who see different aspects of a problem can constructively explore their differences and search for solutions that go beyond their own limited vision of what is possible'.

As discussed above, Dickinson and Glasby (2010) warned about the impact of (the perception of) *coercion* in the context of networking between health and social care organisations, because 'partnership is starting to lose some of its legitimacy within the wider health and social care community' (Dickinson and Glasby 2010: 824). As a result the partnership runs the risk of acquiring negative connotations and being dismissed out of hand due to such connotations (Dickinson and Glasby 2010). I agree with Purdy (2012) that the success of a collaborative process depends on the *sharing* of power rather than on a power struggle to achieve dominance. To enable this, greater attention should be given to assessing (perceived) power in inter-agency collaboration and developing a tool for managing (perceived) power imbalances among participants (Purdy 2012). By doing so, both, the service users, in this case (potential) offenders, and society will benefit (in the long term).

Concluding Observations: Widening the Research on Legitimacy

In this chapter the focus was mainly on the claims for legitimacy of determinative (and conflicting) values by power-holders in the criminal justice as well as in the health and social system. It has become clear that it is worthwhile to empirically study the legitimacy of criminal justice organisations in inter-agency collaboration, not least because professionals from health and social services also interact with (potential) offenders and might influence offenders' opinion of the criminal justice services.

One might fundamentally criticise the use(fulness) of the concepts of legitimacy in the analysis of inter-agency collaboration since the health and social services are no (individual) citizens expected to comply with or obey the law. On the contrary, health and social services act as agents of social control as well, although they may be less visible than the police (Jackson et al. 2012). In fact, care in itself can be a technique of exercising power (Svensson 2003, Scull 2006). However, the analysis can inform law enforcement services in the case of conflicting values both with regard to inter-agency cooperation and with regard to interaction with citizens. As to the latter, the discussion on conflicting values, the use of coercion and negotiating legitimacy can offer guidance for criminal justice organisations as to how best adapt strategies and training in a fast-changing and increasingly cosmopolitan world, characterised by the changing social values (Bottoms and Tankebe 2012).

References

Apostel, L. 1985. Paradoxen van de welzijnszorg: een driefrontenoorlog. In *Interventierecht. Bijdragen tot de studiedag georganiseerd n.a.v. het emeritaat van Prof. Dr. G. De Bock op 5 oktober 1984 ed.* Seminarie en Laboratorium voor Jeugdwelzijn en Volwassenenvorming. Malle: De Sikkel, 29–48.

Bales, W.D. and Piquero, A.R. 2012. Assessing the impact of imprisonment on recidivism. *Journal of Experimental Criminology*, 8, 71–101.

Barton, A. 1999a. Breaking the crime/drugs cycle: The birth of a new approach? *The Howard Journal*, 38(2), 144–57.

Barton, A. 1999b. Sentenced to treatment? Criminal justice orders and the health service. *Critical Social Policy*, 19(4), 463–83.

Barton, A. and Quinn, C. 2006. Risk management of groups or respect for the individual? Issues of information sharing and confidentiality in drug treatment and testing orders. *Drugs: Education, Prevention and Policy*, 9(1), 35–43.

Belgian Criminal Code (Belgisch Strafwetboek) of 8 June 1867 [Online]. Available at: http://www.ejustice.just.fgov.be/cgi_loi/change_lg.pl?language=nl&la=N&cn=1867060801&table_name=wet [accessed: 5 March 2013].

Bellamy, C., Raab, C., Warren, A. and Heeney, C. 2006. Institutional shaping of interagency working: Managing tensions between collaborative working and client confidentiality. *Journal of Public Administration Research and Theory*, 17, 405–34.

Bianchi, E.C. and Brockner, J. 2012. In the eyes of the beholder? The role of dispositional trust in judgments of procedural and interactional fairness. *Organizational Behavior and Human Decision Processes*, 118, 46–59.

Bond, B.J. and Gittell, J.H. 2010. Cross-agency coordination of offender reentry: Testing collaboration outcomes. *Journal of Criminal Justice*, 38, 118–29.

Bottoms, A. and Tankebe, J. 2012. Beyond procedural justice: A dialogic approach to legitimacy in criminal justice. *The Journal of Criminal Law and Criminology*, 102(1), 119–70.

Boyer, R., Carry, C., Chailonick, P., Friess, J., Gerey, N., Lecamp, M., Oddou, A., Roguin, G. and Rome, I. 2002. *Toxicomanies et Lois: Controverses*. Paris: L'Harmattan.

Bull, M. 2005. A comparative review of best practice guidelines for the diversion of drug related offenders. *International Journal of Drug Policy*, 16(4), 223–34.

Bullock, T. 2003. Changing levels of drug use before, during and after imprisonment, in *Prisoners' Drug Use and Treatment: Seven Research Studies*, edited by M. Ramsay. London: Home Office, 23–47.

Chuang, E. and Wells, R. 2010. The role of inter-agency collaboration in facilitating receipt of behavioral health services for youth involved with child welfare and juvenile justice. *Children and Youth Services Review*, 32, 1814–1822.

Colman, C., De Ruyver, B., Vander Laenen, F., Vanderplasschen, W., Broekaert, E., De Keulenaer, S. and Thomaes, S. 2011. *De Drugbehandelingkamer: een Andere Manier van Afhandelen. Het Pilootproject Geëvalueerd.* Antwerpen: Maklu.

Compton, M.T., Neubert, B.N.D., Broussard, B., McGriff, J.A., Morgan, R. and Oliva, J.R. 2011. Use of force preferences and perceived effectiveness of actions among crisis intervention team (CIT) police officers and non-CIT officers in escalating psychiatric crisis involving a subject with schizophrenia. *Schizophrenia Bulletin*, 37(4), 737–45.

Davidov, D.M., Nadroff, M.R., Jack, S.M. and Coben, J.H. 2012. Nurse home visitors' perspectives of mandatory reporting of children's exposure to intimate partner violence to child protection agencies. *Public Health Nursing*, 29(5), 412–26.

De Ruyver, B., Lemaître, A., Schoenaers, F., Vander Laenen, F., Ponsaers, P. and Pauwels, L. 2009. *Onderzoek naar essentiële en bijkomende randvoorwaarden voor interactie justitie en drughulpverlening.* Gent: Academia Press.

De Wree, E., De Ruyver, B. and Pauwels, L. 2009. Criminal justice responses to drug offences: Recidivism following the application of alternative sanctions in Belgium. *Drugs: Education, Prevention, and Policy*, 16, 550–60.

De Wree, E., Pauwels, L., Colman, C. and De Ruyver, B. 2009. Alternative sanctions for drug users: Fruitless efforts or miracle solution? *Crime, Law and Social Change*, 52, 513–25.

Dickinson, H. and Glasby, J. 2010. 'Why partnership working doesn't work'. Pitfalls, problems and possibilities in English health and social care. *Public Management Review*, 12(6), 811–28.

Dirks, K.T. and Ferrin, D.L. 2001. The role of trust in organizational settings. *Organizational Science*, 12(4), 450–67.

Fletcher, B.W., Lehman, W.E.K., Wexler, H.K., Melnick, G., Taxman, F.S. and Young, D.W. 2009. *Drug and Alcohol Dependence, 103S*, 554–64.

Freeman, K. 2002. *New South Wales Drug Court Evaluation: Health, Well-Being and Participant Satisfaction*. Sydney: NSW Bureau of Crime Statistics and Research.

Garland, D. 2001. *The Culture of Control, Crime and Order in Contemporary Society*. Chicago: University of Chicago Press.

Geenens, K., Colpaert, K., Balthazar, T., Vander Laenen, F. and De Ruyver, B. 2005. Samenwerking en communicatie van cliëntinformatie binnen de hulpverlening en met de justitiële sector: wettelijke randvoorwaarden, in *Tussen droom en daad: implementatie van case management voor druggebruikers binnen de hulpverlening en justitie*, edited by K. Geenens et al. Gent: Academia Press, 191–241.

Glasby, J., Dickinson, H. and Smith, J. 2010. 'Creating NHS Local': The relationship between English local government and the National Health Service. *Social Policy and Administration*, 44(3), 244–64.

Hancock, T.U. and Waites, C. 2012. Facing structural inequality: Students' orientation to oppression and practice with oppressed groups. *Journal of Social Work education*, 48(1), 5–23.

Heale, P. and Lang, E. 2001. A process evaluation of the CREDIT (court referral and evaluation for drug intervention and treatment) pilot programme. *Drug and Alcohol Review*, 20(2), 223–30.

Henderson, C.E., Young, D.W., Jainchill, N., Hawke, J., Farkas, S. and Davis, R.M. 2007. Program use of effective drug abuse treatment practices for juvenile offenders. *Journal of Substance Abuse Treatment*, 32, 279–90.

Holloway, K., Bennett, T. and Farrington, D. 2005. *The Effectiveness of Criminal Justice and Treatment Programmes in Reducing Drug-Related Crime: A Systematic Review*. London: Home Office, Research Development and Statistics Directorate.

Huq, A.Z., Tyler, T.R. and Schulhofer, S.J. 2011. Why does the public cooperate with law enforcement? The influence of the purposes and targets of policing. *Psychology, Public Policy and Law*, 17(3), 419–50.

Irvine, R., Kerridge, I., Mcphee, J. and Freeman, S. 2002. Interprofessionalism and ethics: Consensus or clash of cultures? *Journal of Interprofessional care*, 16(3), 199–210.

Jackson, J., Bradford, B., Hough, M., Myhill, A., Quiton, P. and Tyler, T.R. 2012. Why do people comply with the law? Legitimacy and the influence of legal institutions. *British Journal of Criminology*, 52(6), 1051–1071.

Kamer. 2011. Verslag namens de Belgische Kamer van Volksvertegenwoordigers, De behandeling van seksueel misbruik en feiten van pedofilie binnen een gezagsrelatie, inzonderheid binnen de Kerk. *GeDr. St. Kamer*, 31 maart 2011, DOC 53 0520/002.

Kanato, M. 2008. Drug use and health among prison inmates. *Current Opinion in Psychiatry*, 21, 252–4.

Lasker, R.D., Weiss, E.S. and Miller, R. 2001. Partnership Synergy: A practical framework for studying and strengthening the collaborative advantage. *The Milbank Quarterly*, 79(2), 179–205.

Liebling, A. 2011. Distinctions and distinctiveness in the work of prison officers: Legitimacy and authority revisited. *European Journal of Criminology*, 8(6), 484–99.

Liebling, A. and Arnold, H. 2012. Social relationships between prisoners in a maximum security prison: Violence, faith, and the declining nature of trust. *Journal of Criminal Justice*, 40(5), 413–24.

Lough, G. 1997. Law enforcement and harm reduction: mutually exclusive or mutually compatible. *International journal of Drug Policy*, 9(3), 169–73.

Marlowe, D. 2003. Integrating substance abuse treatment and criminal justice supervision. *Science and Practice Perspectives*, 2(1), 4–14.

McGrath, R.J., Cumming, G. and Holt, J. 2002. Collaboration among sex offender treatment providers and probation and parole officers: The beliefs and behaviours of treatment providers. *Sexual Abuse: A Journal of Research and Treatment*, 14(1), 49–65.

Mcleod, J. and Stewart, G. 1999. *Evaluation of the Drug Diversion Pilot Programme: A Report Prepared for the Drugs and Health Protection Services Branch*. Victoria: Public Health Division, Department of Human Services.

McSweeney, T., Stevens, A., Hunt, N. and Turnbull, P. 2007. Twisting arms or a helping hand? Assessing the impact of 'coerced' and comparable 'voluntary' drug treatment options. *British Journal of Criminology*, 47(3), 470–90.

McSweeney, T., Turnbull, P. and Hough, M. 2002. *Review of Criminal Justice Interventions for Drug Users in Other Countries*. London: Criminal policy research unit.

McSweeney, T., Turnbull, P. and Hough, M. 2008. *The Treatment and Supervision of Drug Dependent Offenders: A Review of the Literature Prepared for the UK Drug Policy Commission*. London: UK Drug Policy Commission.

Mears, D.P., Cochran, J.C. and Bales, W.D. 2012. Gender differences in the effects of prison on recidivism. *Journal of Criminal Justice*, 40, 370–78.

Mears, D.P, Winterfield, L., Hunsaker, J., Moore, G.E. and White, R.M. 2002. *Drug Treatment in the Criminal Justice System: The Current State of Knowledge*. Washington D.C.: Urban institute Justice policy center.

Morrissey, J.P., Fagan, J.A. and Cocozza, J.J. 2009. New models of collaboration between criminal justice and mental health systems: Commentary. *American Journal of Psychiatry*, 166(11), 1211–1213.

Nash, B. 2005. *Developing Drug Service Policies. Briefing No. 8: Working in Partnership*. London: Drugscope.

Pavis, S., Constable, H. and Masters, H. 2003. Multi-agency, multi-professional work: Experiences from a drug prevention project. *Health education Research. Theory & Practice*, 18(6), 717–28.

Peters, R. and Wexler, H. 2005. *Substance Abuse Treatment for Adults in the Criminal justice System*. Rockville: US Department of Health and Human Services.

Purdy, J.M. 2012. A framework for assessing power in collaborative governance processes. *Public Administration Review*, 72, 409–17.

Richardson, S. and Asthana, S. 2006. Inter-agency information sharing in health and social care services: The role of professional culture. *British Journal of Social Work*, 36(4), 657–69.

Roach, K. 1999. Four models of the criminal process. *Journal of Criminal Law and Criminology*, 89(2), 671–84.

Robinson, M. and Cottrell, D. 2005. Health professionals in multi-disciplinary and multi-agency teams: Changing professional practice. *Journal of Interprofessional Care*, 19(6), 547–60.

Salmon, G. and Rapport, F. 2005. Multi-agency voices: A thematic analysis of multi-agency working practices within the setting of a child and adolescent mental health service. *Journal of Interprofessional Care*, 19(5), 429–43.

Scull, A. 2006. Power, social control and psychiatry: Some critical reflections, in *Perspectives on Punishment: The Contours of Control*, edited by S. Armstrong and L. McAra. Oxford: Oxford University Press, 197–216.

Seddon, T. 2007. Coerced drug treatment in the criminal justice system: Conceptual, ethical and criminological issues. *Criminology and Criminal Justice*, 7(3), 269–86.

Sidman, M. 1989. *Coercion and its Fallout*. Boston: Authors Cooperative, Inc.

Schwalbe, C.S. and Maschi, T.M. 2012. Probation officers' perspectives on interagency collaboration for juvenile offender with mental health problems. *Psychiatric Services*, 63(8), 830–33.

Sparks, J.R. and Bottoms, A.E. 1995. Legitimacy and order in prisons. *British Journal of Criminology*, 46(1), 45–62.

Stevens, A., Berto, D., Heckmann, W., Kerschl, V., Oeuvray, K., Van Ooyan, M., Steffan, E. and Uchtenhagen, A. 2005. Quasi-compulsory treatment of drug depend offenders: An international literature review. *Substance Use & Misuse*, 40(3), 269–83.

Stuart, H. 2012. United Nations convention on the rights of persons with disabilities: A roadmap for change. *Current Opinion in Psychiatry*, 25(5), 365–9.

Svensson, K. 2003. Social work in the criminal justice system: An ambiguous exercise of caring power. *Journal of Scandinavian studies in Criminology and Crime Prevention*, 4, 84–100.

Taplin, S. 2002. *The New South Wales Drug Court Evaluation: A Process Evaluation*. NSW Bureau of crime and statistics and research.

Todts, S. 2004. De drugwet en de hulpverlening: LAT-relatie of shotgun wedding?, *Orde van de Dag*, 26, 5–18.

Treloar, C., Abelson, J., Cao, W., Brener, L., Kippax, S. and Schultz, L. 2004. *Barriers and Incentives to Treatment for Illicit Drug Users*. Australia: Australian Government.

Turnbull, P., McSweeney, T., Webster, R., Edmunds, M. and Hough, M. 2000. *An Evaluation of Drug Treatment and Testing Orders*. Final Evaluation Report. London: Home Office.

Tyler, T.R. (ed.) 2007. *Legitimacy and Criminal Justice: International Perspectives*. New York: Russell Sage Foundation.

Tyler, T.R. 2012. Justice and effective cooperation. *Social Justice Research*, 25(4), 355–75.

Van Damme, A. and Pauwels, L. 2012. Explaining support for vigilantism and punitiveness: Assessing the role of perceived procedural fairness, ethnocentrism, authoritarianism and anomia, in *Social Conflicts, Citizens and Policing: Governance of Security Research Papers Series*, edited by M. Cools et al. Antwerp-Apeldoorn: Maklu, 31–54.

Vander Laenen, F. 2011. The end of the affair? Het beroepsgeheim in de samenwerking tussen justitie en de hulpverlening. *Panopticon*, 32(4), 1–11.

Vander Laenen, F., Vandam, L. and Colman, C. 2010. Met velen aan de tafel: Goede voorbeelden van een integraal en geïntegreerd drugbeleid. *Tijdschrift Verslaving*, 6(4), 54–71.

Vander Laenen, F. Vander Beken, T. and De Bie, M. 2012. Strafrecht en welzijnswerk, in *Handboek Forensisch Welzijnswerk, Ontwikkeling, Beleid, Organisatie en Praktijk*, edited by R. Roose, F., Vander Laenen, I., Aertssen, I. and L. van Garsse. Gent: Academia Press, 3–25.

Vander Laenen, F., De Ruyver, B., Vanderplasschen, W., Ansseau, M., Smet, V., De Maeyer, J., Buckinx, M. and Van Audenhove, S. 2012. *Analysis and Optimazation of Substitution Treatment in Belgium. Summary (draft report)*. Ghent: Ghent University.

van der Toorn, J., Tyler, T.R. and Jost, J.T. 2011. More than fair: Outcome dependence, system justification, and the perceived legitimacy of authority figures. *Journal of Experimental Social Psychology*, 47(1), 127–38.

Verenging voor Alcohol en andere Drugproblemen (VAD) 2012. *Juridische Handvaten voor de Hulpverlener bij het rapporteren aan politie en justitie bij doorverwijzing van meerderjarige druggebruikers*. Brussels: VAD.

Weiss, I. 2005. Is there a global common core to social work? A cross-national comparative study of BSW graduate students. *Social Work*, 50(2), 101–10.

Wenzel, S.L., Longshore, D., Turner, S. and Ridgely, M.S. 2001. Drug courts – A bridge between criminal justice and health services. *Journal of Criminal Justice*, 29(3), 241–53.

Wenzel, S.L., Turner, S.F. and Ridgely, M.S. 2004. Collaborations between drug court and service providers: Characteristics and challenges. *Journal of Criminal Justice*, 32(3), 253–63.

Williams, I. 2009. Offender health and social care: A review of evidence on inter-agency collaboration. *Health and Social Care in the Community*, 17(6), 573–80.
Wong, K.C. 2001. Federalization of local criminal procedures: A study of conflict in values and process. *International Journal of the Sociology of Law*, 29, 203–35.

Chapter 8

Mutual Recognition in EU Criminal Law and Its Effects on the Role of a National Judge

Anže Erbežnik[1]

Mutual recognition is perceived as the ultimate solution to the creation of a common EU area of freedom, security and justice. However, its practical application in criminal law shows substantial differences in the understanding of criminal law, especially as regards criminal procedure in the Member States. Such differences and their accommodation (in cross-border cooperation) through an automatic mutual recognition system could challenge the classical role of a judge in a modern democracy, as well as his/her legitimacy and the perception of legitimacy of his/her decisions. An uncritical application of mutual recognition bears the danger of transforming the judge into a kind of 'ticking box' automaton checking only pre-established criteria and neglecting his/her duty of a critical assessment and safeguarding fundamental (constitutional) rights of the defendant. Therefore, it is necessary to define a balancing theory of mutual recognition in EU criminal law allowing a national judge to conduct a fair procedure, safeguard fundamental (constitutional) rights, as well as to foster a pro-European understanding allowing efficient mutual cooperation between Member States. Such a theory has to establish equilibrium in a way to keep the fundamentals of legitimacy of a national legal constitutional system untouched, on one side, and to help to transform the idea of an EU criminal law area into a coherent and functioning reality, thus legitimising the EU legal system, on the other side.

The Role of a Judge in Democracy: Separation of Powers and the Concept of Constitutional Fundamental Rights

Any analysis of the role of the judge in a democracy has to start from an understanding that democracy is not merely majority rule and requires also a proper balance between fundamental rights of the individual and the demands of society. It is a kind of synthesis of individual and social utilitarianism, meaning that

1 The views expressed in this chapter are personal ones and do not reflect an official position of the European Parliament.

the majoritarian principle of parliamentary decision-making requires a corrector to protect the individual from the tyranny of the majority (Tocqueville 2007: 190–208). To prevent negative consequences of the majority rule it is necessary to introduce the concepts of limited government and separation of powers enshrined in a constitution (or constitutional tradition) providing fundamental principles of a 'fair game' in a society. A constitution presents a common minimum denominator to which a certain society agreed to for its beneficial functioning. As such, it is not only a rational (contractual) legal document but also an expression of the 'feeling of justice' of a certain society. Consequently, democracy does not mean simply elections and majority rule, but its true nature is in the attitude of the majority towards the minority. This means that the system must be conceived in such a way that it grants an individual certain inalienable rights, regardless of the passing will of changing majorities, which leads directly to a concept of fundamental human rights enshrined in a constitution (constitutional tradition).

In this regard the need for a certain authority arises, which does not represent directly the will of the majority and which is capable of resolving existing antagonisms between the individual and society in a legitimate manner for both sides (Cardozo 1991: 92). The judicial branch proved itself as ideal to reconcile these differences (Hamilton et al. 2003, The Federalist Paper No. 78). As such judges/courts constitute the third branch in the separation of powers doctrine and function as co-creators of law and controllers of majoritarian legislation. The way in which judges are installed proves as a key advantage, as their power, although coming from the people, is at the same time also sufficiently separated from the people. The undetermined tenure of the judicial mandate plays a vital role in that regard, for it guarantees sufficient independence from temporarily vicious passions of the majority (Hamilton et al. 2003, The Federalist Paper No. 51). This means that any demands for the reduction of judicial independence (e.g. time limits on judicial tenure) present an assault against the democratic republic itself.[2]

Judge as 'Modern Aristocrat'

As judges are not directly elected by the people, they do not need to please the majority. The permanence of the function is what allows judges to independently and impartially take a decision, thus forming the basis of their moral and intellectual authority.[3] The role of judges as protectors of democracy even makes Plato's theory of guardians of the state (a dangerous, totalitarian concept of his theory) somewhat

2 The notion of judicial independence plays a key role for a functioning system of mutual recognition as will be elaborated further in the text.

3 See in that regard the 1998 European Charter on the Statute for Judges, the 2010 Recommendation (2010)12 of the Committee of Ministers of the Council of Europe, as well as the 2010 Venice Commission report on the independence of the judicial system (CDL-AD(2010)004).

acceptable (Popper 2003: 127–65). A judge in a democratic society is a kind of modern 'aristocrat', providing benefits of 'aristocracy' (independence and moral excellence), without its attendant injustices and unlimited discretion (Tocqueville 2007). As 'guardians' of democracy judges are also tasked with preventing abuses of the democratic rules by those who wish to participate in the democratic process with the sole purpose of destroying it. Democracy is a system which can only permit the active participation of those who respect its democratic rules. Thus, for example, the German Weimar republic collapsed, as it was a democracy without a critical mass of democrats. The scope of certain individual rights (such as the right of expression and assembly) might be limited where a democracy must protect itself. Of course, such a limitation should never destroy the essence of fundamental individual rights by denying individuals basic human dignity (such as the right to life, prohibition of torture, equality before the law). The judiciary must thus have the prerogatives (as the most suitable of the three branches) to interfere in the political life of a democratic state by banning political parties, which do not recognise democratic rules or (mis)use them with the sole intention to destroy democracy.[4]

(Self-)Limitation of Judges

However, *it was the best of theories, it was the worst of theories*, and the role of the judiciary as 'guardian of the society' may also conceal certain pitfalls. Such a theory, taken to an extreme, would create a kind of judicial dictatorship – 'government by judiciary' (Berger 1997: 457–66). Obviously such an understanding would entail significant dangers, for power corrupts and absolute power corrupts absolutely, as Lord Acton properly stated. Thus the power of judges in a democracy is far from being limitless. They are bound by a constitution, laws adopted by a parliamentarian majority (as long as they are in line with fundamental human rights and democracy), existing legal precedents and the codex of judicial ethics. At the same time they have to be (self)aware of their role in a democracy and understand that a judge is generally qualified to consider the legal policy underlying human rights protection

4 See e.g. the 1952 decision of the German Federal Constitutional Court *BVerFGE 2, 1*, banning the Socialist Party of the Reich (*Sozialistische Reichspartei*) as the heir to the national-socialist ideology, and the 1956 decision *BVerfGE 5, 85*, banning the Communist Party of Germany. The aforementioned also reflects the approach of the European Court of Human Rights (ECtHR) on Article 11 of the European Convention on Human Rights (ECHR). See, e.g., ECtHR, *Refah Partisi (The Welfare Party) and others v. Turkey*, a. nos. 41340/98, 41342/98, 41343/98, 41344/98, Judgment of 31 July 2001, confirmed by the Grand Chamber Judgment of 13 February 2003; *United Communist Party of Turkey and others v. Turkey*, Reports 1998-I, 30 January 1998; *Freedom and Democracy Party (Özdep) v. Turkey*, a. no. 23885/94, Judgment of 8 December 1999; *Socialist Party and others v. Turkey*, a. no. 21237/93, Judgment of 25 May 1998, etc.

and should in principle beware of evaluating complex, polycentric questions of economic or social policy that require specialised expertise and knowledge (Barak 2006). Therefore, judges in a modern democracy cannot do as they please.

Accordingly, democracy moves between two extremes, the danger of the tyranny of the majority, on one side, and the negative consequences of extreme judicial particularism leading to excessive inequality, on the other side. In all this the judge must seek an adequate balance. However, such a guardian role has to be based on the concept of fundamental human rights. Without such a legal and philosophical basis (enshrined in a written constitution or being part of a firm constitutional tradition) judicial law-making turns into something negative, into judicial despotism with grave consequences for the rights of the individual, as shown by the US Supreme Court case *Dred Scott*, 60 U.S. 393 (1856). And yet, fundamental rights of an individual must be adequately counter-balanced against the rights of others, as criminal law clearly illustrates.

The Role of a Judge in Criminal Law

Legality v. Legitimacy of Criminal Law

Security corresponds, according to Maslow, to one of the basic needs, being placed immediately after physiological needs (Maslow 1987). Consequently, social control, also in the form of criminal law, is a normal part of human nature as well as part of a diversified modern society. In criminal law, as the most visible part of formal social control, the conflict between the interests of the individual and society reaches its peak. Consequently, criminal law presents a kind of litmus paper of the self-limitation of the state. It presents a testing sample of the immune system of a certain society – its reaction to attacks against its fundamental moral/legal values. Serious crime, for example terrorism, and the fight against it provide a good example in that regard as in such circumstances an individual can be quickly sacrificed at the altar of common interest.[5] Societies at different levels of their moral development react differently to such challenges. A modern democratic state based on the rule of

5 Winston Churchill said in that regard that '[the] mood and temper of the public in regard to the treatment of crime and criminals is one of the most unfailing tests of the civilisation of any country. A calm and dispassionate recognition of the rights of the accused against the State, and even those of convicted criminals against the State, a constant heart searching by all charged with the duty of punishment, a desire and eagerness to rehabilitate in the world of industry all those who have paid their dues in the hard coinage of punishment, tireless efforts towards the discovery of curative and regenerating processes, and an unfaltering faith that there is a treasure, if you can only find it, in the heart of every man – these are the symbols which in the treatment of crime and criminals mark and measure the stored-up strength of a nation and are the sign and proof of the living virtue in it'. W. Churchill, UK House of Commons, 20 July 1910.

law limits itself to take into account certain fundamental rights of the individual. Such a society is not only legal – *law and order*, but also legitimate – *rule of law* (Zupančič 2008: 31–5). The legal (constitutional) frame of a modern democratic state could be compared with post-conventional morals (Kohlberg et al. 1995) and presents a society based on certain fundamental principles (Dworkin 2001: 208–16). However, recent developments as regards the violations of fundamental rights by democratic states in the fight against terrorism (institutional use of torture, unlimited detentions without a fair trial, targeted killings, mass surveillance, etc.) showed that such a frame is not as strong as we thought. Bauman's finding should be recalled, which states that modern society without proper safeguards is even capable of an industrially managed genocide, as shown by the horrific events of Second World War (Bauman 2005: 83). Zimbardo's Stanford experiment on the situational/system influence confirms this. A deviant institutional framework can make average normal individuals to participate in the most horrifying behaviour (Zimbardo 2007).

Consequently, respect for fundamental (constitutional) rights and the role of a judge, which is shown in the limitations, placed on the omnipotence of the legislator and on the discretion of the executive branch, play an elementary role in safeguarding democracy. The criminal procedure (as the most intense form of formal social control) is a kind of visible 'moment of truth' as regards the respect for the rule of law in a certain society (Zupančič 1990: 94–9). The reality shown in a criminal procedure is a sort of Janus' second face of a society due to the fact that a criminal procedure is an artificial dispute with an equilibrium being established between the parties through self-limitation of the state. Today the real democratic nature of a criminal procedure does not show itself in the historical[6] notions of the accusatorial, inquisitorial and mixed procedure, but in the respect for the suspect's rights guaranteeing equality of arms between him/her and the state. Therefore, in a democratic modern state it is not enough for a criminal procedure to be only perceived as legal but it has to be also legitimate in the meaning of a fair trial and safeguarding basic fundamental (constitutional) rights. As such a criminal procedure cannot be separated from the fundamental understanding of the notion of justice valid in a certain society, as fundamental criminal procedural rights are also fundamental constitutional rights and form a substantial part of the rule of law concept. This applies also to actions based on a request by another state. If a state is required to use coercive powers, it should be obliged to justify the use of those powers to its population, even if those powers are exercised at the behest of another state (Peers 2004).

Phases of Criminal Procedure

The role of the judiciary varies through the different phases of the criminal procedure. In the pretrial phase a judge should prevent arbitrariness as regards the

6 For a general overview of the different historical types of criminal procedure see, e.g., the classical work of Esmein (1913) and Langbein (2003).

use of coercive law-enforcement measures (for example, pretrial detention, house-searches, wiretappings, etc.) as well as with respect to the start of the criminal procedure as such (either through a decision based on a special remedy against the start of a police/prosecutorial investigation or through a decision regarding the start of a judicial investigation). A judicial body also verifies the justification for the charge before the trial itself. At trial the judge has to perform the role of an impartial and unbiased arbiter for adjudicating the case. He also has to decide, in case no decision was taken before, upon admissibility of evidence gathered in previous phases or evidence based on such evidence (the so-called fruit of the poisonous tree doctrine). In the legal remedies phase a judge also functions as a controller and corrector of possible subordinate judicial legal and factual errors. However, different phases of a criminal procedure form an organic unity, and the best and the fairest trial amounts only to an appeal if law-enforcement authorities do not respect the basic rights of the suspect in the pretrial phase.[7]

In that regard it is interesting to compare two main trends in Europe as regards the organisation of criminal justice, a police/prosecutorial investigation and a judicial investigation (investigating magistrate). Several EU Member States changed in the past their system (or are debating such a change) by abolishing the model of judicial investigation, based, inter alia, on the claim that such a procedure is inquisitorial (the same person being judge and investigator) and often tainted by the so-called 'psychological contamination' of the investigation judge. Some of such claims present an oversimplification of the real dynamics in a criminal procedure. As mentioned above, criminal procedure is not a 'fight' between equal parties but an artificially created dispute (through self-limitation of the state) whereby equality of the parties has to be created and maintained in an artificial way through the whole process. A system in which a suspect has contacts in the pretrial stage only or predominantly with the other party to the procedure (as regards the collecting of evidence) is much more prone to expose the suspect to psychological pressure.[8] In that regard the possibility of a judicial presence and intervention already in the pretrial phase can be an important safeguard against arbitrariness, as well as a guarantor of equality of arms and the presumption of innocence (prosecutorial burden of proof, the right to remain silent and the requirement of *in dubio pro reo*). Therefore, the role and presence of a judge in pretrial procedure is considered in several systems as a legitimising element of

7 See Judge Goldberg's comment in *Escobedo v. Illinois*, 378 U.S. 478 (1964): 'The rule sought by the State here, however, would make the trial no more than an appeal from the interrogation, and the right to use counsel at the formal trial would be a very hollow thing if, for all practical purposes, the conviction is already assured by pre-trial examination'. See also the ECtHR judgment in *Imbroscia v. Switzerland*, a. no. 13972/88, Judgment of 11 September 1992, para. 36.

8 A recent Austrian research as regards the introduction of a police/prosecutorial investigation (BGBl I 19/2004) being applied from 2008 showed that the police was actually the *dominus litis* of the procedure, not the prosecutor (Birklbauer et al. 2011).

criminal law action *in concreto* and also of the system as such (as a fundamental principle). This has been recently highlighted, for example, by the Croatian Constitutional Court as regards the abolition of judicial investigation in Croatia.[9]

At the same time the important question of the role of the prosecutor in a national system has to be answered. It is logical that a prosecutor, being a party to the procedure, cannot be impartial (although he can and should be independent from the executive branch).[10] The situation becomes even more complicated if the police or the prosecutor can authorise certain coercive investigative measures (for example, house searches).[11] At the same time a fair procedure is usually also reflected in the attitude towards admissibility of evidence and the exclusionary rule, whereby a whole variety of solutions exists in EU Member States with only a common minimum in ECtHR case law as regards admissibility of evidence obtained by torture or inhuman or degrading treatment and as regards a fair trial in general.[12] Whatever the particular national solution, the perception of fairness of a criminal procedure is also a cultural phenomenon based on past national experience and legal culture (Damaška 1991). The above mentioned does

9 The Croatian system provides an interesting example, as it was historically based on the mixed type of procedure, but was 2008 changed in line with an accusatorial concept with a prosecutorial/police investigation. The Croatian Constitutional Court questioned (case U-I-448-2009, Judgment of 19 July 2012) several solutions as adopted by the legislator in the new Croatian Criminal Procedural Code (*Narodne novine*, No. 152/08) and highlighted the importance of judicial control in the pretrial procedure (para. 39.2), although falling short of re-introducing the investigating judge.

10 See, e.g., ECtHR, *Medvedyev v. France*, a. no. 3394/03, Judgment of 10 July 2008, and *Mouline v. France*, a. no. 37104/06, Judgment of 23 November 2010, as regards the role of the prosecutor in detention procedures as a violation of Article 5 ECHR. See also Hodgson (2010: 1361–1411). See also, the decision of the Slovenian Constitutional Court No U-I-42/12 of 7 February 2013 clearly stating that the public prosecutor, although a judicial body in the broad sense, is not part of the constitutional separation of powers doctrine (Article 3 of the Slovenian Constitution), and hence is not a court body but a prosecutorial executive body.

11 What I have in mind here is a normal authorisation of a house search, not an authorisation or execution of a house search in urgent circumstances (for example, if somebody calls for help, hot pursuit, etc.).

12 For a comparison between some EU Member States (Ireland, Germany, France, Belgium, Italy, Netherlands, Spain, Greece, UK) see Thaman et al. (2013). Although the ECtHR does not deal in principle with admissibility of evidence as such, it nevertheless developed a clear theory on admissibility as regards violations of Article 3 ECHR (see, e.g., *Gäfgen v. Germany*, a. no. 22978/05, Judgments of 30 June 2008 and 1 June 2010 (Grand Chamber)), and only a general balancing theory based on fairness as regards violations of Article 6 (right to remain silent and right to a lawyer) and Article 8 ECHR (right to privacy) taking into account the nature of the violation, the probative value of evidence, the possibility of redress and even public interest (*Schenk v. Switzerland*, a. no. 10862/84, Judgment of 12 July 1988, *Khan v. UK*, a. no. 35394/97, Judgment of 12 May 2000, *Bykov v Russia*, a. no. 4378/02, Judgment of 10 March 2009, etc.).

not address only nuances of justice but goes to the core of a particular national understanding of fairness, with whole generations of lawyers trained to follow such basic programming, despite public expectations for certain (usually convicting) judicial outcomes. In that regard an uncritical application of mutual recognition based on 'commanded' mutual trust, not taking account of the differences in national constitutional identity (as guaranteed by Article 4(2) TEU), bears the danger of overlooking fundamental differences between national systems and their perception of justice, and to unnecessarily create resistance and mistrust against cooperation in criminal matters in the EU.

Mutual Recognition in Criminal Law

Meaning and Origins of Mutual Recognition

The concept of mutual recognition in EU criminal law was not initially part of the Treaties[13] and was introduced only by the 1999 Tampere European Council,[14] based on the logic of the 'country of origin principle' developed by the Court of Justice (the *Cassis de Dijon* case) within the framework of free movement of goods under the former first pillar and subsequently extended to the other freedoms.[15] However, what was overlooked was that decisions in a criminal procedure are not 'goods' in the usual sense but relate to fundamental (constitutional) rights as basic concepts of the rule of law and legitimacy of a national system (Mitsilegas 2006). Mutual recognition was used under the former first pillar to enhance freedoms of EU citizens in the common market and more broadly. However, the introduction of such a principle in the area of criminal law, without prior substantial harmonisation of defence rights (such a harmonisation is only in progress based on

13 The concept was given an explicit basis in the Treaties only with the adoption of the Lisbon Treaty (Article 82 TFEU).

14 The Tampere European Council conclusions, 15–16 October 1999, pp. 33–7, referred to mutual recognition as the 'cornerstone of judicial co-operation in criminal matters'. See also the 2000 Programme of measures to implement the principle of mutual recognition of decisions in criminal matters (OJ C 12, 15.1.2001, p. 10), the 2004 Hague Programme (OJ C 53, 3.3.2005, p. 1), and the 2009 Stockholm Programme (OJ C 115, 4.5.2010, p. 1).

15 CJEU, case 120/78, *Rewe-Zentral AG/Bundes-monopolverwaltung für Branntwein*, [1979] ECR 649. The 'country of origin principle' is based on two rules: (a) presumption of mutual recognition of products being placed legally on the market; (b) 'rule of reason' allowing certain limited grounds for refusal ('mandatory requirements'), such as fairness of commercial transactions, public health, protection of consumers, etc. An extension followed to the other freedoms (persons – CJEU, case C-415/93 (Bosman) [1995] ECR I-4921, and case C-55/94 (Gebhard), [1995] ECR I-4165; services – CJEU, case C-76/90, (Säger/Dennemeyer), [1991] ECR I-4221; and capital – CJEU, case C-98/01, (Commission/United Kingdom), [2003] ECR I-4641).

the 2009 Roadmap)[16], benefited mostly law-enforcement authorities (Möstl 2010). There was also a democratic deficit at work putting the defendant as regards his/her rights in an unclear position ('journey into the unknown') as regards legal certainty (Mitsilegas 2006: 1281, 1288). When introduced in the area of criminal law, mutual recognition was a product of intergovernmental cooperation of a kind of commanded social engineering, and not an evolutionary creation based on a proper democratic debate.[17] Neither has a prior analysis being carried out to determine its nature, consequences and possible preconditions (possible needs of prior harmonisation of the rights of suspects). Nevertheless, a whole raft of far-reaching instruments based on mutual recognition has been adopted covering different phases of the criminal procedure,[18] and new ones are being adopted.[19]

---

16 Resolution of the Council of 30 November 2009 on a Roadmap for strengthening procedural rights of suspected or accused persons in criminal proceedings (OJ C 295, 4.12.2009, p. 1).

17 Articles 34 and 39 of the former TEU limited the role of the European Parliament to the issuing of an opinion, and the 1997 Protocol on the role of national parliaments in the European Union provided only for an obligation to inform them on legislative proposals.

18 Council Framework Decision 2002/584/JHA of 13 June 2002 on the European arrest warrant and the surrender procedures between Member States (OJ L 190, 18.7.2002, p. 1), Council Framework Decision 2003/577/JHA on the execution in the EU of orders freezing property or evidence (OJ L 196, 2.8.2003, p. 45), Council Framework Decision 2005/214/JHA on the application of the principle of mutual recognition for financial penalties (OJ L 76, 22.3.2005, p. 16), Council Framework Decision 2006/783/JHA on the application of the principle of mutual recognition for confiscation orders (OJ L 328, 24.11.2006, p. 59), Council Framework Decision 2008/909/JHA of 27 November 2008 on the application of the principle of mutual recognition for judgments imposing custodial sentences or measures involving deprivation of liberty (OJ L 327, 5.12.2008, p. 27), Council Framework Decision 2008/947/JHA of 27 November 2008 on probation decisions and alternative sanctions (OJ L 337, 16.12.2008, p. 102), Council Framework Decision 2008/978/JHA of 18 December 2008 on the European evidence warrant for the purpose of obtaining objects, documents and data for use in proceedings in criminal matters (OJ L 350, 30.12.2008, p. 72), Council Framework Decision 2009/829/JHA of 23 October 2009 on the application, between Member States of the European Union, of the principle of mutual recognition to decisions on supervision measures as an alternative to provisional detention (OJ L 294, 11.11.2009, p. 20), and Council Framework Decision 2009/299/JHA of 26 February 2009 amending Framework Decisions 2002/584/JHA, 2005/214/JHA, 2006/783/JHA, 2008/909/JHA and 2008/947/ JHA, thereby enhancing the procedural rights of persons and fostering the application of the principle of mutual recognition to decisions rendered in the absence of the person concerned at the trial (OJ L 81, 27. 3. 2009, p. 24).

19 Initiative of the Kingdom of Belgium, the Republic of Bulgaria, the Republic of Estonia, the Kingdom of Spain, the Republic of Austria, the Republic of Slovenia and the Kingdom of Sweden for a Directive of the European Parliament and of the Council regarding the European Investigation Order in criminal matters (OJ C 165, 24.6.2010, p. 22), providing for mutual recognition of possibly all investigative measures.

Practical Problems with Mutual Recognition

A sound functioning of mutual recognition is based on the idea of coherent standards as regards fundamental rights protection in criminal proceedings of the Member States, thus based on the notion of mutual trust of compatible criminal law systems. However, an 2008 EU-wide research clearly showed anomalies in criminal procedures of several Member States and came to the following overall conclusion: 'A striking finding is the fact that fundamental rights such as the right to remain silent, to have access to the file and to call and/or examine witnesses or experts, which are basic requirements of a fair trial in the ECHR, are not provided for in the legislation of all the Member States' (Spronken et al. 2009: 14).[20] Such a conclusion destroyed the myth of a sound convergence of criminal procedural fundamentals between EU Member States, based only on a common ECHR framework without carrying out prior extensive harmonisation at EU level. The mentioned anomalies appear mostly during the pretrial procedure (the investigation phase). This means that the earlier in the procedure mutual recognition is being applied, the more sensitive it is. Consequently, the more we move towards mutual recognition of final court decisions, the less problematic an automatic application of the concept becomes. Also, through the application of mutual recognition, any national anomalies in a criminal procedure tend to become a common problem. The basic precondition of mutual recognition, i.e. the existence of an independent and impartial judiciary in all the EU Member States as a *sine qua non* condition, already becomes a common point of interest, significantly expanding the role and prerogatives of the EU in that regard.[21]

At the same time the practical application of the European Arrest Warrant (EAW), as the first adopted mutual recognition instrument in criminal law, showed deficiencies and differences in its application in the Member States. In several of them the question of compatibility between EU law and national constitutions was raised – leading even to changes of national constitutions (Pollicino 2008). Some Member States (UK, Ireland, Belgium, Austria)[22] transposed the EAW with an

20 The study showed a divergence as regards initial warnings about the right to remain silent and the right to a lawyer before and during pretrial interrogations, posing questions, inter alia, about conformity of such practices with the ECtHR *Salduz* case-law – *Salduz v. Turkey*, a. no. 36391/02, Judgment of 27 November 2008.

21 See, e.g., EP working document 904760 stating that 'any doubts in the independence and impartiality of judges based on systematical flaws in the Constitution and national laws could have a significant impact on the on-going cooperation in the common area on freedom, security and justice based on the principle of mutual recognition as enshrined in Articles 81 TFEU (civil matters) and 82 TFEU (criminal matters)'. In that regard also the question of EU fundamental rights protection outside the application of EU law arises, whereby Article 2 TEU seems an additional broader source of EU competence in comparison with the limitation of Article 51(1) of the Charter (von Bogdandy et al. 2012: 489–520).

22 See, e.g., the UK *Extradition Act 2003*, Part 1, Section 21; the Irish *European Arrest Warrant Act 2003*, Part 3, Section 37; the Belgian *Loi du 19 décembre 2003 relative*

additional 'human rights violation' non-recognition clause, although such clause is not explicitly mentioned in the EAW Framework Decision, clearly showing that they felt uncomfortable with a fully automatic application. In addition, other issues have been raised such as proportionality (issuing of EAWs for minor offences) leading to a change in the EAW's Handbook;[23] problematic prison conditions, triggering a possible application of Article 3 ECHR;[24] dual criminality; as well as the definition of 'judicial authorities', issuing an EAW.[25]

Judicial Authorities as a Factor of Legitimacy

The question of the definition of judicial authorities is a horizontal issue as regards mutual recognition in criminal law. It is particularly sensitive as regards certain coercive investigative measures where substantial differences between Member States exist in relation to two types of coercive measures – wiretappings and house-searches. The authorising national authorities for these measures in some Member States are not judges/courts, but prosecutors and police. For example, in the UK,[26] it is the Home Secretary who authorises wiretappings, as the information gathered by them is perceived as only police/intelligence information and is not admissible as evidence in a criminal trial.[27] In some other Member States, the prosecutor (Italy)[28] or even the police itself (Finland)[29] can order house searches. The problem with the definition of 'judicial authority' stems already from the 1959 MLA Council of Europe Convention, which leaves such a definition in the

---

au mandat d'arrêt européen, Article 4; or the Austrian *Bundesgesetz über die justizielle Zusammenarbeit in Strafsachen mit den Mitgliedstaaten der Europäischen Union*, § 19.

23 Council doc. 17195/1/10.

24 Irish Supreme Court, *MJELR v. Rettinger*, [2010] IESC 45, Judgment of 23 July 2010.

25 See, e.g., Julian Assange v Swedish Prosecution Authority, UK Supreme Court [2012] UKSC 22, and High Court, 2011 EWHC 2849 (Admin), and also post-Assange case-law on the question of ministries as judicial authorities – Bucnys, Sakalis and Lavrov, 2012 EWCH 2771 (Admin), where the High Court differentiated between conviction and accusation EAWs and considered ministries as judicial authorities for conviction EAWs if courts participated in the issuing procedure. In that regard it considered the Lithuanian ministry as a judicial authority, but not the Estonian one.

26 The *Regulation of Investigatory Powers Act 2000*, whereby recent changes introduced judicial control as regards the prerogatives of local authorities – see the UK *Protection of Freedoms Act 2012*.

27 For criticism of the current system as regards the rights of the defence see Oxford Pro Bono Publico (2006).

28 See, e.g., Article 244 of the Italian *Codice di procedura penale*.

29 See the Coercive Measures Act (pakkokeinolaki, Act no. 646/2003), and ECtHR judgments in cases *Harju v. Finland*, a. no. 56716/09, Judgment of 15 February 2011, and *Heino v. Finland*, a. no. 56720/09, Judgment of 15 February 2011, as regards a violation of Article 8 ECHR.

hands of Contracting Parties.[30] The 2000 EU MLA Convention[31] built on this. The problem persisted with the introduction of mutual recognition measures, whereby, for example, the EAW left the choice of issuing authorities to Member States (Article 6) leading to a situation whereby in some Member States even ministries are perceived as judicial authorities.[32] It was in the Assange case, relating to an EAW request from Sweden to the UK, where this issue has been prominently raised. The High Court, although granting the Swedish EAW, was of the opinion that administrative authorities could not be perceived as judicial authorities, and tied the acceptance of a request by a prosecutor to a pre-existing court decision in the issuing state.[33] On the other hand, the UK Supreme Court based its reasoning on a mainly historical evaluation of the EAW drafting process and considered prosecutors as judicial authorities.[34] As regards evidence gathering, Framework Decision 2008/978/JHA on the European Evidence Warrant (EEW), trying to solve the issue, introduced (a) a special non-recognition ground in cases where the issuing authority was not a judge or a prosecutor (or has not been validated by such an authority) for searches and seizures (Article 11(4)), and (b) the possibility of such non-recognition (by a special declaration by the Member State) in all cases where the measures necessary to execute the EEW would have to be ordered or supervised by a judge, a court, an investigating magistrate or a public prosecutor under the law of the executing state in a similar domestic case (Article 11(5)). A

30 European Convention on Mutual Assistance in Criminal Matters, 20 April 1959.

31 Council Act of 29 May 2000 establishing in accordance with Article 34 of the Treaty on European Union the Convention on Mutual Assistance in Criminal Matters between the Member States of the European Union (OJ C 197, 12.7.2000, p.1).

32 Final report on the fourth round of mutual evaluations, The practical application of the European Arrest Warrant and corresponding procedures between Member States, Council doc. 8302/1/09Rev 4.

33 2011 EWHC 2849 (Admin). In that regard it stated: '47. For example, if a warrant was issued by a Ministry of Justice which the Member State had designated as an authority under Article 6, it would not, in our view, be a valid EAW under the Framework Decision. The principles of mutual recognition and mutual confidence which underpin the common area for justice would not require the recognition of such a warrant, as it would self evidently not have been issued by a body which, on principles universally accepted in Europe, was judicial ... public confidence in the EAW would only be undermined by the recognition of an EAW issued by a Ministry of Justice in contradistinction to an EAW issued by a judge or prosecutor ...'.

49. Although in our view no challenge can be made to the validity of the EAW issued by the Prosecutor, it is necessary to consider whether the EAW should be accorded more intense scrutiny as a warrant issued by a party to the proceedings. That might be the case where it had not been subject to the impartial scrutiny of a judge in the Member State of issue. Although a prosecutor would ordinarily act independently in the decision to issue the EAW and in pursuance of what would in the terms of the Framework Decision be regarded as a judicial function, the decision is that of a party to the proceedings which has not been subjected to the impartial scrutiny of a judge'.

34 [2012] UKSC 22.

special validation procedure has been also provided in the Council general approach on the proposed Directive on the European investigation order.[35] However, this did not solve the problem of prosecutors as issuing authorities if a court authorisation in the executing state is legally (constitutionally) obligatory.[36]

The definition of 'judicial authority' should not be underestimated, as such a notion refers to the basic legitimacy of a certain measure and consequently even of a criminal procedure as such. National constitutional requirements of a court authorisation form in some Member States part of their 'national identities, inherent in their fundamental constitutional structures' (Article 4(2) TEU) and should also be understood in the light of the nature of a constitution, laying the foundation of values, commitments and orientations of a society, reflecting events in the past and determining its future, philosophy, politics and law all in one (Barak 2006). Therefore, in my opinion, a purely result-oriented approach, i.e. one based only on the intention of law enforcement and not on the type of authority, is not enough. It is not only the result that legitimises a certain measure but also the way of reaching the result.[37]

An EU Miranda Warning System and the Exclusionary Rule

Differences exist between Member States as regards the understanding of the right to remain silent and the right to a lawyer. Several Member States did not have a 'Miranda' warning system in place and did not comply with the *Salduz* case law. The situation has been recently partly remedied by the introduction of a common EU 'Miranda' system (Article 3 of Directive 2012/13/EU on the right to information in criminal proceedings).[38] However, the understanding of the absolute nature of the right to remain silent still varies and in some Member States negative consequences are being inferred from the silence of the defendant. At the same time both harmonisation measures are only half-hearted solutions if not coupled with a common understanding regarding the admissibility of evidence and the exclusionary rule in the case of violations. Admissibility rules and the exclusionary rule are not only technical tools to achieve a correct judgment (as regards the

35 Council doc. 18225/1/11. See Articles 1 and 5a.

36 This could be easily solved by referring in EU criminal law mutual recognition instruments as regards the execution of a request to the national rules of the executing state, such as a court authorisation. Such a solution would guarantee that internal constitutional standards (like a court authorisation) in the executing state are respected, while at the same time the evaluation itself in the executing state would be limited by the agreed non-recognition grounds, including a human rights non-recognition ground (giving enough leverage for conducting court prerogatives).

37 As certain criteria are necessary to legitimise the criminalisation of certain behaviour *in abstracto* (see in that regard Peršak 2007), also certain preconditions have to be fulfilled (depending on the system) to justify a law enforcement measure *in concreto* (such as reasonable doubt, proportionality, judicial authorisation, etc.).

38 OJ L 142, 1.6.2012, p. 1.

establishing of truth) but refer to the basic understanding of fairness in a criminal procedure. The more a society perceives a defendant as a person endowed with fundamental procedural rights, the stronger it regulates admissibility of evidence and applies the exclusionary rule. For the moment, no common binding EU rules on admissibility exist[39] (they are national prerogatives) and it seems that Member States are reluctant to accept such rules.[40] It is also not fully clear whether and how Member States are respecting the ECtHR case law in that regard.[41]

Human Rights Violation Non-Recognition Clause

Respect for human rights is an essential element of democracy. Take human rights out of democracy and democracy loses its soul; it becomes an empty shell, whereby the task of a judge is to protect and uphold such rights (Barak 2006: 81). It has to be clear that the respect for human rights is also an essential part of mutual recognition whereby such rights must be ensured for individuals, regardless of whether a single Member State, two or more Member States, or even the EU itself is acting (Klip 2012). At the moment a human rights non-recognition ground is not explicitly included in the existing mutual recognition instruments, with the exception of Council Framework Decision 2005/214/JHA on the application of the principle of mutual recognition to financial penalties (Article 20(3)). In that regard the instruments refer only in a general way to the protection of fundamental rights and prohibit discriminatory prosecution on the grounds of sex, race, religion, ethnic origin, nationality, language, political opinions or sexual orientation. However, several Member States, as mentioned above, transposed the EAW Framework Decision in way that includes such a special non-recognition ground.[42] Such a ground has been also explicitly demanded by the European Parliament[43] and was

39 Only a non-binding Green paper on obtaining evidence in criminal matters (COM(2009)0624) exists.

40 Compare the initial Commission proposal on access to a lawyer (COM(2011)0326) that would introduce a common admissibility rule (Article 13(3)) with the Council general approach (Article 11) excluding such a common rule.

41 See footnote 12.

42 As regards fundamental rights protection a significant change took place in the perception of the Commission from being 'disturbed' by additional national non-recognition grounds based on fundamental rights (2005 Report (COM(2005)0063)) to highlighting the need of harmonisation of fundamental rights in the criminal procedure and the importance of the 2009 Roadmap (2011 Report (COM(2011)0175)). It is also interesting that the JHA Council in 2005 did not oppose to a fundamental rights non-recognition ground but stated only that 'several politically important questions came to light' including an additional fundamental rights non-recognition ground (Council doc. 8849/05). See also Mitsilegas (2006: 1292–1294).

43 http://www.europarl.europa.eu/document/activities/cont/201205/20120523ATT45657/20120523ATT45657EN.pdf.

acknowledged by Advocate General Sharpston in the case C-396/11 (*Radu*).[44] The introduction of such an explicit ground in secondary EU legislation would send a clear message that the protection of human rights is an essential part of mutual recognition. Additionally, the possible misuse of it could be prevented through the initial burden of proof, whereby an unreasoned claim by a defendant would not suffice, but would have to be accompanied by a certain level of convincing proof in order to trigger the burden of proof of the issuing State. In this way, mutual recognition in criminal law (as one of the most sensitive legal areas) would be put in line with the existing mutual recognition systems in other fields, providing for additional *ordre public* exceptions.[45]

Primacy of EU Law and the Solange Debate

Criminal procedures relate directly to basic fundamental constitutional rights. As regards the relationship between national constitutions and EU law, the Court of Justice clearly took the view of primacy of EU law,[46] an opinion only tolerated by some national constitutional courts.[47] Consequently, the principle

---

44 Paragraph 108: '… The competent judicial authority of the Member State executing a European arrest warrant can refuse the request for surrender without being in breach of the obligations authorised by the founding Treaties and the other provisions of European Union law, where it is shown that the human rights of the person whose surrender is requested have been infringed, or will be infringed, as part of or following the surrender process. However, such a refusal will be competent only in exceptional circumstances. In cases involving Articles 5 and 6 of the Convention and/or Articles 6, 47 and 48 of the Charter, the infringement in question must be such as fundamentally to destroy the fairness of the process. The person alleging infringement must persuade the decision-maker that his objections are substantially well founded. Past infringements that are capable of remedy will not found such an objection'. A special non-recognition ground based on a fundamental rights violation (as regards inhuman and degrading treatment) was acknowledged by the Court of Justice in the field of transfers of asylum seekers (*N.S. and others*, Joined Cases C-411/10 and C-493/10). However, the Court missed the opportunity to clarify this issue as regards criminal law in the mentioned *Radu* case, although it recognised that the Charter applies.

45 Limitations to four freedoms (see, e.g., Article 36 TFEU and the mandatory exceptions introduced by the '*Cassis de Dijon*' case-law), mutual recognition of civil judgments (see, e.g., Article 34 of Council Regulation 44/2001 on jurisdiction and the recognition and enforcement of judgments in civil and commercial matters), driving licences (e.g., Joined cases C-329/06 and 343/06, *Wiedemann and Funk*), diplomas (e.g., case C-311/06, *Consiglio Nazionale degli Ingeneri*), etc.

46 *Flaminio Costa v ENEL* [1964] ECR 585 (6/64).

47 See, e.g., the judgments of the *Bundesverfassungsgericht* – BVerfGE 37, 271, Judgment of 29 May 1974 (Solange I), and BVerfGE 73, 339, Judgment of 22 October 1986 (Solange II), BVerfGE 89, 155 (1993), Judgment of 12 October 1993 (Maastricht Treaty), and BvE 2/08, 2 BvE 5/08, 2 BvR 1010/08, 2 BvR 1022/08, 2 BvR 1259/08 and 2 BvR 182/09, Judgment of 30 June 2009 (Lisbon Treaty).

of primacy has not been directly included into the Treaties but has been defined only in Declaration No. 17. At the same time Article 4(2) TEU states, inter alia, that 'the Union shall respect the equality of Member States before the Treaties as well as their national identities, inherent in their fundamental structures, political and constitutional, inclusive of regional and local self-government'. Furthermore, Articles 82(3) and 83(3) TFEU allow a Member State to oppose a criminal law measure where it considers that they 'would affect fundamental aspects of its criminal justice system'. This could be perceived as overcoming the idea of absolute primacy of EU law and as an endorsement of a pluralistic vision of the relationship between EU law and national constitutional identity – composite constitutionalism, *Verfassungsverbund* (von Bogdandy and Schill 2011). Therefore, mutual recognition instruments should avoid triggering a direct conflict between EU law and fundamental national constitutional law.

However, recently the question of primacy of EU law arose directly in the case C-399/11 (*Melloni*),[48] where the Spanish Constitutional Court requested, inter alia, an interpretation of Article 53 of the EU Charter of Fundamental Rights on the possibility of the application of stricter national constitutional rules.[49] The case related to an EAW request by Italy based on a judgment rendered *in absentia* and to a dichotomy between stricter Spanish constitutional rules as regards obligatory retrial and Article 4a of the FD EAW (introduced by FD 2009/299/JHA) providing a lower standard. Advocate General Bot (in para. 100) highlighted primacy of EU law (even secondary EU law) and denied the application of higher national constitutional fundamental rights standards in a legislated EU legal area. However, he referred also to the notion of national identity (Article 4(2) TEU) stating that the present case did not raise such an issue (paras 138–42). His opinion was followed by the Court of Justice stating that FD 2009/JHA harmonised the conditions if execution of an EAW in the event of a conviction rendered *in absentia*, and that Article 53 of the Charter has to be interpreted in a way that the primacy, unity and effectiveness of EU law are not thereby compromised. Such an answer does not take fully into account the sensitivities regarding criminal law and does not clarify the notion of national constitutional identity. A better way forward would be to give fundamental human rights a special status as regards the question of primacy of EU law. Consequently, EU common standards from the Charter should always represent very high standards of protection of fundamental human rights (and not only a common minimum denominator based on the understanding of the

48 CJEU, *Melloni*, case C-399/11, Judgment of 26 February 2013.

49 Article 53 of the Charter (Level of protection): 'Nothing in this Charter shall be interpreted as restricting or adversely affecting human rights and fundamental freedoms as recognised, in their respective fields of application, by Union law and international law and by international agreements to which the Union or all the Member States are party, including the European Convention for the Protection of Human Rights and Fundamental Freedoms, and by the Member States' constitutions'.

ECHR).[50] At the same time EU secondary law should introduce an *ordre public* non-recognition ground based on human rights per analogy with the existing exceptions to mutual recognition in other areas of EU law.[51] From the perspective of legitimacy of EU law it would be odd to allow an *ordre public* non-recognition ground in other areas of mutual recognition, but not in the field of criminal law as the most intrusive form of social control that may significantly (and detrimentally) impact the (fundamental) rights of the individual.

This would avoid another *Solange* debate as well as prevent the lowering of the level of protection of human rights in the EU by forcing Member States with higher national standards to use lower common standards. In this way a de-alienation of EU criminal law mutual recognition instruments from national constitutions could be avoided, taking into account that the development of law must maintain normative coherence within a legal system and must reflect the fundamental values of the legal system (Barak 2006). On the other side, national courts have to be fully aware that they are part of a common EU ('federal') legal area and bound by the sincere cooperation principle (Article 4(3) TEU). Therefore, the starting point in applying mutual recognition instruments has to be mutual trust (enhanced by the harmonisation of procedural rights), putting the initial burden of proof as regards claims of human rights violations on the defendant. Consequently, national courts have to understand that non-recognition is an exception, not the rule, and that therefore it should not be used lightly.

How Mutual Recognition Could Work and Respect the Classical Role of a Judge

Mutual recognition is a proper way forward in a non-harmonised environment. However, the system should include at least the following elements:

- All existing third-pillar mutual recognition instruments should be replaced by new legislation, adopted in the ordinary legislative procedure (Article 294 TFEU), thereby guaranteeing full democratic legitimacy.
- A human rights non-recognition ground should be a standard part of EU criminal law mutual recognition instruments contributing to the avoidance of any *Solange* disputes.
- An additional *ordre public* non-recognition ground should be applied for certain coercive investigative measures (wiretappings, covert investigations, controlled deliveries) – 'a measure would not be approved in a similar domestic case'.
- A basic and common EU understanding of 'judicial authorities' has to

50 In line with the possibility provided for in Article 52(3) of the Charter to adopt higher standards that the ones guaranteed by the ECHR, taking into account the Court's extensive interpretation of the applicability of the Charter – see case C-617/10 (*Åklagaren v. Hans Åkerberg Fransson*).

51 See footnote 46.

be introduced, excluding police authorities and recognising that court authorisation for certain coercive investigative measure can form part of national constitutional identity in some Member States.

- The abolishment of dual criminality for the already agreed category of 32 offences should be applied in the framework of usual shared meaning of an offence, taking into account the level of existing EU material criminal law harmonisation.[52]
- Further harmonisation of procedural rights based on the 2009 Roadmap and beyond is necessary (presumption of innocence, *ne bis in idem* and admissibility of evidence).
- The Court of Justice should take into account the sensitivities and special status of criminal law as regards human rights and the notion of legitimacy.[53]

Conclusions

Mutual recognition in EU criminal law relates to essential questions as regards the legal structure of the EU constitutional order and interrelates to concepts such as primacy of EU law, national constitutions, fundamental human rights, and last but not least the role of a judge in democracy. Consequently, it is not a pure technical rule but demands a careful and thought-through design, providing a fine equilibrium between the different tasks that it has to fulfil. A defective concept of mutual recognition, disregarding the seriousness of the questions connected with its application, bears the danger of causing significant legal and constitutional anomalies, thus creating a possible legal vacuum as regards legal certainty of individual rights and even causing mistrust. Therefore, mutual recognition instruments drafted on the basis of Article 82 TFEU have to be structured in a way to continue legitimising the existing national constitutional identities of the Member States and at the same time legitimise the necessity and added value of EU measures and a common European Union. An essential 'legitimiser' of modern democratic legal systems is the respect for fundamental rights, as guaranteed by national constitutional traditions, the ECHR and the Charter, whereby national and EU judges act as guardians of such

---

52 It should be considered that the dual criminality requirement is not fulfilled if a Member State uses an atypical definition of an offence from the list. See also Vermeulen et al. (2012: 27–8, 106–84).

53 In that regard it should adopt a high standard of protection of the Charter rights (not only the ECHR minimum) as well as evaluate mutual recognition cases in coherence with fundamentals of national constitutional systems. See also Klip (2012). The current Court's 'optimistic' mutual trust approach, as highlighted in *Gözütok and Brügge* (Joined cases C-187/01 and 385/01), is not sufficient and a more tolerant approach towards national constitutional concerns is necessary. An important step in that regard would be a further clarification of the concept of national constitutional identity as enshrined in Article 4(2) TEU following the *Sayn-Wittgenstein* case-law (C-208/09).

rights. Consequently, mutual recognition should not change the classical role of a judge to safeguard such rights, nor should it trigger a race to the bottom approach, as regards the level of their protection, or create a dangerous rift in the common EU judicial structure by creating a variety of *Solange* disputes. In the present text it was tried to provide an intelligent design of mutual recognition avoiding the mentioned problems and being based mainly on a commonly acceptable definition of judicial authority, a human rights non-recognition ground and necessary additional harmonisation measures. The proposed system can be achieved by a combination of legislative measures (secondary EU legislation and national rules transposing it) and judicial decisions, remedying possible negative anomalies associated with mutual recognition, in which the Court of Justice and national courts should work together in mutual respect based on the power of logic and not on the logic of power (Zupančič 2003).[54]

References

Barak, A. 2006. *The Judge in a Democracy*. Princeton: Princeton University Press.

Bauman, Z. 2005 (orig. 1989). *Modernity and the Holocaust*. Cambridge: Polity Press.

Berger, R. 1997. *Government by Judiciary*, 2nd edn. Indianapolis: Liberty Fund.

Birklbauer, A., Stangl, W., Soyer, R., Weber, C., Starzer, B., Hirtenlehner, H., Gombots, R., Hammerschick, W., Luef-Kölbl, H. and Hotter M. 2011. *Die Rechtspraxis des Ermittlungsverfahrens nach der Strafprozessreform*. Vienna: Neuer Wissenschaftlicher Verlag.

Bogdandy, A. von and Schill, S. 2011. Overcoming absolute primacy: Respect for national identity under the Lisbon Treaty. *Common Market Law Review*, 48(5), 1417–53.

Bogdandy, A. von, Kottmann, M., Antpöhler, C., Dickschen, J., Hentrei, S. and Smrkolj, M. 2012. Reverse Solange – Protecting the essence of fundamental rights against EU Member States. *Common Market Law Review*, 49(2), 489–519.

Cardozo, B.N. 1991 (orig. 1921). *The Nature of the Judicial Process*. New Haven: Yale University Press.

Damaška, M. 1991 (orig. 1986). *Two Faces of Justices*. New Haven: Yale University Press.

Dworkin, R. 2001 (orig. 1986). *Law's Empire*. Cambridge: Harvard University Press.

54 It is not only about the level of judicial authority (Court of Justice v. national constitutional courts) but also about the ability to provide logically coherent judicial decisions guaranteeing the highest possible level of human rights protection in a common EU criminal law area and thus being perceived as legitimate.

Esmein, A. 1913. *A History of Continental Criminal Procedure with Special Reference to France*. Boston: Little, Brown, and Company.

Hamilton, A., Madison, J. and Jay, J. 2003. *The Federalist Papers*. New York: Bantam Classic.

Hodgson, J.S. 2010. The French Prosecutor in Question. *Washington and Lee Law Review*, 67(4), 1361–1411.

Klip, A. 2012. *European Criminal Law: An Integrative Approach*, 2nd edn. Cambridge/Antwerp: Intersentia.

Kohlberg, L., Levine, C. and Hewer, A. 1995 (orig. 1984). Zum gegenwärtigen Stand der Theorie der Moralstufen, in *Die Psychologie der Moralentwicklung*, edited by L. Kohlberg. Frankfurt am Main: Suhrkamp, 217–372.

Langbein, J.H. 2003. *The Origins of Adversary Criminal Trial*. Oxford: Oxford University Press.

Maslow, A.H. 1987. *Motivation and Personality*, 3rd edn. New York: HarperColins.

Mitsilegas, V. 2006. The constitutional implications of mutual recognition in criminal matters in the EU. *Common Market Law Review*, 43(5), 1277–1311.

Möstl, M. 2010. Preconditions and Limits of Mutual Recognition. *Common Market Law Review*, 47(2), 405–36.

Oxford Pro Bono Publico. 2006. *Legal Opinion on Intercept Communication* [Online]. Available at: http://www2.law.ox.ac.uk/opbp/OPBP%20Intercept%20Evidence%20Report.pdf [accessed: 15 January 2013].

Peers, S. 2004. Mutual recognition and criminal law in the European Union: Has the Council got it wrong? *Common Market Law Review*, 41(1), 5–36.

Peršak, N. 2007. *Criminalising Harmful Conduct: The Harm Principle, Its Limits and Continental Counterparts*. New York: Springer.

Pollicino, O. 2008. European arrest warrant and constitutional principles of the member states. *German Law Journal*, 9(10), 1313–54.

Popper, K. 2003 (orig. 1945). *Open Society and Its Enemies, Volume One: The Spell of Plato*. Routledge.

Spronken, T., Vermeulen, G., de Vocht, D. and van Puyenbroeck, L. 2009. *EU Procedural Rights in Criminal Matters*. Antwerp: Maklu Publishers. Available also online at: www.eulita.eu/eu-procedural-rights-criminal-proceedings [accessed: 15 January 2013]

Thaman, S.C. (ed.) 2013. *Exclusionary Rules in Comparitive Law*. Heidelberg/New York/London: Springer.

Tocqueville, A. 2007 (orig. 1835). *Democracy in America*, vol. 1. Stilwell: Digireads.

Vermeulen, G., De Bondt, W. and Ryckman, C. 2012. *Rethinking International Cooperation in Criminal Matters in the EU*. Antwerp: Maklu Publishers.

Zimbardo, P. 2007. *The Lucifer Effect*. London/Auckland/Johannesburg: Rider.

Zupančič, B.M., 1990. *Pravo in prav*. Ljubljana: Cankarjeva založba.

Zupančič, B.M., 2003. Adjudication and the rule of law, 'power of logic' v. 'logic of power', 'rule of law' v. 'law and order'. *European Journal of Law Reform*, 5(1/2), 23–126.

Zupančič, B.M. 2008. *The Owl of Minerva*. The Hague: Eleven International Publishers.

Case Law

BVerfGE 37, 271, Judgment of 29 May 1974 (Solange I)
BVerfGE 73, 339, Judgment of 22 October 1986 (Solange II)
BVerfGE 89, 155 (1993), Judgment of 12 October 1993 (Maastricht Treaty)
BvE 2/08, 2 BvE 5/08, 2 BvR 1010/08, 2 BvR 1022/08, 2 BvR 1259/08, 2 BvR 182/09, Judgment of 30 June 2009 (Lisbon Treaty)
CJEU, *Åklagaren v. Hans Åkerberg Fransson*, case C-617/10
CJEU, *Bosman*, case C-415/93, [1995] ECR I-4921
CJEU, *Commission/United Kingdom*, case C-98/01, [2003] ECR I-4641
CJEU, *Flaminio Costa v ENEL* [1964] ECR 585 (6/64)
CJEU, *Gebhard*, case C-55/94, [1995] ECR I-4165
CJEU, *Gözütok and Brügge*, Joined cases C-187/01 and 385/01
CJEU, *Melloni*, case C-399/11
CJEU, *Rewe-Zentral AG/Bundes-monopolverwaltung für Branntwein*, [1979] ECR 649
CJEU, *Säger/Dennemeyer*, case C-76/90, [1991] ECR I-4221
ECtHR, *Bykov v Russia*, a. no. 4378/02, Judgment of 10 March 2009
ECtHR, *Gäfgen v. Germany*, a. no. 22978/05, Judgments of 30 June 2008 and 1 June 2010
ECtHR, *Harju v. Finland*, a. no. 56716/09, Judgment of 15 February 2011
ECtHR, *Heino v. Finland*, a. no. 56720/09, Judgment of 15 February 2011
ECtHR, *Imbroscia v. Switzerland*, a. no. 13972/88, Judgment of 11 September 1992
ECtHR, *Khan v. UK*, a. no. 35394/97, Judgment of 12 May 2000
ECtHR, *Medvedyev v. France*, a. no. 3394/03, Judgment of 10 July 2008
ECtHR, *Mouline v. France*, a. no. 37104/06, Judgment of 23 November 2010
ECtHR, *Schenk v. Switzerland*, a. no. 10862/84, Judgment of 12 July 1988
Irish Supreme Court, *MJELR v. Rettinger*, [2010] IESC 45, Judgment of 23 July 2010.
UK Supreme Court, *Julian Assange v Swedish Prosecution Authority*, [2012] UKSC 22
High Court, *Julian Assange v Swedish Prosecution Authority*, 2011 EWHC 2849 (Admin)
Croatian Constitutional Court, case U-I-448-2009, Judgment of 19 July 2012

Chapter 9
Flaws and Contradictions in the Mutual Trust and Recognition Discourse: Casting a Shadow on the Legitimacy of EU Criminal Policy Making and Judicial Cooperation in Criminal Matters?

Gert Vermeulen

Introduction

Legitimacy is a much-used notion in political theory and social science; however 'concealing widely different [and often inconsistent] accounts of the reasons why human beings obey political authority or accept social norms' (Marquez 2012). Most probably, the concept needs to be abandoned for 'more precise accounts' thereof 'in particular contexts' (Marquez 2012). In the very context of the EU's criminal policy making and judicial cooperation in criminal matters – in which the mutual trust and mutual recognition nexus is key – the position taken is that, philosophically speaking, legitimacy will depend of whether the EU through its mutual trust and mutual recognition discourse puts forward 'putative good reasons' (Knowles 2010) for its criminal policy and cooperation in criminal matters to be acceptable. Its discourse on mutual trust and mutual recognition must then at least display the quality of '*a priori* credibility'. Even if the validity of the putative reasons is not 'a matter of strict logical or conceptual necessity' (Knowles 2010), it will be clearly prohibited for any account 'to be based on lies, myths … or falsehoods generally'. To phrase it positively, trustworthiness requires 'a moral commitment to honesty' (Rose-Ackerman 2001).

Along the same lines, the credibility of the EU's discourse on the matter (and therefore its moral authority, which is grounded on it) will undeniably be significantly compromised when it is marked by manifest contradictions or illogicality, flagrant ambiguousness or plain conceptual incoherence. Following up on the latter notion, especially in complex argumentations such as about EU mutual trust and mutual recognition, 'coherence [as a positive characteristic] between different justifications is an important legitimising factor' (Lerch and Schwellnus 2006). Further, the legitimacy of (criminal) policy and rule-making (on cooperation in criminal matters) seems to be dependent on a sufficient degree in stability of the discourse underlying them: 'Legitimacy involves a balance between the deliberative ideal in which the rules themselves must be redeemable in discourse and the need to ensure that the rules are not up for grabs every single time' (Parkinson 2003).

Hence, legitimacy will be used hereafter as an umbrella notion, associated with either the presence of characteristics having a positive normative connotation (i.e. when arguments or policies are credible, honest, logical, coherent or stable) or the absence of characteristics having a negative normative connotation (i.e. when they are contradictory, false, ambiguous), for which the EU criminal policy making and cooperation in criminal matters will be tested. The result of this exercise will be largely negative in that the EU's mutual trust and mutual recognition discourse (underlying the criminal policy and rules on cooperation in criminal matters) often proves to lack the above-mentioned positive characteristics and to problematically suffer from the negative ones.

For European cooperation instruments in criminal matters to work there has to exist mutual trust between member states, and between competent authorities from different member states, in the sense that they feel confident relying on each other's decisions in criminal matters and executing them without further requirements or conformity control vis-à-vis their own substantive and procedural criminal law standards (Vermeulen 2008, Vernimmen-Van Tiggelen and Surano 2009). Since its official policy introduction in 1999 as the new cornerstone or bedrock of EU judicial cooperation in criminal matters, the principle of mutual recognition has been linked up with either the (assumed) existence or the (perceived) lack of mutual trust. Mutual recognition, even if much branded as an unambiguous, stable and coherent notion that is harmoniously balanced vis-à-vis the approximation of criminal law, has many faces – as many as mutual trust in the EU's and the member states' discourse(s). Drawing on over a decade of mutual trust and mutual recognition related research (Vermeulen 2002a, Vermeulen 2006, Vermeulen 2008, Vermeulen, De Bondt and Van Damme 2010, Vermeulen and van Puyenbroeck 2010, Vermeulen 2011a, Vermeulen, De Bondt and Ryckman 2012), the below analysis unravels the EU's mutual trust and mutual recognition discourse, unveiling its often contradictory, illogical, false – and sometimes even discriminatory, biased, one-sided or merely instrumental – underlying assumptions or agendas and policy outcomes or implications.

This exercise is intrinsically normative and value-loaded in nature, the point of departure being whether the discourse is a priori credible or putatively good. From this perspective, it is basically irrelevant whether the EU criminal policy and cooperation in criminal matters is perceived or felt as legitimate (as a basis for having trust in it). Primarily, the task of our analysis is to analyse the legitimacy of the principle of mutual recognition as the basis for enhanced EU judicial cooperation in criminal matters.

Since its introduction at the Tampere Summit (October 1999), the principle of mutual recognition (hereafter: MR) of judicial decisions in criminal matters in the EU, which is said to build on mutual trust between the EU member states, has served as the main vehicle to enhance judicial cooperation in criminal matters between them. The Lisbon Treaty, which entered into force on 1 December 2009, has even officialised MR as the principle on which judicial cooperation in criminal matters in the Union shall be based (Article 82 TFEU). Fundamentally, the question arises whether there is a sufficient, genuine and unambiguous 'mutual trust' basis in place? If not, the entire basis for MR is obviously seriously compromised. That seems to actually be the case: on some occasions the existence of mutual trust is politically assumed as a justification for MR, while on other occasions trust-building initiatives (primarily approximation measures in the sphere of procedural criminal law) are taken as the so-called 'flanking measures' in support of MR. In the latter case, MR has apparently been introduced without a sufficient trust basis, hence lacking credibility until such measures have been taken. Before embarking with a detailed analysis of both scenarios outlined, it needs to be stressed that, logically speaking, they are fundamentally incompatible and contradictory. In the first scenario (detailed under the next heading), trust (even if merely assumed) is the point of departure and MR the (alleged) legitimate result. In the second scenario, MR (tangibly reflected in newly adopted legal cooperation instruments in criminal matters) is the point of departure, constituting the legitimisation for ex-post trust-building or enhancing measures. Logically, it ought to be the one or the other: either trust as a lead-up to MR, or MR as a lead-up to trust. Not both. In reality, though, it is neither one, since both scenarios are crooked. In the first, trust is simply assumed (non-existing or at least not proven); in the second, it must be that the required level of trust for instigating MR was lacking. This allows us to conclude that trust is unproven or non-existing, which consequently renders MR lacking a sufficient, genuine and unambiguous legitimacy basis.

(Assumed) Trust as a Legitimisation for Mutual Recognition-Based Judicial Cooperation

Trust as a legitimisation for MR-based judicial cooperation instruments suffers from a series of flaws, inconsistencies and contradictions. They are systematically addressed hereafter, albeit not necessarily in an exhaustive fashion.

On the Origin of Species: MR as the Lesser Evil

MR recognition of criminal judgments was far from being a new concept when it was officially introduced at the Tampere Summit in 1999. The principle of MR had already been established in a (large) number of – traditionally Council of Europe (hereafter: CoE) – conventions, which, however, owing to a lack of ratification had not prompted the success that was hoped for (Vermeulen 2002a). Frustration with the slowness and formalities (e.g. distrust-based exequatur and conversion procedures) of traditional judicial cooperation in criminal matters, which characterise the said conventions, paved the way for the EU's decision to construct 'a European legal area' on the 'cornerstone' of MR of judicial decisions in criminal matters (Vermeulen 2002a). Building on the conclusions of the Cardiff and Vienna Summits of June and December 1998, respectively, it was on the occasion of the Tampere Summit that the European Council formally stated 'that enhanced mutual recognition of judicial decisions and judgments and the *necessary* [emphasis added] approximation of legislation would facilitate cooperation between authorities and the judicial protection of individual rights'. In doing so, the Tampere European Council endorsed the principle of MR, which, it stated, should become the cornerstone of judicial cooperation in criminal matters within the Union. Following the adoption of the 'Programme of measures to implement the principle of mutual recognition'[1] by the JHA Council of November 2000, the MR principle has been systematically employed in a series of Framework Decisions (hereafter: FDs), replacing the former CoE mother conventions on judicial cooperation in criminal matters. With the Lisbon Treaty, MR was finally given a proper treaty basis in Article 82(1) TFEU, recapitulating that the principle shall be the primary basis for judicial cooperation in criminal matters, with Article 82(2) TFEU – at least formally – reaffirming the subsidiary role of (procedural criminal law) approximation, even if only to the extent necessary to facilitate MR of judgments, judicial decisions, and police and judicial cooperation in criminal matters that have a cross-border dimension).

The principal importance of the above historical note lies in the clarity it provides to the relation between approximation and MR (as originally intended and formally confirmed later in the Lisbon Treaty): approximation was to be pursued only to the extent that MR would not be feasible without a certain degree of approximation. In other words, the choice for MR was a fundamental choice in favour of mutual respect for the diverging criminal law approaches of the member states – approximation being marginalised to scenarios in which, because of too drastic divergences, it would not be acceptable for member states to give effect to foreign judicial decisions in criminal matters. In particular, as the respect for the original finality of approximation has been of little or no concern in the 2000s (with the adoption of very many, especially substantive criminal law, approximation instruments, having an autonomous approximation function (Weyemberg 2004)), it is all the more important to bring the original MR-approximation nexus into the spotlight. In the lead-up to the 1998 Cardiff and Vienna Summits and the 1999 Tampere Summit, it were notably the resurfacing worries of (mainly UK) sceptics about self-standing criminal law unification processes, which paved the way to MR as a new leading principle for judicial cooperation. They perceived the unification idea underlying the so-called *Corpus Juris* concept[2] as particularly threatening, as 'another brick in the building of a single, centralised European State, robbing

1 *OJ* C 012, 15.01.2001, 10–22.

2 *Corpus Juris*, even if confined to fraud against the EU budget only, namely implied the creation of a single body of substantive and procedural criminal law to be applied in all Member States (Delmas-Marty 1997).

nations of their ancient freedoms' (Hall and Bhatt 1999: 34–5, Tupman 1998), in need of being neutralised. MR – with approximation in a subsidiary, facilitator function only – was suggested as the answer. Although the UK had never been keen on MR when it had been introduced before in various CoE conventions (as revealed in its blunt non-ratification thereof), but some step 'forward' was due. MR, compared to unification, harmonisation or unification, was simply the lesser evil. The trust-discourse (trust being the justification for MR) was essentially instrumental in nature – a political attempt to cutting unification and approximation tendencies short: I will trust you, you will trust me and we will trust each other just as we are. MR did not expect trust to be real.

Invalidity of the EU–CoE Trust Divide

Obviously, the assumed trust needed some underpinning in order for it to at least appear justified. The aforementioned 'Programme of measures to implement the principle of mutual recognition' stated that the trust which MR presupposes and which member states must have in each other's criminal justice systems 'is grounded, in particular, on their shared commitment to the principles of freedom, democracy and respect for human rights, fundamental freedoms and the rule of law'. The ideal justification seemed to have been found. But, are not these principles shared among all CoE states – the same CoE the EU wanted to distinguish itself from by overcoming traditional distrust clauses and hindrances that marked the CoE conventions? Does one distinguish oneself from another by stressing what is shared with the other? No. One does not. It seems that the very foundation of the EU common trust basis was fundamentally invalid from the onset. It still is today.

Reality Check

A reality check followed soon. Not even a year had lapsed since the entry into force[3] of the European Arrest Warrant (EAW) Framework Decision (as the first MR-based judicial cooperation instrument), when the European Council already endorsed the Hague Programme (November 2004),[4] stressing that reinforcing mutual trust was the key to making MR operate smoothly. The Commission followed up by issuing in May 2005 its communication 'on the mutual recognition of judicial decisions in criminal matters and the strengthening of mutual trust between member states'.[5] It admitted that 'the first endeavours to apply the MR principle, in particular with the EAW, revealed a series of difficulties which could to some extent be resolved if the Union were to adopt harmonisation legislation'. Distrust proved to be a real problem, well-reflected already in the British implementing of the Act of the EAW,

3 As per 1 January 2004.

4 The Hague Programme: Strengthening freedom, security and justice in the European Union, *OJ* 2005 C 53/1, 3.3.2005.

5 Brussels, 19.5.2005, COM/2005/0195 final.

which 'provides (in effect) that the judge must in every case consider whether the proposed surrender would be compatible with his [of the person concerned] Convention rights [referring to the ECHR], and block it unless he is satisfied that it is' (Spencer 2004). Ironical. Notably the core of the putative foundation for mutual trust – the ECHR – became the EAW's very Achilles' heel even before it was ever applied.

Both jurisprudence of the ECtHR (ECtHR 2012) (in cases like *T.I.*[6] and more recently *M.S.S.*[7] and *Radu*[8]) and of the CJEU (see in particular the *N.S.*[9] case, referring to the *M.S.S.* case) as well as NGO reports (e.g. Fair Trials International 2011) and scholars (e.g. Billing 2012; Tinsley 2012) have confirmed that human rights compliance assumptions in transferring people to EU member states, either in the event of their removal (*refoulement*) pursuant to the Dublin Regulation or – analogously – in the context of their surrender under the EAW, are unacceptable. The main focus therein has especially been on the risk of ill treatment or torture-like detention circumstances, either in the member states themselves or in third countries to which they may be sent back to or surrendered to. Moreover, even the European Commission itself[10] has acknowledged serious problems with the EAW in relation to human rights concerns.

Yet another example (besides in the event of risk for degrading and inhumane treatment) where the (initial) human rights assumption underlying the MR-based EAW has proved wrong is with respect to *in absentia* judgments. Not only did member states initially wrongfully assume that they could trust one another when it came to preliminary procedural guarantees before issuing an EAW for *in absentia* judgments (leading them to amend the EAW FD in 2009[11] by limiting non-execution on this account to situations where such guarantees had not convincingly been given), the practice ever since actually shows that member states frequently

6 *T.I. v. The United Kingdom*, No. 43844/98, decision on admissibility, 7 March 2000.

7 *M.S.S. v. Belgium and Greece*, No. 30696/09, judgment, 21 January 2011.

8 *Radu Pop v. Romania*, No. 14337/04, final judgment, 17 October 2012.

9 *N.S. v Secretary of State for the Home Department*, C-411/10, 21 December 2011, in which the CJEU has pointed out that there cannot be a 'conclusive presumption' that the EU member states 'observe the fundamental rights of the European Union'.

10 Report from the Commission to the European Parliament and the Council on the implementation since 2007 of the Council Framework Decision of 13 June 2002 on the European arrest warrant and the surrender procedures between Member States, Brussels, 11.4.2011, COM/2011/175 final.

11 FD 2009/299/JHA of 26 February 2009 amending Framework Decisions 2002/584/JHA, 2005/214/JHA, 2006/783/JHA, 2008/909/JHA and 2008/947/JHA, thereby enhancing the procedural rights of persons and fostering the application of the principle of mutual recognition to decisions rendered in the absence of the person concerned at the trial, *OJ* 2009 L 81/24.

still do not give sufficient guarantees in this respect before issuing and EAW, prompting quite some EAW execution refusals.[12]

Dual Criminality Bubble

In line with the archetypical EAW FD, MR-based legal instruments typically drop former dual criminality requirements for a list of 32 offence types. The official rationale given therefore is (or, back then, was) that these offence types had/ have been criminalised throughout the EU, rendering the traditional requirement obsolete. However, this reasoning is invalid for two reasons. First, if a consensus on criminalisation really exists (or existed) around the specific set of 32 offences, the steps taken since the adoption of the EAW FD towards approximation of the member states' substantive criminal law provisions would not have been necessary for these offences. Yet, for numerous crime types on the list, approximation instruments were adopted. Second, assuming for a while that such a broad criminalisation *acquis* would have been a reality, this would have implied that the very dual criminality requirement had been met, ruling out the need for the latter to be suppressed in MR instruments. Notwithstanding this double validity failure in the core MR discourse, the further developing of MR, including the dropping of dual criminality as a precondition where it used to exist and grounding it on the fact that member states can trust one another that MR will not be forced upon them for offences that they have not criminalised themselves still continues today. The trust assumption underlying the 32-list and the suppression of dual criminality as a standard feature of MR is thus nothing more than a soap bubble – nice on the outside, yet nothing but air on the inside.

Additionally, by identifying the substantive criminal law definition of the issuing member state as the definitional point of reference for the crimes included in the 32-list – instead of the common notion of the particular offence (or at least of the part of it that member states have jointly defined as criminal) in cases where dual criminality is a fact – the EU is barking up the wrong tree. Referring to the issuing state's definition does by no means build on the points where states can trust one another, i.e. where they have effectively commonly criminalised certain behaviour. On the contrary, the sole reference to the issuing member state's law will in these situations merely force the executing member state to trust the offence scope and definition of the former member state, no matter how much wider or broader it is than its own conception of the given offence.

It was stated above that MR-based legal instruments, based on alleged mutual trust, typically drop former dual criminality requirements for offences in the 32-list. Let us assume for a moment that mutual trust would be legitimate in this matter, in that all member states would share the very same conception and definition

12 Council of the European Union, Replies to questionnaire on quantitative information on the practical operation of the European arrest warrant – Year 2011, 9200/7/12 REV 7 COPEN 97 EJN 32 EUROJUST 39, Brussels, 15 January 2015.

of this exact set of 32 offence types (which they do not, as shown above). The argumentation would seem valid then. Still, validity requires a stable and coherent stand. Occasionally and/or randomly altering premises fundamentally underlying rule-making seems incompatible therewith. Yet, this is exactly what has happened. In a single instance, the 32-list has been extended to a 37-list: in FD 2005/214/JHA of 24 February 2005 on the application of the principle of mutual recognition to financial penalties (hereafter: FD financial penalties). On other occasions, the dual criminality rule has exceptionally been lifted altogether, i.e. for whichever offence (in the case of FD 2008/675/JHA of 24 July 2008 on taking account of convictions in the Member States of the European Union in the course of new criminal proceedings). On yet other occasions member states have been allowed to opt-out from the principal lifting of dual criminality for the offences in the 32-list, either totally (in FD 2008/909/JHA of 27 November 2008 on the application of the principle of mutual recognition to judgments in criminal matters imposing custodial sentences or measures involving deprivation of liberty for the purpose of their enforcement in the European Union (hereafter: FD custodial sentences)) or partially (like Germany in FD 2008/978/JHA of 18 December 2008 on the European evidence warrant for the purpose of obtaining objects, documents and data for use in proceedings in criminal matters (hereafter: EEW), below). If there is trust, it must be characterised by at least some degree of stability, mustn't it? And trustworthiness (for the sake of argument, based on a common criminalisation *acquis* coinciding with the 32 offence types concerned) must show some coherence throughout the various MR-based judicial cooperation instruments, mustn't it?

The German opt-out possibility in the EEW, referred to in the previous paragraph, further illustrates that even the mutual trust *assumption* that relates to dual criminality issues was unaccounted for. In the negotiations on the EEW, Germany successfully (cf. the general approach reached on the instrument in June 2006)[13] insisted on being given the right to make the execution of an EEW subject to verification of dual criminality in cases relating to terrorism, computer-related crime, racism and xenophobia, sabotage, racketeering and extortion or swindling, if it proved necessary to carry out a search or seizure for the execution of the warrant. Such dual criminality checks will not be performed, however, in cases where the issuing authority has officially declared that its definition of one of the stated offences reflects the criteria set out in the German declaration, which – unsurprisingly – reflects the constituent elements the latter requires for the offence concerned. In other words, the EU has agreed to allow Germany to return to the traditional system of dual criminality for at least some of the core crime categories featured in the 32-list, such as terrorism, by granting it the possibility of opting-out. In being forced (due to the pre-Lisbon unanimity rule) to allow the opt-out clause, which itself was triggered by the growing distrust of at least one of the member states, the EU has officially unveiled the trust myth around

13 Council of the European Union, European Evidence Warrant (EEW): Council reached a general approach, No 10081/06, Luxembourg, 1 June 2006.

dual criminality. The proclaimed mutual trust model, on which MR is based, was confronted by a new realism. The momentum that 9/11 had created, was – at least temporarily – exhausted. The 'bubble' has imploded.

Further Illogical Trust Derivatives

Further, the immediate post 9/11 climate was also taken advantage of by the European Commission and certain member states to finally and formally get rid of both the political offence exception and the non-discrimination rule in extradition law. Instead of explicitly spelling out the human and fundamental rights conditions required for allowing simplified hand-over procedures between the EU member states, both human rights-based exceptions were simply abolished altogether in the EAW (Vermeulen 2002b). They were seen as distrust-based hindrances for smooth surrender rather than inherent to the system of checks and balances that characterise EU democracies. Given their foundation in distrust in member states' compliance with the principle of protection against discriminatory prosecution, abolishing them on the basis of the trust assumption underlying the early MR discourse, was another illogical trust derivative: if effectively trustworthy, the member states should not have feared (and stepped away from) exceptions that could only be triggered in case they would prove to be non-trustworthy (by initiating discriminatory prosecutions).

Boomerang Effects

Ironically, the 'trust-based' removal of both human rights-inspired 'barriers' has in the meantime been contradicted by the adoption of 'trust-building' approximation measures in the sphere of procedural criminal law in support of MR. On 30 November 2009, the Council unanimously adopted a so-called 'Roadmap for strengthening procedural rights of suspected or accused persons in criminal proceedings' (hereafter: Procedural Rights Roadmap; further elaborated on below) in response to the observed 'need for enhanced mutual trust between the judicial authorities in the member states' (recital 9). Whilst the core of the putative foundation for mutual trust had been the EU's superior compliance with the ECHR (rendering the exceptions that found their origin in distrust in the member states' compliance with key human rights notions such as the protection against discriminatory prosecution and *non-refoulement* redundant), it was later on declared 'important that, complementary to the [ECHR], there exist European Union standards for the protection of procedural rights which are properly implemented and applied in the member states'. Speaking of the 'boomerang effect'.

MR was not only introduced to do away with distrust-based human rights-inspired exceptions like the political offence and non-discrimination exceptions, but also with distrust and sovereignty-based exequatur and conversion procedures that characterised the CoE mother conventions in judicial cooperation in criminal matters. Distrust had officially cleared the way for trust. Boomerang effects followed suit.

A perfect illustration of the resurrection of practices and concepts that, until quite recently, were perceived as incompatible with the MR principle, at least in its initial interpretation (i.e. when the archetypical EAW FD was designed), can be found in the context of the MR of custodial sentences. In the case of deprivation of liberty, member states were required – according to the initial interpretation given to MR – to have blind confidence in each other's decisions involving deprivation of liberty. Consequently, the executing member state should not be put in a position in which it should opt for the *lex mitior* (the mildest applicable law) principle, as it was traditionally supposed to do under e.g. the European Convention of 28 May 1970 on the international validity of criminal judgments, or the Convention of 21 March 1983 on the transfer of sentenced persons – both CoE conventions. Instead, it should simply take account of the sentence and execute it without attaching any further requirements. In this respect, it suffices to refer to the explanatory memorandum (2001) to the initial EAW Commission proposal.[14] Under Article 4, paragraph 6 of the EAW FD, it is possible for the executing member state, where surrender is sought for the purpose of executing a sentence, to execute the sentence itself instead of surrendering the person concerned to the member state issuing the EAW (*aut dedere aut exequi* rule), which means MR of the sentence pronounced in the issuing member state. Back then, the Commission pointed out that, in such a case, the executing member state would not be allowed to adapt the sanction imposed to bring it in line with its domestic law. The text of the memorandum (ibid.: 18–19) is crystal clear: 'Where this Article is applied, the amount of the penalty cannot be amended, even if it is different from what would have been ordered in the executing State. The text does not take over Article 10 (2) of the 1983 Convention, the implementation of which is basically incompatible with the principle of mutual recognition. The executing State's system of execution of sentences will apply'. Contrary to the initial Commission standpoint in designing the EAW as the first MR-based EU instrument, according to which the executing member state enjoyed no discretion whatsoever to convert or adapt the sentence imposed by the issuing member state, the FD custodial sentences, adopted in late 2008, reintroduced the traditional CoE possibility for the executing member state to apply the *lex mitior* principle after all by lowering the sentence to the maximum sanction the facts concerned could incur according to its own law. This adaptation provision, moreover, *mutatis mutandis* even applies in the very EAW-case when the executing member state chooses to execute itself the sentence in the context of applying the *aut dedere, aut exequi* principle referred to above. As beneficial as the (unfortunately only optional) *lex mitior* rule may be, it is conceptually not compatible with the MR theory in the way the latter was dogmatically introduced

14 Proposal for a Council Framework Decision on the European Arrest Warrant and the surrender procedures between the Member States, Brussels, 25.9.2011, COM(2001) 522/final/2.

in its conception phase. This constitutes not just a minor, unimportant diversion in the course of the process, but a diametric change of stance. We are back to where we were: to the domestic legal system (of the executing member state) as the point of reference, to the distrust and national sovereignty era which MR precisely aimed to overcome. It has not worked. The trust is lacking, even if the EU continues to uphold its stereotype discourse.

Ironically, the trust climate even prompted a series of additional grounds for non-execution of MR-based warrants or orders. In other words, trust seems to have triggered new obstacles for judicial cooperation in criminal matters in comparison with traditional CoE cooperation mechanisms. The first new ground for non-execution is the situation in which an immunity or privilege under the law of the executing member state makes it impossible to execute the issuing member state's decision (see elaborately in Vermeulen, De Bondt and Ryckman 2012). The ground for non-execution concerned has been inserted in the EAW (it was non-existent in former extradition law) during the December 2001 negotiations on the instrument for the sole reason of convincing Italy and thus reaching unanimous support for adoption of the EAW. Italy did not want to run the risk that Italians under a national (political) immunity or privilege would become eligible for surrender under the EAW (Italy has not ratified the 1996 EU Extradition Convention,[15] which had already introduced the principle of extradition of own nationals in the relationship between the other then member states). Whilst it should already be regretted that this was the price to be paid for reaching consensus at the level of the JHA Council on the EAW, copying the ground for non-execution from the EAW (erroneously considered to be the archetypical standard to which all later MR instruments must be modelled) into the sphere of mutual legal assistance (FD 2003/577/JHA of 22 July 2003 on the execution in the European Union of orders freezing property or evidence (hereafter: FD freezing orders), FD EEW and the proposed directive on the European Investigation Order[16] (hereafter: EIO)) and into the sphere of execution of foreign sentences[17] counts for a systematic step back compared to traditional CoE judicial cooperation conventions, neither of which allowed calling upon immunity or privilege under national law to refuse cooperation. It seems

15 Convention drawn up on the basis of article K.3 of the Treaty on European Union, of 27 September 1996, relating to Extradition between the Member States of the European Union, *OJ* C 313, 23.10.1996.

16 Council of the European Union, Initiative of the Kingdom of Belgium, the Republic of Bulgaria, the Republic of Estonia, the Kingdom of Spain, the Republic of Austria, the Republic of Slovenia and the Kingdom of Sweden for a Directive of the European Parliament and of the Council regarding the European Investigation Order in criminal matters, Brussels, No. 18918/11, 21 December 2011.

17 FD financial penalties, FD 2006/783/JHA of 6 October 2006 on the application of the principle of mutual recognition to confiscation orders, FD custodial sentences, FD 2008/947/JHA of 27 November 2008 on the application of the principle of mutual recognition to judgments and probation decisions with a view to the supervision of probation measures and alternative sanctions.

that the EU member states have installed a reverse CoE–EU divide, with more hindrances among themselves than between themselves and CoE member states. Possible counter-arguments, such as the introduction of a national immunity exception in the MR instrumentarium only constituting a formal change, since the exception was also formerly applied based on international law, or the immunity exception formerly being included in the catch-all *ordre public* exception, are invalid. If the latter were true, explicitly inserting an immunity refusal ground would be redundant. The argument that the immunity refusal ground follows from international public law is incorrect. The immunity exception in the MR cooperation instruments has been phrased in a very open fashion, encompassing also purely national immunities. Surely, diplomatic immunity follows from (customary) public international law.[18] However, it is regulated strictly in the Vienna Convention on Diplomatic relations and applies only to clearly defined persons.[19] It does not, for example, cover parliamentarians. State officials as defined in the Convention performing in their official capacity are exempt from foreign law when the acts and transactions being carried out are directly correlated to their official function. This immunity can be circumvented; as regards core crimes, modern state practice and *opinio juris* (e.g. Wirth 2002) deny immunities for core crimes to all former and incumbent state officials with the sole exception of the highest state representatives such as Heads of State or ministers for foreign affairs, and even the latter are being protected only while in office.[20] The above shows that international law provides immunity only for clearly defined 'State officials', under the condition that they acted in their official capacity and that the actions have been carried out in direct correlation with their official function. Hence, there is no public international law basis that would protect just any official to whom a member state wishes to grant immunity, let alone protecting them without functional or time restrictions.

The second ground for non-execution, which notably did not exist in the sphere of mutual legal assistance, is the so-called extraterritoriality exception (Vermeulen, De Bondt and Ryckman 2012). The refusal ground, which can be invoked where the facts concerned have been committed outside the territory of the issuing member state and the executing member state does not allow prosecution for the same offences committed outside its territory, has traditionally always taken a prominent place in CoE conventions relating to extradition, transfer of proceedings and transfer of the execution of sentences. It did not form part, though, of the mutual legal assistance regulations, neither at the level of the CoE (1959 Convention) or the EU (2000 Convention). Yet, the 2003 FD freezing orders (mistakenly modelled after the EAW) introduced the refusal ground in the

18 Report of the International Law Commission on the work of its 32nd session, UN GAOR, 35th Session, Supp. No. 10, UN Doc. A/35/10 (1980) at 344.

19 Art. 2, Vienna convention on diplomatic relations, 1961.

20 ICJ, 14 February 2000, *The Arrest Warrant (Democratic Republic of Congo v. Belgium)*.

sphere of mutual legal assistance, followed later by the 2008 FD EEW and the proposed EIO. Apparently, the historical (Thomas 1980) and present-day (Watney 2012) fundamental distinction between mutual legal assistance as a secondary form of judicial cooperation in criminal matters[21] and primary cooperation forms, involving the transfer and taking over of procedural responsibility, such as the transfer of criminal proceedings and of the execution of sentences, including the transfer of prisoners and the confiscation (and prior seizure) of assets, has been set aside without justification or perhaps even without awareness of its existence. It seems that the EU has once more 'advanced' in cooperation by walking backwards.

The final example is the almost generic call for a merits or proportionality test in executing MR-based warrants or orders. Practical evaluation of the EAW,[22] for example, has shown that there is a 'general agreement among member states that a proportionality check is necessary to prevent EAWs from being issued for offences which, although they fall within the scope of Article 2(1) of the [EAW], are not serious enough to justify the measures and cooperation which the execution of an EAW requires'. However, the EAW (apart from the 32 offences, for which the sanction threshold was even raised from one to three years) has not lowered the sanction threshold required for offences to lead to surrender or extradition in comparison with the 1996 EU Extradition Convention (it remained identical), and only slightly lowered it on the side of the executing/requested member state (to six months instead of one year) in comparison with the 1957 CoE Convention on extradition (keeping the threshold at 12 months/one year on the side of the issuing/requesting member state) (Vermeulen and Vander Beken 1997). Clearly, the much-pleaded-for introduction of a merits or proportionality test on the side of the executing member state would come down to a largely undefined refusal ground, giving too much discretion to the latter, thus undermining the principal obligatory character of judicial cooperation instruments in criminal matters. A merits or proportionality exception would most definitely mark yet another step backwards compared to the cooperation predating MR, which apparently was more good-faith (trust) based. Surely, MR has reduced the margin of non-consent on behalf of the executing/requested member states, but that was the whole point in introducing MR, was it not? The abolition of the refusal ground for own nationals (in EAW context) and of dual criminality for 32 offences (almost generically) seems to have in particular prompted a call for a new defence line – in the form of a merits or proportionality non-execution ground. The latter clearly lacks credibility. Own nationals do not deserve more or better protection than

21 Together with extradition, which has traditionally been regarded as more far-reaching than mutual legal assistance that has been looked upon as a 'minor' or 'accessory' cooperation only ('*entraide mineure*'; '*entraide accessoire*'; '*sonstige Rechtshilfe*' (Thomas 1980)).

22 Report from the Commission to the European Parliament and the Council on the implementation since 2007 of the Council Framework Decision of 13 June 2002 on the European arrest warrant and the surrender procedures between Member States, Brussels, 11.4.2011, COM/2011/175 final, 7.

other EU nationals and if the abolition of dual criminality for 32 offence types was a mistake (as I claim above), the answer does not lie in a vague, discretionary compensation through a merits or proportionality test, but in reintroducing dual criminality. Proportionality must be guaranteed by mechanisms built-in into the instruments themselves (Vermeulen, De Bondt and Ryckman 2012).

Mutuality Bubble: Non-Reciprocity, Self-Centredness, Discrimination and One-Directionality

The above analysis also provides proof that trust is currently being rather non-mutual instead of mutual. The mutuality discourse has been largely contradicted by the self-centred, one-sided or even flagrantly discriminatory positions that member states have taken. A perfect example of trust being non-reciprocal and purely self-centred is the above-mentioned German partial opt-out from the 32-list, which allows Germany to demand for 6 offences from the 32-list to reflect the same constituent elements as the corresponding offences under German law. The basis for trust is here therefore found in one's very own legal point of reference alone.

Another – possibly even more flagrant – example can be found in the discriminatory and self-centred difference in stances taken by member states when it comes to deplorable prison conditions. In the context of the EAW (especially when the surrender of own nationals or residents is sought) such conditions are very much perceived as a human rights-based legitimisation for non-execution (the executing member state even having the possibility to make surrender for the purpose of prosecution abroad dependent on a transfer back home of one's own national or resident in view of serving the sentence), whilst the very same conditions are looked upon as a priori good and equal, legitimising the discriminatory 'export' of non-national or non-resident convicts to prison in the member state of their nationality on the basis of the FD Custodial. Or, to put it bluntly, exposing a British national to the Polish prison conditions is a no-go; exposing a Polish EU citizen, convicted in the UK, to the Polish prison conditions, by sending him back to Poland to serve his sentence, even against his will, is OK, save perhaps when the conditions are so much torture-like that a clear *non-refoulement* obligation would result from it. Clearly, the FD custodial has little or nothing to do with the social rehabilitation it putatively seeks to promote (Vermeulen et al. 2011), but everything to do with being tough on crime by non-nationals or non-residents (cf. itinerant groups and the like; Vermeulen 2011b) through an internal readmission mechanism designed to that end.

Another example is related to the FD custodial sentences yet again and to the proposed EIO. Mutuality should not only be reciprocal and non-discriminatory. MR also entails mutual trust in the sense that the executing member state is supposed to trust the issuing member state's decision (in that it will execute it in its territory as if it was its own decision) and that the issuing member state entrusts the execution of its decision to the executing member state in the way the latter would execute a similar decision of its own. In that sense, mutual trust is traditionally also being considered as two-directional. As far as the FD custodial sentences is concerned, however, a clear distrust-based option for the issuing member state is in the possibility, offered by the MR-based instrument, to withdraw the certificate jointly sent with its decision (thereby revoking its request), when the member state is dissatisfied with the sentence execution rules under which its decision would be executed by the executing member state (for it believes the latter to be too lenient; Vermeulen et al. 2011). Hence, trust can be limited to a one-directional issue only: the executing member state must trust the issuing member state, but not vice versa. The proposed EIO incorporates an analogous anomaly in that it copies the *forum regit actum* principle from the EEW, which copied it from the EU 2000 Convention on mutual legal assistance without due respect for the two-directionality that has characterised most MR instruments. When it was introduced in the EU over 10 years ago (in the EU 2000 Convention), the *forum regit actum* principle was supposed to accommodate concerns of admissibility of evidence that resulted from foreign evidence gathering along the formerly known cooperation principles. Originally, mutual legal assistance between the EU member states had its sole legal basis in the 1959 CoE Convention on mutual assistance. According to that 'mother treaty', the requested state would execute a mutual assistance request in accordance with its own rules and regulations, i.e. according to the *locus regit actum* principle: the location where the investigative measure would take place (*locus*) was the decisive element in determining applicable law. However, as a result of differences between national procedures, information and evidence gathered in the requested member state could sometimes not be used (declared inadmissible) in the requesting member state, as the way in which the information had been obtained did not fit the national procedural requirements of the requesting state that was the *forum* of the trial (Vermeulen 1999). Hence, when developing an EU instrument (2000 Convention) to complement the existing CoE instrument (1959 Convention), a solution was found through the introduction of the so-called *forum regit actum* principle in the former instrument. Since, the requesting member state has been allowed to ask the requested member state to comply with the formalities or procedural requirements the former deems essential under its national legislation, the latter, however, not being required to violate fundamental principles of its legal system in doing so. That very same principle, no matter how handy it may be in a one-on-one situation (Vermeulen 2011a, Vermeulen, De Bondt and Ryckman 2012) in order to limit evidence admissibility problems, is fundamentally illogical when departing from a mutual trust perspective, which has been traditionally characterised by a two-directional trust between executing (trusting the issuing) and issuing (trusting the executing) member state. The only logical solution would be in the genuine MR of evidence, even beyond the one-on-one situation between an issuing and executing member state – in a real and multi-directional 'free movement of evidence' regime, which can probably be based only on common minimum standards for all investigative evidence gathering measures and techniques (Vermeulen 2011a).

Mutual Recognition as a Legitimisation for Trust-Building Procedural Criminal Law Approximation Measures

Putting the Carriage before the Horse

The Procedural Rights Roadmap, already referred to above, was adopted on 30 November 2009, on the eve of the entry into force of the Lisbon Treaty. It lists several procedural rights measures which the EU has undertaken to implement step-by-step as 'flanking measures' in support of MR. While the MR proved to lack the trust foundation that was initially said to underlie it, these flanking measures do find their legitimisation in the need to underpin the trust basis required for MR. The historical official rationale for the Roadmap can best be captured by referring to the explanatory memorandum to the (failed) preceding (pre-Lisbon) proposal for a FD on certain procedural rights in criminal proceedings throughout the EU:[23] 'If common minimum standards are applied to basic procedural safeguards throughout the EU, this will lead to increased confidence in the criminal justice systems of all the member states which in turn will lead to more efficient judicial cooperation in a climate of mutual trust'. Mutual trust had been declared. MR had built upon in. Yet real trust still needed to be created, it seems.

Confusing Carriage Racing and Jumping

But what really is the linkage between the measures envisaged in the Roadmap and the trust required for MR-based judicial cooperation in criminal matters? Has anyone tried to explain in a precise way why would the sort of measures envisaged actually be helpful in taking away the member states' unease in applying MR? It follows from the above analysis that the main obstacles for MR to work are likely to be the member states' sovereignty-based self-centredness and the abolition of the dual criminality requirement for 32 offence types, of several distrust-based grounds for refusal and of adaptation or exequatur procedures capable of securing compliance with member states' own legislation and procedures. That the right to translation and interpretation in criminal matters, the right to information on the charges and about the dossier, the right to legal assistance, to consular assistance and to contact with family members and one's employer are granted throughout the EU is nice and important – most probably even needed. The same applies to preferential procedural rights for vulnerable persons (such as mentally ill or minors as suspects and offenders) and to limiting pretrial detention and raising pretrial detention standards. However, how can such measures tangibly take away MR-triggered problems? Distrust in MR-based cooperation contexts seems to have little or nothing to do with respect or non-respect of these rights. Recital 10 of the Roadmap makes it rather clear what its true ambitions are: 'Efforts should be deployed to strengthen procedural guarantees and the respect of the rule of law

23 European Commission, COM(2004) 328 final, Brussels, 28.4.2004, 2, recital 9.

in criminal proceedings, *no matter where citizens decide to travel, study, work or live in the European Union*' (emphasis added). More and better justice for all, throughout the EU: that is the real goal. But what sense is there in upgrading procedural rights (no matter how good and just a cause that is) if these are largely irrelevant or at least non-functional for solving the MR-linked trust problem? Why train a carriage-racing horse to jump over a series of 'procedural rights' hurdles? There is no point in it.

From Lesser Evil to Trojan Horse?

The truth may very well be that MR has evolved from the lesser evil (above) to the Trojan Horse – the vehicle for attacking the member states' domestic legal order from within, unleashing the 'approximation' enemy by surprise. Even if, according to Article 82(2) TFEU, the Roadmap's procedural criminal law measures ought to be taken only to the extent necessary to facilitate MR of judgments and judicial decisions and police and judicial cooperation in criminal matters *having a cross-border dimension*, the three directives that the Roadmap so far has delivered (directives on the right to interpretation and translation[24] and on the right to information)[25] or is in the process of delivering (the directive on the right of access to a lawyer)[26] are all *domestic* in scope, with marginal or even no direct or indirect relevance for the application of cross-border MR instruments altogether. It seems that creating a proper trust basis for MR, which is indeed necessary (Spronken et al. 2009), has simply become the perfect pretext for enacting approximation measures in the sphere of procedural rights as an autonomous policy goal, largely disconnected from MR, yet instrumentalising it as an ideal vector. Procedural rights lobby groups and NGOs do not worry about facilitating MR; the real or at least primary added value sought is in the domestic effect of the Roadmap measures (Amnesty International EU Office et al. 2010).[27] The same goes for the European Commission: creating more and better justice for all will shape the

24 Directive 2010/64/EU of 20 October 2010 on the right to interpretation and translation in criminal proceedings, *OJ* 2010 L 280/1, 26.10.2010.

25 Directive 2012/13/EU of 22 May 2012 on the right to information in criminal proceedings, *OJ* 2012 L 142/1, 1.6.2012.

26 Council of the European Union, Proposal for a Directive of the European Parliament and of the Council on the right of access to a lawyer in criminal proceedings and on the right to communicate upon arrest [First reading] – Progress report, No. 16521/12, Brussels, 3 December 2012.

27 '... Given that neither the Stockholm Programme nor the Roadmap mention a restriction in the scope of the measures, we consider that the question of limitation to cross border cases has been settled. Notwithstanding, we observe that any future measure must be adopted in accordance with the fundamental values of the European Union, taking account of the Charter of Fundamental Rights and the ECHR. No differential treatment between citizens of the EU, on account of the limitation of procedural safeguards to cross border cases, could be entertained in the post Lisbon Treaty era ...'.

legacy. The European Parliament is on the same page. Only (some of) the member states keep calling Article 82(2) to mind, even if they seem to have lost all hope: in adopting the Directive on the right to information in criminal proceedings (second Roadmap measure), the Council stressed that its domestic scope did 'not necessarily constitute a precedent in the framework of discussions concerning other proposals for measures contained in the [Roadmap]', but that 'however, overall consistency with the remaining measures provided for by the Roadmap shall be ensured'.[28]

Roadmap Bubble and the Shifting of Distrust

It was challenged already that the sort of measures the Roadmap envisages are likely to be helpful in sorting out the MR-triggered trust problems. More fundamentally, the question arises whether the Roadmap does not even create new or fake obstacles for MR-based judicial cooperation in criminal matters. Being mindful of the very essence of MR – i.e. that executing member states should execute judicial decisions in criminal matters originating from other member states as if it were their own decisions, trusting the decisions of other member states as their own decisions – the question arises, for example, whether the MR-based FD custodial sentences requires more trust on behalf of the executing member state than the formerly applicable 1983 CoE Convention on the transfer of prisoners and the 1997 Additional Protocol thereto? Clearly not. The traditional CoE sanction adaptation and conversion mechanism is back (back to normal, that is) in and member states have even managed to negotiate an opt-out possibility from the abolition of dual criminality for the 32-list.

There is no MR-linked trust problem with the instrument that would not suffer from other problems though. Essentially these relate to the legal position of the person concerned and the possibly poor detention conditions in the executing member state. With the FD custodial sentences, the person concerned may be transferred back to his member state of nationality and residence against his will, even if he is an EU citizen and is therefore in principle enjoying free movement of persons after having served his sentence. This situation differs from the one of a (possibly even illegal) third-country national, who would be under immigration legislations usually expelled, deported or asked to leave the territory of the convicting member state and for whom serving his sentence back home (following a transfer based on the 1983 Convention and 1997 Protocol) would at least theoretically be in the interest of his social rehabilitation, given that he would have to return to his home country after having served his sentence anyway. This problem is not MR-triggered or trust-linked at all. Does the Roadmap address it? Not to the least extent. On the contrary, the Roadmap has merely announced a Green

28 Council of the European Union, Proposal for a Directive of the European Parliament and of the Council on the right to information in criminal proceedings: Declaration on the scope, No. 18702/11, Brussels, 19 December 2011, 2.

Paper on pretrial detention (condition) 'problems' (van Kalmthout, Knapen and Morgenstern 2009), allegedly arising in the context of the application of the EAW. The only reason therefore was that executing member states worried about having to expose their own nationals or residents to poor pretrial detention conditions in the issuing member state. Actual detention in the sentence execution phase was not so much an issue, given that executing member states could save their nationals or residents from having to actually serve a custodial sentence that would be imposed upon them abroad, by making their surrender for prosecution purposes conditional on their re-surrender in order to serve such sentence at home through the *aut dedere aut exequi* mechanism (Vermeulen 2008). The ultimate Green Paper[29] only broadened its perspective to detention (condition) problems in general (though still largely focusing on pretrial detention), because additional worries had arisen about deplorable detention conditions also becoming an unforeseen obstacle for the smooth operation of the FD custodial sentences: 'If people are detained in conditions bad enough to be considered degrading punishment, what judicial authority would authorise the transfer of a detainee to a place where he or she would face a substantial risk of being ill-treated?' (Reding 2010: 4). The agreed prisoner export instrument needed to be kept on the rails, at all price. If that could possibly entail upgrading detention conditions, it was wise to consult about it. Did any tangible measure follow, even after indeed the major detention condition problems observed had been meticulously mapped and reported (Vermeulen et al. 2011) to the Commission? Of course not. Both the Commission and the member states went back to business.[30] It can be concluded therefore that the problems that were newly created by the MR-based FD custodial have not been addressed, and are not bound to be addressed, neither in the context of the Roadmap (which never intended to do so) nor alongside the Roadmap. The latter, on the contrary, has only focused on detention-related problems in the context of the application of the EAW. Only the (pretrial) detention (condition) problems were about to undermine trust in the issuing member state. Raising doubts about the detention conditions in the executing member state in the context of the FD custodial sentences would come down to the shifting of distrust, i.e. from the issuing member state (EAW) to the executing member state (FD custodial sentences). This was not a real concern (and it is still not), because it is unlinked to MR (theoretically requiring enhanced trust in the issuing member state) and only a potential threat – which seems to be under control now – to the envisaged internal prisoner readmission mechanism. Hence, there was no need for action. The Procedural Rights Roadmap did never intend to address real cross-border procedural rights problems prompted by the MR instruments. From that perspective, it is another bubble. Moreover, the Roadmap's

29 European Commission, Strengthening mutual trust in the European judicial area – A Green Paper on the application of EU criminal justice legislation in the field of detention, COM/2011/0327 final, Brussels, 14 June 2011.

30 European Commission, Workshop on the implementation of the framework decisions on the transfer of prisoners and on probation, Brussels, 20 March 2012.

focus on EAW-linked pretrial detention problems is plainly illogical, since MR has only improved the situation if compared with pretrial problems linked with traditional extradition.

Precisely in order to counter the member states discriminatory use of pretrial custodial measures against non-nationals or non-residents (non-custodial measures awaiting trial are likely to be granted predominantly to own nationals and residents), the EU has adopted FD 2009/829/JHA of 23 October 2009 on the application, between Member States of the European Union, of the principle of mutual recognition to decisions on supervision measures as an alternative to provisional detention, allowing member states that envisage issuing an EAW for prosecution purposes to not immediately do so. Instead they may order the home member state, in which the person they want for trial has his residence and/or and is willing to return to, to take a non-custodial supervision measure, with just-in-time delivery for the trial through an EAW (thereby avoiding unnecessary pretrial detention in the issuing member state). Honestly, has this worsened extradition-linked pretrial detention problems or rather dramatically improved them?

EU–CoE Divide Sequel: The Azerbaijan Contradiction

Can we apply a Surveillance-order-like instrument when extradition is sought by a non-EU CoE member state, say Azerbaijan? Hence, is the pretrial detention issue not a bigger problem in the relation with non-EU–CoE member states than between EU member states? Won't we extradite to Azerbaijan or grant it mutual legal assistance because we have doubts that suspects and defendants have their the right to interpretation and translation in criminal matters, to information about the charges or access to the dossier, to assistance by a lawyer, or their being granted preferential rights if mentally ill or under-aged? No. Its seems that the Roadmap – given the official (obviously false) discourse that its measures are needed to pump up trust levels between MS in order to safeguard MR – creates only new obstacles for EU cross-border cooperation vis-à-vis cooperation with non-EU CoE member states. Where has the logic gone, really? The Roadmap is (apart from some specific clauses in the directives adopted or under negotiation) largely counterproductive for EU judicial cooperation in criminal matters.

Its real goal (and effect) is in shaping a better EU, with more and higher criminal procedural rights for all, through the setting of domestic minimum standards in all member states. This is a just cause, legitimate to strive for as an autonomous policy goal. However, it rather works against member states' historical aversion towards domestic approximation when the latter is not necessary for cross-border cooperation in criminal matters (as enshrined in Article 82(2) TFEU). Yet, the Trojan Horse is in, and the MR mechanism was the gate through which it has entered.

References

Amnesty International EU Office, European Criminal Bar Association, Irish Council for Civil Liberties, Open Society Institute-Brussels and Open Society Justice Initiative. 2010. *Open letter to European Commissioner for Justice Viviane Reding*. Brussels, 29 June 2010.

Billing, F. 2012. The parallel between non-removal of asylum seekers and non-execution of a European Arrest Warrant on human rights grounds. The CJEU case of N.S. v. Secretary of State for the Home Department. *European Criminal Law Review*, 2, 77–91.

Delmas-Marty, M. 1997. *Corpus Juris Introducing Penal Provisions for the Purpose of the Financial Interests of the European Union*. Paris: Economica.

ECtHR. 2012. Factsheet – Expulsions and Extraditions [Online]. Available at: http://www.echr.coe.int/NR/rdonlyres/211A6F9C-A4EC-4CF7-AB2E-42E9D49FB2EF/0/FICHES_Expulsions_et_extraditions_EN.pdf [accessed: 31 January 2013].

Fair Trials International. 2011. *The European Arrest Warrant Seven Years on – The Case for Reform*. London.

Hall, B. and Bhatt, A. 1999. *Policing Europe: EU Justice and Home Affairs Co-operation*. London: Centre for European Reform (CER), 34–5.

Knowles, D. 2010. *Political Obligation: A Critical Introduction*. Abingdon and New York: Routledge, 56–78.

Lerch, M. and Schwellnus, G. 2006. Normative by nature? The role of coherence in justifying the EU's external human rights policy. *Journal of European Public Policy* (Special Issue: What Kind of Power? European Foreign Policy in Perspective), 13(2), 304–21. Available at: 10.1080/13501760500452665 [accessed: 31 January 2013].

Marquez, X. 2012. *The Irrelevance of Legitimacy* [Online]. Available at: 10.2139/ssrn.2027249 [accessed: 31 January 2013].

Parkinson, J. 2003. Legitimacy problems in deliberative democracy. *Political Studies*, 51(1), 180–96. Available at: 10.1111/1467-9248.00419 [accessed: 31 January 2013].

Reding, V. 2010. *The Future of European Criminal Justice under the Lisbon Treaty*. European Law Academy, Trier, 12 March 2010. Available at: https://www.era.int/upload/dokumente/10928.pdf [accessed: 31 January 2013].

Rose-Ackerman, S. 2001. Trust, honesty, and corruption: Reflection on the state-building process. *European Journal of Sociology*, 42, 27–71. Available at: 10.2139/ssrn.283429 [accessed: 31 January 2013].

Spencer, J. 2004. The European Arrest Warrant, in *The Cambridge Yearbook of European Legal Studies 2003–4*, 201–17.

Spronken, T., Vermeulen, G., de Vocht, D. and van Puyenbroeck, L. 2009. *EU Procedural Rights in Criminal Proceedings*. Antwerp, Apeldoorn and Portland: Maklu.

Thomas, F. 1980. *De Europese Rechtshulpverdragen in Strafzaken*. Gent: Story-Scientia.

Tinsley, A. 2012. The case Radu: When does the protection of fundamental rights require non-execution of a European Arrest Warrant? *European Criminal Law Review*, 2, 338–52.

Tupman, W. 1998. Supranational investigation after Amsterdam, the Corpus Juris and Agenda 2000. *Information & Communications Technology Law*, 7(2), 85–101.

van Kalmthout, A., Knapen, M. and Morgenstern, C. 2009. *Pre-Trial Detention in the European Union*. Nijmegen: Wolf Legal Publishers.

Vermeulen, G. 1999. *Wederzijdse Rechtshulp in Strafzaken in de Europese Unie: Naar een Volwaardige Eigen Rechtshulpruimte voor de Lid-Staten?* Antwerp and Apeldoorn: Maklu.

Vermeulen, G. 2002a. Where do we currently stand with harmonisation in Europe?, in *Harmonisation and Harmonising Measures in Criminal Law*, edited by A. Klip and H. Vander Wilt. Amsterdam: Royal Netherlands Academy of Arts and Sciences, 65–76.

Vermeulen, G. 2002b, Criminal policy aspects of the EU's (internal) asylum policy. *Law and European Affairs*, 2001–2002(5), 602–12.

Vermeulen, G. 2006. Wederzijdse erkenning van straffen in de Europese Unie en België, in *L'exécution des Peines*, edited by A. Masset et al. Brussels: La Charte, 141–94.

Vermeulen, G. 2008. Mutual recognition, harmonisation and fundamental (procedural) rights protection, in *Crime, Rights and the EU: The Future of Police and Judicial Cooperation*, edited by M. Maik. London: Justice, 89–104.

Vermeulen, G. 2011a. *Free Gathering and Movement of Evidence in Criminal Matters in the EU: Thinking Beyond Borders, Striving for Balance, in Search of Coherence*. Antwerp and Apeldoorn: Maklu. Available at: http://www.ejtn.net/PageFiles/6335/Vermeulen%20Free%20gathering%20and%20movement%20of%20evidence.pdf [accessed: 31 January 2013].

Vermeulen, G. 2011b. Oost, West. Thuis Best? Twijfelachtige vertrouwensbasis voor gedwongen terugkeer veroordeelde EU-onderdanen naar gevangenis in thuislidstaat. *Panopticon*, 2011(6), 1–5.

Vermeulen, G. and van Puyenbroeck, L. 2010. Approximation and mutual recognition of procedural safeguards of suspects and defendants in criminal proceedings throughout the European Union, in *EU and International Crime Control: Topical Issues*, edited by M. Cools et al. Antwerp, Apeldoorn and Portland: Maklu, 4, 41–62.

Vermeulen, G. and Vander Beken, T. 1997. New conventions on extradition in the European Union: Analysis and evaluation. *Dickinson Journal of International Law*, 1997(2), 265–300.

Vermeulen, G., De Bondt, W. and Van Damme, Y. 2010. *EU Cross-Border Gathering and Use of Evidence in Criminal Matters: Towards Mutual Recognition of*

Investigative Measures and Free Movement of Evidence? Antwerp, Apeldoorn and Portland: Maklu

Vermeulen, G., De Bondt, W. and Ryckman, C. 2012. *Rethinking International Cooperation in Criminal Matters in the EU: Moving Beyond Actors, Bringing Logic Back, Footed in Reality*. Antwerp, Apeldoorn and Portland: Maklu. Available at: https://biblio.ugent.be/record/2125289 [accessed: 31 January 2013].

Vermeulen, G., van Kalmthout, A., Paterson, N., Knapen, M., Verbeke, P. and De Bondt, W. 2011. *Cross-Border Execution of Judgements Involving Deprivation of Liberty in the EU: Overcoming Legal and Practical Problems Through Flanking Measures*. Antwerp, Apeldoorn and Portland: Maklu. Available at: http://ec.europa.eu/justice/news/consulting_public/0012/JLS-DC-FinalReport_en.pdf [accessed: 31 January 2013].

Vernimmen-Van Tiggelen, G. and Surano, L. 2009. Quel futur pour la reconnaissance mutuelle en matière pénale?, in *The Future of Mutual recognition in Criminal Matters in the European Union*, edited by G. Vernimmene-Van Tiggelen, L. Surano and A. Weyembergh. Brussels: Éditions de l'Université de Bruxelles, 549–82.

Watney, M. 2012. A South African perspective on mutual legal assistance and extradition in a globalized world. *Potchefstroomse Elektroniese Regsblad – Potchefstroom Electronic Law Journal* [Online], 15(2), 292–318. Available at: 10.4314/pelj.v15i2.11 [accessed: 31 January 2013].

Weyembergh, A. 2004. *L'Harmonisation des Législations: Condition de l'Espace Pénal Européen et* Révélateur *de Ses Tensions*. Brussels: Éditions de l'Université de Bruxelles.

Wirth, S. 2002. Immunity for core crimes? The ICJ's Judgment in the Congo v. Belgium case. *European Journal of International Law*, 13(4), 877–93.

PART III
Concluding Thoughts

Chapter 10

Diverging Perspectives, Converging Thoughts? Common Themes and Prospects in Legitimacy Research

Nina Peršak

> Creative thinking about legitimacy requires a deepening of thought about the epistemic circumstances within which the modern problem of legitimacy is located. (Connolly 2000: 280)

This book has provided a series of analyses that highlight the complexities and challenges in understanding various aspects of legitimacy as they are reflected in the criminal law and criminal policy as well as in the organisation and practice of the judiciary (be it at national, international or EU level). Analytical, descriptive, normative and jurisprudential approaches from academics and practitioners attempted to reveal existing problems and their underlying causes of the present-day legitimacy challenges that can be found in the broad area of criminal justice.

At various points of the colloquium that preceded this volume a sort of frustration with the concept of legitimacy surfaced, as the discussion on legitimacy often tended to open more questions than provide answers, which is exacerbated by the fact that legitimacy has various aspects, so that by focusing on one or some of them one often or necessarily neglects the others. Yet, despite the occasional seeming 'cacophony', several prima facie different themes 'harmonised' or converged on several points. Although the chapters speak for themselves and the reader should consider the ideas fleshed out therein independently, it may be useful to highlight some of these convergence points or common themes that emerged from this project.

Norms, Procedures, Outcomes

All these three dimensions need to be equally accounted for in criminal justice. As regards *norms*, firstly, the shared moral norms and values form a basis for trust. Inferences about shared core values are central in our attributions of trust: we tend to consider those whom we perceive as having a similar value system as more trustworthy (Cvetkovich, in Breakwell 2007). When the law complies with the shared salient values of the people, this also contributes towards the law's legitimation. The normative aspect is, secondly, crucial for assessing legitimacy independently from its sociological meaning, where legitimacy is measured as public acceptance or consent of the governed. Norms are, thirdly, important in the sense of norm defining 'normality' or prevailing standards, which consequently define deviance from the 'norm' – conduct that is likely to be criminalised, punished. And, lastly, norms are important also in the sense of legal norms, the content and form of criminal law norms.

Law should be considered as an independent entity, an authority that independently requires legitimacy. Furthermore, it is an additionally important agent as it grants legitimacy to other authorities and agents through legality, i.e. through making their actions legal. The legitimacy of the justice system (and consequently of trust therein) thus flows firstly from the legitimacy of the legal system, of which it forms part. Crawford (2000) distinguishes between four inter-related forms or aspects of trust: trust in people, trust in expertise, trust in abstract systems (procedures and rules) and trust in symbolic tokens. Applying this distinction to criminal law, one may argue that when people trust criminal law, they have trust in the abstract system that law (procedure and rules) represents but perhaps as well in the symbolic token that criminalisation (or criminal law) in particular represents. Criminal law has a symbolic dimension that lies in the fact that it represents a declaration on the part of society or state that a certain conduct is wrong and will be punished if committed.

In the area of criminal law, all begins with criminalisation, with the making of criminal law norms and the consequently with the question of the legitimacy of state intervention in the individual autonomy and human conduct through criminal law (broadly conceived). The enactment of the criminal legislation is from the individual's standpoint one of the most intrusive forms of social control and repressive acts of state power, for it not only restricts one's freedom of action but also punishes infringements, often with deprivation of the individual's liberty and may significantly (and detrimentally) impact on the (fundamental) rights of the individual (Erbežnik). In today's liberal democratic societies, governed by the rule of law, it is understood the state does not (and should not) have a completely free hand in proscribing conduct of its citizens. In addition to other types of limitations on the state, such as the system of checks and balances (the separation of powers), 'civil society' and the requirement of governmental transparency, the state's power in the sphere of criminalisation should equally be restricted by requiring that criminalisation takes place only if legitimate or good reasons for criminalisation exist (Peršak) and only if certain well-established principles of criminal law are followed (Elholm).

In today's rule of law-governed societies, it is also assumed that the everyday interaction between the individual and the state follows (and ought to follow) certain prearranged rules of fair play, and this concerns also how the individual is treated in *procedures* or in the application of criminal law and criminal policy. Here, issues such as fairness but also accessibility and communication as well as respect for different goals of agents involved in the process (Vander Laenen) come to the fore. Justice is administered through a variety of arrangements and institutions (Goodall, Malloch and Munro 2012) and when relevant agents are not being 'heard', justice will necessarily suffer. Criminal law procedural measures are legitimised not (only) by the result but also (or predominantly) by the way the result has been reached (Erbežnik). While illegally obtained evidence may be 'correct' in that it represents a testimony of what had actually happened, it is nonetheless illegitimate, as it has been obtained in a legally unacceptable way (e.g. by torture).

However, *outcomes* are not to be neglected either, particularly when assessing legitimacy of the judiciary. In other words, once it comes down to the law's application or practice, it is about how you are treated, but also about the results, the quality of judicial decisions, impartiality, distributive justice concerns, proportionality issues in sanctioning and effectiveness (Peršak and Štrus). In the case of law, its consequences (whom the law 'captures') may be a source of much greater concern to people than the lack of the law's formal integrity, as the case of administrative sanctions in Belgium seems to show (Vander Beken and Vandeviver). When it comes to EU criminal law, in particular, another much-desired outcome is coherence (Elholm), which could perhaps be understood as an outcome-oriented principle of criminal law. Assessing outcomes in the EU criminal law, moreover, includes assessing the impact of (arguably imperfect and somewhat confused) mutual recognition system on the current state of affairs in judicial cooperation (Vermeulen). Here it is worth bearing in mind that the law and legal instruments can affect trust and legitimacy in both ways. They may build it, but they may also jeopardise it. As Vermeulen has shown, the mutual recognition mechanism (i.e. legal instruments containing it) that is progressively being used in the area of home and justice has many countries distrusting it or displaying suspicion towards it, and perhaps rightfully so. The mechanism has, however, also repercussions for the national judiciary and its legitimacy, as executing judgments not based on the independent reasoning and deliberation by the judge herself but rather based on automatic recognition procedures reduces the scope of her original, 'classic' functions (Erbežnik).

Although outcomes of police work and of criminal policy are understood differently and measured differently, possible injustices resulting from it, e.g. from uneven application of law, discrimination in police practices, can be construed as another problematic outcome that needs to be addressed when evaluating legitimacy of the agent or institution or policy behind it (Van der Leun and Van der Woude). What is critical here is to recognise that there are marked differences between groups of citizens that come to be 'processed' by the criminal justice agents. Complex, two-directional sociological processes that take place may, for some, run deeper than the interaction might at first glance indicate. Van der Leun and Van der Woude fittingly describe the situation: '[i]f, for instance, a migrant is stopped by the police in the streets time and again and if he or she experiences exclusion or discrimination in several domains of life, a concrete interaction may be polite and procedurally right, but the person may still start to question the right of the police to rule'.

Multiple Rationalities, Multiple Expectations

In law making, multiple rationalities are reflected in different interest groups, lobbyists putting pressure or exerting influence on the legislator, but the multi-directional communication and importance of 'being heard' is perhaps even more salient in concrete cases of law application, where different institutions, different actors meet in search for dispute resolution and justice. Here, it is particularly crucial that the existence of different stakeholders, power groups and their different goals, as well as the interaction between them and consequent 'dialogicality' of legitimacy (Bottoms and Tankebe 2012) is properly acknowledged. Institutions are, after all, people and groups of people, and the bigger the institution, the more and more diverse groups and people it will host. All these different actors have multiple goals, multiple agendas – internally or externally determined – but with them different expectations come, which is important to realise, as our expectations tend to be underpinning our claims that something or someone is or is not legitimate. Considering trust is 'a positive feeling of expectation regarding another's future actions' (Barbalet 2009: 375), expectations are trust's building bricks.

Although law and legal standards may provide a basis for legitimacy of an institution and its role, in concrete circumstances, it is often about people or 'the human factor'. Despite the rules in place enabling the sharing of information between police, for example, for a police officer in some country, who needs some information it often comes down to whom he or she personally knows in some other country that might help and how they approach this person. Knowing someone, sharing similar values or having the same goals generates trust and fuels cooperation – and this applies across institutions (Vander Laenen) as well as across countries (Vermeulen). The question of communication and acceptance of the other's goals as legitimate, even if they differ from yours, is challenging, as Vander Laenen has shown in the case of information sharing in the courtroom. Being 'on the same side' (as judges tend to see themselves and social care workers as being) does not guarantee that their goals are identical. Overcoming such obstacles in communication can pose quite a challenge for justice, the justice system and consequently its legitimacy.

The heterogeneity of agents and multifaceted communication also necessarily leads to the question of the entitlement over claims or to the question 'of whom' and 'by whom': whose definition of legitimacy is important (and whose trust)? Of the general public? Of experts (e.g. legal experts, lawyers, legitimacy researchers)? The academic elite? Who is asking the question? Who is defining what legitimacy is? Who is the power-holder in defining legitimacy? If the public or people (as the sovereign) are not the main yardstick then who is or ought to be? Here it is worth recalling that in a democracy the support of at least a majority of its citizens is particularly important, as 'without the granting of legitimacy by the people, a democracy would lose its authority' (Dogan 2003: 117). However, for Weber (1978), democracy is not a necessary condition for the establishing of legitimacy: legitimacy can be established through codified laws, customs and cultural principles, it does not require popular vote. Even when formal elements of democracy are met they may not produce necessarily good outcomes or best decisions. The majority may prefer ineffective rather than effective policy decisions (Mayntz 2010) or favour outcomes that infringe human rights of minorities.

Trust Comes into Play at Various Points

Mutual trust is not just a central concern for communitarians (Crawford 2000) but very relevant whenever cooperation is required between agents, agencies or states – be it at the national or at the EU level. For the legal instruments enabling cooperation to work, mutual trust between the two (or several) parties – authorities and services in the different Member States – is essential. Now, within EU mutual trust is more or less assumed, but this assumption only works to a certain point (as some recent cases show) and moreover, even when it is not challenged, the cooperation may be undermined by agents or authorities de facto refusing to provide information or 'losing' the requests in the drawer. Trust affects legitimacy, but legitimacy conversely affects trust, as the more legitimate authorities are, the more they are willing to trust each other (Fichera 2009). In fact, one could argue that this is how it ought to be; legitimacy should produce trust, while deducing legitimacy from the perceived (citizen-reported) trust in it should not be sufficient for conferring legitimacy on such an institution. Arguing for this would of course necessarily mean supporting or arguing for the conception of legitimacy as an internal, objective value of an authority, not legitimacy as being derived (merely) from public acceptance or perception.

When we have no data on actual functioning of e.g. courts, it is customary to use people's perceptions (measure their trust in courts) as an indication or approximation of the actual functioning, effectiveness or legitimacy. However, the approximation may be very skewed (some have no experience, never been to court, other have but got an unfavourable result which affects their general view on judiciary, etc.). This highlights the conceptual gap between trust and legitimacy, noted also by Bottoms and Tankebe (2012: 164): while legitimacy is present-oriented or 'concerned with the recognition of the moral rightness of claims to exercise power here and now', trust is future-oriented.

And future-oriented should also be policy and legislative modifications of existing instruments, when mistrusted. While national courts are bound by sincere cooperation principle and therefore the starting point has to be mutual trust, a defective concept of mutual recognition, disregarding the seriousness of the questions connected with its application, bears the danger of causing significant legal anomalies and even causing mistrust (Erbežnik). The EU mutual recognition mechanism, currently far from being unproblematic (Vermeulen), has to be structured in a way to continue legitimising the existing national constitutional identities of the Member States and at the same time legitimise the necessity and added value of EU measures and a common European Union. The respect for fundamental rights, safeguarded by national and EU judges, is the one that essentially legitimises modern democratic legal systems. Erbežnik argues that mutual recognition should not change the classic role of a judge to safeguard such rights or create a dangerous rift in the common EU judicial structure. Respecting the role of a national judge could help increase the legitimacy of EU criminal law legislation and when the legitimacy of EU criminal law legislation is increased, the level of trust among Member State authorities in cross-border criminal law cooperation is also likely to increase. This suggests an important political-strategic dimension of trust. Increased trust among authorities using the law in transnational cases is perhaps the strongest political argument in support of the view that EU legislation should consistently observe the widely agreed criminal law principles, which will increase its chances of being accepted and seen as legitimate (Elholm).

Background, History and Cultural Nuances

In today's world of insecurities and threats, to what extent can trust be assumed at all? The answer here may also depend on the countries in question. Distrust can partly arise out of a legacy of post-Communist states, although distrust is not unknown to Western European nations either. In fact, 'liberal democracy is also based on distrust, but in the opposite direction: it is founded upon the suspicion that the powerful will be tempted to abuse their power, and so must be subject to checks and balances' (Kohn 2008: ix). The sources of (mis)trust, however, differ, as do outcomes of this lack of trust. Considering trust is context- and place-specific (Crawford 2000), attention should be paid to the background, historical and cultural nuances, which have to be appreciated, for example, for the EU to merit legitimacy and generate compliance, mutual respect or mutual trust.

According to Art. 4(2) of Treaty on European Union (TEU), the EU must respect the 'national identities' (similarly Art. 82(2) of the Treaty on the functioning of the European Union (TFEU), which refers to judicial cooperation in criminal matters: the EU must take different national legal traditions into account). Elholm reminds us that the EU should pay attention to this aspect, consider 'the special nature of criminal law and the close link to a country's culture and history', and allow the Member States to adapt EU legislation to their own systems, suggesting that this may incorporate allowing a Member State to refrain from introducing a new criminalisation of a certain conduct if it finds such criminalisation unnecessary, the punishment for it unsuitable or the violation not serious enough.

Damaška (1991) has reminded us of the culturally calibrated yardstick of not only trust but also of perception of fairness of criminal procedure, which is also a cultural phenomenon based on past national experience and legal culture. Erbežnik links this observation with his argument that in this respect 'an uncritical application of mutual recognition based on "commanded" mutual trust, not taking account of the differences in national constitutional identity (as guaranteed by

Article 4(2) TEU), bears the danger of overlooking fundamental differences between national systems and their perception of justice, and to unnecessarily create resistance and mistrust against cooperation in criminal matters in the EU'.

Differences should be acknowledged but not overestimated, or left unquestioned. Much of a country's criminal law regulation does not involve the country's specific historical, cultural and ethical basis (Elholm) nor should they be always, without a good reason, followed. While additional principles of criminalisation such as the offence principle – which is particularly susceptible to taking into account cultural or regional variability – may be more justified in the area of disorder regulation than in the area of criminal law proper, sailing away from the harm principle or 'wrongful harm' as the basis for criminalisation entails risks of overreach and reduced legal certainty (Peršak).

The Need for an Improved Conceptualisation and Objective Criteria of Legitimacy

The concept of legitimacy is multidimensional and elusive, perhaps even an essentially contested one, which increases the danger of reductionist, piecemeal approaches to legitimacy but at the same time requires us to try and broaden the debate or, conversely, object to narrowing it down when the tunnel vision comes at the expense of neglecting important, relevant elements of legitimacy. To some extent, improved conceptualisation therefore means the widening of the concept, i.e. including issues of legitimacy that are relevant for other institutions (which have their own particularities), for example, social care services and other authorities interacting with courts, other audiences and power-holders (Bottoms and Tankebe 2012), but also including all aspects of legitimacy (or as many as possible) in the definition, taking into account perspectives of different social sciences and humanities disciplines.

For this purpose, it is, firstly, useful to delineate which legitimacy (normative or citizen-conferred) do we have in mind when speaking. When talking about normative or more objective one, we should probably not refer to trust (based on citizens' perceptions) in its definition and mix apples and oranges. Secondly, more attempts need to be made at fleshing out some normative criteria of legitimacy, more objective, less trust-based, but eventually contributing to trust (Peršak and Štrus). While we have something similar to them in the area of criminal law, namely principles of criminalisation (see chapters by Elholm and Peršak), such normative criteria are still in need of full development in the area of criminal justice. These criteria may not only help assess the functioning of justice systems, but may also help pave the way for mutual recognition instruments (Vermeulen) and their recognition as being legitimate. Improved conceptualisation may therefore also mean more focused and in that sense perhaps a narrowing exercise – particularly relevant if one is trying to make the concept or its criteria measurable, more objective and less dependent on actual (subjective, forward-looking) trust and people's perceptions. Although justice also needs to be seen to be done, it foremost needs to be done.

In the absence of objective normative indicators of legitimacy, the grey areas or borderline cases – practices 'at the margin' seem to be, however, the best litmus test of legitimacy (legitimacy in the objective sense, i.e. as internal characteristic of *x*), the best proxy. These grey areas and practices at the 'margin' include shady application of laws and practices toward the weakest members of society, such as ethnic profiling (by police) and criminalisation of illegal residence (Van der Leun and Van der Woude), criminalisation of youth, etc. In criminal law (and policy), this can mean inspecting the activity at the borderline of criminal law, i.e. in violations or administrative sanctions (Vander Beken and Vandeviver, Peršak), which remains much less visible to the critical eye of scholars and the public. Similarities can be observed even here: as Van der Leun and Van der Woude note, just being on the street (not doing anything in particular) but being a non-Western immigrant makes one a high-risk category. Similarly, as issued ASBOs show, just 'hanging about', being on the street, in front of the block of flats, not doing anything in particular, just being young, in a group and out there – visible, makes one fall in a high-risk category for anti-social behaviour (and become vulnerable to getting an ASBO).

Some Ideas for Future Research

In addition to the re-conceptualisation and broadening of the notion of legitimacy, mentioned above, there is still plenty of room for empirical work as well. For this, it would first be useful to break legitimacy down into different (more measurable) components (Vermeulen). While a lot has been done on formulating social-empirical indicators of trust and justice (Jackson et al. 2011), *normative indicators* need further exploration. There is clearly a need for measurement of normative and objective (not just perceived) criteria of legitimacy, for example, of justice systems (Peršak and Štrus): in addition to the lack of formulation of several indicators of judicial legitimacy, some of the existing indicators of justice currently rely only on citizens' perceptions of a certain quality of justice, e.g. of judicial independence. People's subjective assessments may be, however, very much misaligned with the actual state of affairs, the actual independence, much like measured fear of crime often is with the actual levels of crime.

Furthermore, the *empirical research* on legitimacy could be widened, as Vander Laenen proposes, by looking at the interaction between courts as 'power-holders' in the criminal justice system and other agencies, such as health and social care providers. Owing to conflicting values and goals, courts represent not only an arena where justice is being sought but also a field in which diverse legitimacy claims and power games are being played out as well as issues of recognition and self-verification.

Considering *historical and cultural nuances* have been shown to play an important role in the perception and evaluation of trust, legitimacy, justice, fairness and so forth, to 'taint' the measurements of these concepts and to protrude in the principles of criminal law and criminalisation, they should be further inspected. Homogeneity is too often assumed, not only when it comes to institutions but also when it comes to Western countries or even European countries. Studying cultural differences, cultural understandings and their background assumptions includes also the studying of differences in research cultures, their actions and omissions. Why do, for example, some cultures invest in studying mainstream discriminatory practices, while others do not even recognise it as a topic? Is the blindness or unwillingness to examine such aspects due to pragmatic problems, e.g. the lack of funding (or unlikeliness of getting national funding for research on such a sensitive topic), or are there (also) some self-censuring aspects of the research culture at play or something else?

What may also be worth studying in terms of criminal policy is the geographical-political dimension of social control, as revealed, for example, in the expansive trend in the regulation of disorder across Europe. A chronological comparison between various countries' disorder regulation may reveal that some (and which) countries are the 'countries of origin' or trend-setters in social control mechanisms and others that are mostly 'receiving countries', indicating certain '*geopolitics of social control*'. The same could be done with other research topics: who dictates research topics? Who defines what legitimacy or 'legitimate' is?

Our analysis also revealed that more detailed examination of legitimacy perceptions or *further unpacking of trust* is required. The legitimacy of EU criminal policy making and cooperation in criminal matters as well as of EU institutions in general is, for example, constantly yet contradictorily assessed by policy makers, practitioners, NGOs, academia and citizens. Vermeulen observed that EU policy-making actors tend not to question it too much, which is understandable considering their EU integration focus. National prosecutors seem to predominantly support mutual recognition, for it facilitates getting things done abroad, while judges tend to have more mixed feelings about it, sometimes feeling uncomfortable with mutual recognition as they feel confined to their own legal system and constitutional principles (which may pull them the other way). Citizens' trust in EU criminal law cooperation, however, seems to be surprisingly high, notwithstanding all the flaws and weaknesses in the EU's and Member States' discourses (Vermeulen). The latter in particular raises some questions. When citizens report higher trust in EU institutions than in national parliaments and governments (see Eurobarometer 2012), do they truly 'trust' them or simply do not care and evaluate them highly as they have no interaction with them – EU institutions are not seen to be intervening in their lives directly and hence do not evoke any emotion? If the latter is true, then the bigger the citizen–EU gap may mean the more uninformed and disinterested the citizen, and, consequently, the more positive the citizen's perception of, and higher trust in, the EU institutions and their policies. The above expert observations on differences in perceptions between the mentioned groups require further empirical testing but they also, as do Eurobarometer findings, clearly underline the need to further unpack 'trust', i.e. explain what these groups (and citizens in particular) mean when they say 'they trust' some authority.

These are just some issues or questions on which the broadening of research and ultimately of our knowledge may help to address the challenge of creative thinking about legitimacy, mentioned by Connolly (2000) above, and deepen the thought on epistemic circumstances surrounding the modern problem of legitimacy. The complexity of all issues and factors involved, including temporal, spatial and cultural distinctions that play a role in the attribution of legitimacy to an agent or institution, requires continuing effort; however, the topic is attracting more and more attention from legal, criminological, philosophical, psychological and socio-legal circles, which all importantly contribute to this increasingly relevant debate on legitimacy and trust in criminal law, policy and justice.

References

Barbalet, J. 2009. A characterization of trust, and its consequences. *Theory and Society*, 38(4), 367–82.

Bottoms, A. and Tankebe, J. 2012. Beyond procedural justice: A dialogic approach to legitimacy in criminal justice. *The Journal of Criminal Law and Criminology*, 102(1), 119–70.

Breakwell, G.M. 2007. *The Psychology of Risk*. Cambridge: Cambridge University Press.

Connolly, W.E. 2000. Legitimacy, in *The Blackwell Encyclopaedia of Political Thought*, edited by D. Miller, J. Coleman, W. Connolly and A. Ryan. Oxford: Blackwell, 279–80.

Crawford, A. 2000. Situational crime prevention, urban governance and trust relations, in *Ethical and Social Perspectives on Situational Crime Prevention*, edited by A. von Hirsch, G. Garland and A. Wakefield. Oxford: Hart, 193–215.

Damaška, M. 1991 (orig. 1986). *Two Faces of Justices*. New Haven: Yale University Press.

Dogan, M. 2003. Conceptions of legitimacy, in *Encyclopedia of Government and Politics*, 2nd edn, ed. M. Hawkesworth and M. Kogan. London: Routledge, 116–26.

Eurobarometer. 2012. *Standard Eurobarometer 78*, Autumn 2012. Brussels: European Commission.

Fichera, M. 2009. Mutual trust in European criminal law, in *Working Paper Series 2009/10*. Edinburgh: University of Edinburgh.

Goodall, K., Malloch, M. and Munro, B. 2012. Social and legal transitions and criminalisation, in *Building Justice in Post-Transition Europe? Processes of Criminalisation within Central and Eastern European Societies* (Routledge

Frontiers of Criminal Justice 2), ed. K. Goodall, M. Malloch and B. Munro. London: Routledge, 3–21.

Jackson, J., Bradford, B., Hough, M., Kuha, J., Stares, S., Widdop, S., Fitzgerald, R., Yordanova, M. and Galev, T. 2011. Developing European indicators of trust in justice. *European Journal of Criminology*, 8(4), 267–85.

Kohn, M. 2008. *Trust: Self-Interest and Common Good*. Oxford: Oxford University Press.

Mayntz, R. 2010. *Legitimacy and Compliance in Transnational Governance* (MPIfG Working Paper 10/5). Cologne: Max Planck Institute for the Study of Societies.

Weber, M. 1978. *Economy and Society*, edited by G. Roth and C. Wittich. Berkley: University of California Press.

Index

For Product Safety Concerns and Information please contact our EU
representative GPSR@taylorandfrancis.com
Taylor & Francis Verlag GmbH, Kaufingerstraße 24, 80331 München, Germany

www.ingramcontent.com/pod-product-compliance
Ingram Content Group UK Ltd.
Pitfield, Milton Keynes, MK11 3LW, UK
UKHW021304190926
475701UK00009B/697

* 9 7 8 1 1 3 8 2 7 0 5 9 6 *